# HARBRA
# COLLEGE
# WORKBOOK
## FORM 11B

# HARBRACE
# COLLEGE
# WORKBOOK
## FORM 11B

## Larry G. Mapp
Middle Tennessee State University

HARCOURT BRACE JOVANOVICH, PUBLISHERS
San Diego   New York   Chicago   Austin   Washington, D.C.
London   Sydney   Tokyo   Toronto

Acknowledgment   NATURAL HISTORY MAGAZINE   For "Beasts Before the Bar" by Frank A. Beach. Reprinted with permission from *Natural History*, Vol. 59, No. 8; Copyright the American Museum of Natural History, 1950.

Student's Edition
ISBN: 0-15-531881-0

Printed in the United States of America

# TO THE INSTRUCTOR

The three forms of the *Harbrace College Workbook* are designed to be used either independently or in conjunction with the Eleventh Edition of the *Harbrace College Handbook*. Each form is unique, however, because each develops a particular theme throughout its examples and exercises. Form 11A examines the cosmos, Form 11B explores the balance between humankind and nature, and Form 11C focuses on writing for the world of work. For Form 11B, all of the explanations in the previous edition have been examined and, at least in part, rewritten; many of the exercises have been completely rewritten.

**Arrangement**   The materials in Form 11B are arranged in sections that parallel the sections in the *Harbrace College Handbook*, Eleventh Edition. The numbers and letters denoting subdivisions within the sections also correspond to those of the *Handbook*.

Section **1** of Form 11B covers the main points of grammar and punctuation; it is, in other words, a practical minicourse in the grammar and punctuation of sentences. Some students may be able to move directly from section **1** to the later sections that treat word choice and sentence effectiveness (sections **20** through **30**) or even to the sections that go beyond the sentence to longer units of composition (sections **31** through **33**). Other students will need additional review of basic areas—such as agreement, tense, and the uses of the comma and apostrophe—that is supplied in the intervening sections (**2** through **19**). Of course, the needs of the class or the individual student will determine how much time is devoted to sections **2** through **19** and how many of the exercises in each section are assigned.

**Exercises**   The subject matter of the examples and exercises is the balance between humans and nature. For example, the text includes discussions of El Niño, the wonderfully complex phenomenon that periodically unbalances the ecosystems of much of the Pacific Ocean; of the Mississippi River's history of changing its course and thereby changing the lives of all creatures in its path; and of genetic engineering, a procedure that forces us to define very carefully our relationship to all living things. The topics, then, are varied and thought-provoking and should keep students interested in the explanations and exercises. I also have tried to present information that will stimulate students to write and to read and, I hope, to understand that reading and writing are the halves of the double helix.

**Writing**   Form 11B includes sections on writing paragraphs (**32**) and essays (**33**). There is enough material in the examples and exercises within each of the chapters to provide a starting point for student writing. Students might be asked to respond to particular questions raised by their reading, perhaps even doing parallel reading in other sources to gather extra material; or they could be encouraged to respond to what they have read in less structured, more expressive writing.

**The Dictionary**   Use of the dictionary is stressed throughout Form 11B: in the study of nouns, adjectives, adverbs, and verbs, and in the sections on capitalization, abbreviations, italics, and numbers. Unless each member of the class is already familiar with the dictionary, the best place to begin teaching and learning dictionary skills might be section **19**, "Good Usage and the Dictionary."

**Spelling**   Although most students receive little formal instruction in spelling after elementary school, correct spelling is important to success in college and in other work. Form 11B does not presume to be a complete spelling manual, but it does emphasize throughout the use of the dictionary to avoid various kinds of misspellings, and it covers all major spelling rules. In addition, it presents a list of words that are frequently misspelled in professional writing. Perhaps even more important, the "Individual Spelling List" at the end of the *Workbook* offers a chart on which students can record the words they misspell in their writing assignments and the reasons for the misspellings.

**Note:**   Each of the forms of the *Harbrace College Workbook* is available in an Instructor's Edition as well as a Student Edition. The Instructor's Edition is an exact replica of the Student Edition, with answers to all exercises overprinted in a second color.

**Acknowledgments**   I thank Loris D. Galford and Cheryl Ware of McNeese State University, Suzanne S. Webb of Texas Woman's University, and John N. Snapper for their perceptive comments and suggestions.

I am grateful to the staff of Harcourt Brace Jovanovich for helping with this book: Stuart Miller, acquisitions editor; Sarah Smith, manuscript editor; Michael Biskup, production editor; Don Fujimoto, designer; and Lynne Bush, production manager.

My colleagues at Middle Tennessee State University are a constant source of support. I wish especially to thank Bob Petersen and Loisteen Kirkman, whose good will has often lifted me "above the ground with cheerful thoughts." Dixie Highsmith has contributed substantially to the contents and to the tone of sections **32** and **33**; I enjoyed sharing these sections with her. And I thank my typist and friend, Cynthia Duke: how much harder all this would have been without her.

Finally, my thanks to Ann, Anna, and Sarah, whose love and support are unconditional.

Larry G. Mapp

# TO THE STUDENT

You learn how to write chiefly by revising your own work. Corrections made for you are of comparatively little value. Therefore the instructor points out the problem but allows you to make the actual revision for yourself. The instructor usually indicates a necessary correction by a number (or a symbol) marked in the margin of your paper opposite the error. If a word is misspelled, the number **18** (or the symbol **sp**) will be used; if there is a sentence fragment, the number **2** (or the symbol **frag**); if there is a faulty reference of a pronoun, the number **28** (or the symbol **ref**). Consult the text (see the guides on the inside covers), master the principle underlying each correction, and make the necessary revisions in red. Draw one red line through words to be deleted, but allow such words to remain legible in order that the instructor may compare the revised form with the original.

**The Comma**   After the number **12** in the margin you should take special care to supply the appropriate letter (**a**, **b**, **c**, **d**, or **e**) from the explanatory sections on the comma to show why the comma is needed. Simply inserting a comma teaches little; understanding why it is required in a particular situation is a definite step toward mastery of the comma. (Your instructor may require that you pinpoint each of your errors by supplying the appropriate letter after every number written in the margin.)

## Specimen Paragraph from a Student Theme

### Marked by the Instructor with Numbers

| | |
|---|---|
| 3 | Taking photographs for newspapers is hard work, it is not the |
| 12 | romantic carefree adventure glorified in motion pictures and novels. For |
| 18 | every great moment recorded by the stareing eye of the camera, there are |
| | twenty routine assignments that must be handled in the same efficient |
| 28 | manner. They must often overcome great hardships. The work continues |
| 24 | for long hours. It must meet deadlines. At times they are called on to |
| | risk their lives to obtain a picture. To the newspaper photographer, get- |
| 2 | ting a good picture being the most important task. |

# TO THE STUDENT

## Marked by the Instructor with Symbols

*cs*       Taking photographs for newspapers is hard work, it is not the

*,/*     romantic carefree adventure glorified in motion pictures and novels. For

*sp*     every great moment recorded by the stareing eye of the camera, there are

    twenty routine assignments that must be handled in the same efficient

*ref*    manner. They must often overcome great hardships. The work continues

*sub*    for long hours. It must meet deadlines. At times they are called on to

    risk their lives to obtain a picture. To the newspaper photographer, get-

*frag*   ting a good picture being the most important task.

## Corrected by the Student

*3*       Taking photographs for newspapers is hard work; it is not the

*12 C*   romantic, carefree adventure glorified in motion pictures and novels. For

*18*     every great moment recorded by the ~~stareing~~ *staring* eye of the camera, there are

    twenty routine assignments that must be handled in the same efficient

*28*   manner. *Newspaper photographers must overcome* ~~They must often overcome great hardships. The work continues~~

*24*   *great hardships and work long hours to meet deadlines.* ~~for long hours. It must meet deadlines~~. At times they are called on to

    risk their lives to obtain a picture. To the newspaper photographer, get-

*2*     ting a good picture *is* ~~being~~ the most important task.

# CONTENTS

## GRAMMAR

# MECHANICS

# PUNCTUATION

# SPELLING AND DICTION

# CONTENTS

# EFFECTIVE WRITING

# SENTENCE SENSE ss 1

# 1

**Develop your sentence sense.**

You probably have more sentence sense than you realize. As proof, what is your response to this group of words?

> When the waters of the Pacific Ocean occasionally become warmer in the winter.

Probably you will say, almost without thinking, that something is missing from the sentence.

What would you write instead of "When the waters of the Pacific Ocean occasionally become warmer in the winter"? Maybe you would add words.

> When the waters of the Pacific Ocean occasionally become warmer in the winter, scientists refer to the change as El Niño.

In that case your sentence sense tells you to add another subject (*scientists*) and another verb (*refer*). Or maybe you would simply omit a word.

> The waters of the Pacific Ocean occasionally become warmer in the winter.

Your instinct tells you that without the word *when*, a subordinator, the group of words is a sentence. Whether you add another subject and verb or omit the subordinator, you are responding to your sense of what is needed to make the group of words into a complete thought.

As you have learned to speak and write, you have become aware of what a sentence is. But to develop this awareness fully, you must know the basic parts of a sentence and how they can be put together in clear and varied patterns. An understanding of this section, then, is necessary to the study of almost all the other parts of this text.

All sentences have a stated or an implied *subject*, someone or something spoken about or to, and a *predicate*, something said (predicated) about or to the subject.

> SUBJECT    +              PREDICATE
>
> Scientists   +    monitor the Earth's atmosphere.

The predicate may be subdivided into two parts: the *verb* and the *complement*. The verb states an action, an occurrence, or a state of being; and the complement receives the action of the verb or expresses something about the subject.

> SUBJECT    +    VERB    +              COMPLEMENT
>
> Scientists   +   have recorded   +   eight significant El Niños
>                                                since World War II.

> [The complement receives the action of the verb.]

The 1982–83 El Niño    +    was    +    a maverick.

[The complement expresses something about the subject.]

Most of the sentences that we write have all three of these basic parts. Subject–Verb–Complement (S–V–C). In the examples that follow, the subject is underlined once; the verb, twice; and the complement, three times. (This is the pattern that you will be asked to follow when working the exercises in this section of the *Workbook*.)

S–V–C  We studied El Niño.

But some sentences have only the subject and verb.

S–V  In the fall of 1982, El Niño arrived.

To write clearly and simply, we make most of our sentence patterns follow the normal order—that is, Subject–Verb–Complement or Subject–Verb. But sometimes, for variety or for emphasis, we vary from the usual order.

NORMAL ORDER

S–V–C  The effects of the last El Niño were spectacular

EMPHATIC ORDER

C–V–S  Spectacular were the effects of the last El Niño.

We also vary from normal order when we write most questions.

V–S–V–C  Do you know the causes of El Niño?

C–V–S–V  How much effect did El Niño have on humans?

And we vary from normal order when we write a sentence that begins with *there* or *it*.

V–S  There were droughts in Australia because of El Niño.

V–S  It is surprising that El Niño caused droughts in Australia and floods in California.

[When *it* introduces a sentence, the subject is usually more than one word. Here the subject is a clause, a structure discussed in **1b** and **1c**.]

Each of these basic sentence parts, along with the modifiers that may accompany them, is fully discussed in the following pages.

**1a  Learn to recognize verbs.**

Although the verb is usually the second main part of the sentence, you should master it first because the verb is the heart of the sentence. It is the one part that no sentence can do without. Remember that a trainer can communicate with a dog using only verbs: *Sit. Stay. Fetch.*

*Function*     The verb, as the heart of the sentence, says something about the subject; it expresses an action, an occurrence, or a state of being.

<blockquote>

ACTION              Temperatures *increased* across the Pacific Ocean.

OCCURRENCE          Some scientists *consider* El Niño to be impossible to predict.

STATE OF BEING  "El Niño"—the child—*sounds* like a name for an innocent phenomenon.

</blockquote>

The verb also determines what kind of complement the sentence will have: either a word or words that will receive the action of the verb or a word or words that will point back to the subject in some way. If the verb is *transitive*, it transfers or passes along its action to a complement called a *direct object*.

<blockquote>

TRANSITIVE   Scientists keep careful records of each occurrence of El Niño.

[The transitive verb, *keep*, passes its action along to its complement, the direct object *records*.]

</blockquote>

If the verb is *intransitive*, it does not pass its action along to a complement. One kind of intransitive verb is complete in itself; it has no complement.

<blockquote>

INTRANSITIVE   The temperatures soared.

[The verb, *soared*, is complete in itself; it does not need a complement.]

</blockquote>

Another type of intransitive verb is the *linking verb*, which links the subject with a complement that refers back to the subject. The most common linking verbs are *be* (*is, are, was, were, has been, have been, will be*, and so on), *seem*, *appear*, and verbs that are related to the senses, like *feel*, *look*, and *taste*.

<blockquote>

INTRANSITIVE   Scientists seem frustrated by El Niño.

[The linking verb, *seem*, calls for a complement that refers back to the subject.]

</blockquote>

*Position*     The verb (underlined twice) is usually the second main part of the sentence, but in questions, in emphatic sentences, and in sentences that begin with *there* or *it*, the verb may come first or before the subject (underlined once).

USUAL ORDER    Scientists have predicted some El Niños.

QUESTION    Have scientists predicted some El Niños?

EMPHATIC    Rare is an accurate prediction.

*THERE*    There are few accurate predictions.

Always look for the verb first when you are trying to match it with its subject. This practice will help you to avoid agreement errors (the use of a plural verb with a singular subject and vice versa). If you look for the subject first, you may easily choose the wrong word in a sentence like this: "The scientists in the research institute (*is, are*) *studying* weather patterns." You are much less likely to choose "institute" as the subject if you first locate the verb (*is, are*) *studying*, and then determine whom or what the verb is speaking about: the institute is not studying; the *scientists* are studying.

*Form*    The verb may be recognized not only by its function and its position but also by its endings. Verbs ending in *d* or *ed* are in the past tense: he tried, she jumped, it required. (Sometimes, however, the verb changes its form altogether in the past tense: he rides, he rode; she lies down, she lay down; it comes, it came.) In the third person, verbs ending in *s* or *es* are singular in number: he tries, she jumps, it requires.

**Auxiliaries (Helping Verbs)**    The verb may be one word or several words. The main part of the verb—the word that actually expresses the action, occurrence, or state of being—may be accompanied by auxiliaries or helping verbs—words like *has, have, should,* and *can* and forms of *be* (see the Appendix for a list of auxiliary verbs). This cluster of verbs is referred to as a *verb phrase.* Often the parts of the verb phrase are separated.

Scientists do not understand the effects of El Niño on world weather patterns.

[*Not* often comes between the auxiliary and the main verb; it is a modifier, not a part of the verb, even when it appears in contractions like *don't.*]

Have you seen the results of a flood?

[In a question parts of the verb phrase are usually separated.]

Often, extensive damage has been done.

**Phrasal Verbs**    The main verb may also be accompanied by a word like *up, down,* or *in* that functions as a part of the verb. This part of the verb is called a *particle;* the particle usually changes or adds to the meaning of the main verb.

VERB        I passed a model of a rain forest in the museum.

VERB WITH    I passed up a good opportunity to photograph a model of a rain forest
  PARTICLE

        in the museum.

The particle ordinarily follows immediately after the main verb, but it may sometimes be separated from the main verb.

    I passed the opportunity up.

# SUMMARY

**Function**   The verb expresses an action (*throw, run, talk*), an occurrence (*prevent, criticize, modify*), or a state of being (*be, seem, appear, become*).

**Position**   The verb is usually the second main part of the sentence ("We photographed a model of a rain forest."), but it may come elsewhere, especially in questions ("May we photograph inside the museum?").

**Form**   The verb shows past tense by a *d* or an *ed* ending (solve*d*, walk*ed*, carri*ed*). Sometimes, however, the verb changes form completely in the past tense: *run, ran; buy, bought; choose, chose.* The verb may be only one word (*turned*) or several words (*has turned, will be turning, should turn in*). In the third person (*he, she, it*), the verb shows singular number by an *s* or *es* ending (feed*s*, come*s*, carrie*s*).

**1b(1) Learn to recognize subjects of verbs.**

All sentences except those that issue commands have a stated subject. And even in a command, the subject—*you*—is understood.

[You] Write a paper about the causes of El Niño.

*Function*     The subject is who or what the sentence is about. Once you have located the verb in the sentence, you need only to ask who or what is *doing*, *occurring*, or *being*. Your answer will be the complete subject. To find the simple subject, ask specifically who or what the verb is talking about.

Everyone in our class is writing a paper about the causes of El Niño.

[Who is writing? *Everyone in our class.* Who specifically is writing? Not *in our class*, but *everyone.*]

My topic, unlike the others, has been assigned by the instructor.

[What has been assigned? *My topic, unlike the others.* What specifically has been assigned? Not *my* or *unlike the others*, but *topic.*]

As in these examples, a word or a group of words usually comes before and/ or after the simple subject. Do not confuse one of these other words with the subject. If you do, you may fail to make the subject and the verb work together well; you may use a singular subject with a plural verb or vice versa. As was suggested in the discussion of verbs, always identify the verb before you try to locate the subject to avoid this kind of agreement mistake.

The students in our class are studying the causes of El Niño.

[The verb, *are studying*, is plural; therefore the subject must be plural too. *Students*, not *class*, is the plural subject; it is the word that answers the question "Who are studying?"]

*Position*     In most sentences the subject is the first main part of the sentence. But in questions, in emphatic sentences, and in sentences that begin with *it* or *there*, the subject follows the verb or comes in the middle of the verb phrase.

USUAL ORDER     Scientists carefully catalog all changes in Pacific Ocean currents.

QUESTION     Do scientists keep records of changes in Pacific Ocean currents?

EMPHATIC     Careful and detailed are a scientist's records.

*THERE*     There are careful scientific records of changes in Pacific Ocean currents.

*Form*　　Because the subject tells who or what the sentence is about, it must be either a *noun* or a *pronoun*—the two parts of speech that name people and things—or a cluster of words that functions as a noun. (Word clusters that may be substituted for a noun or pronoun are explained in Section **1d**.)

Nouns are words that name individuals or classes of people (*Fred Colvin, tribe, jury*), places (*New Zealand, parks, Earth*), things (*Kleenex, candy, watch*), activities (*Little League, basketball, festival*), and concepts (*divine right of kings, endurance, conclusion*). Pronouns are words used in the place of nouns; they take their meaning from the nouns that they replace.

NOUNS　　　*Scientists* sought water *samples* from the warming currents.

PRONOUNS　　*They* brought *them* from the warming currents.　[*They* replaces *scientists; them* replaces *samples.*]

Some pronouns—such as *we, he,* and *she*—refer only to people; some—such as *it, something,* and *which*—refer only to things; and some—such as *each, many,* and *some*—refer to either people or things.

Like verbs, nouns have certain endings that help you to identify them. But unlike verbs, nouns show the plural by an *s* or an *es* ending (key*s*, cave*s*, tomato*es*). Some nouns completely change their form when they are made plural (*man→men; leaf→leaves; child→children*). Nouns may also be recognized by the articles that frequently accompany them (*a* chair, *an* error, *the* person) and by their ability to form the possessive (child*'s* shoe, people*'s* choice, boys*'* dates).

Somewhat like verbs, nouns may consist of more than one word when all the words are necessary to name the person, place, or thing being spoken of: *Dr. Frank Field, Peck Hall, fishing rod.*

# SUMMARY

**Function**　　The subject is who or what the sentence is about. Thus when we ask who or what specifically is responsible for the action, the occurrence, or the state of being that the verb expresses, the answer will be the simple subject.

**Position**　　The subject is usually the first main part of the sentence ("*Ecuador* was the first country to feel the effects of El Niño."); however, in questions, emphatic sentences, and sentences that begin with *there* or *it*, it may come after the verb or in the middle of the verb phrase ("When did *Ecuador* first feel the effects of El Niño?").

**Form**　　Most nouns and pronouns that function as subjects undergo various changes to show plural number (*hurdle→hurdles; woman→ women; I→we*). Noun subjects are frequently preceded by articles (*a* storm, *an* exception, *the* currents), and both noun and pronoun subjects are often followed by words that limit their meaning (a month *without a day of rain;* each *of the farmers;* someone *in our class*). A noun subject is often made up of more than one word, especially if the noun is naming a particular person, place, or thing (*A. Conan Doyle, Galapagos Islands, Great Barrier Reef*).

## Subjects and Verbs in Simple Sentences

Exercise 1–5

NAME _____ SCORE _____

DIRECTIONS    Here are ten sentences about the impact of El Niño on Australia written without people-related subjects. Rewrite each sentence with a person or people (or a personal pronoun like *he, she,* or *they*) as the subject. Underline the subject of your revised sentence with one line and the verb with two lines. When you have finished revising the sentences, decide which version you think is more interesting and easier to read.

EXAMPLE
Nowhere did El Niño hit harder than in Australia.

*Australians were hit hardest by El Niño.*

1. Two and a half billion dollars of Australian property was lost to El Niño.

2. Much of the loss was to farmers.

3. Drought, heat, dust storms, and nightmarish brushfires tormented the farmers.

4. On February 8, 1983, the impact of El Niño on Australians reached its climax.

5. There was a darkening of the sky, a stilling of the breeze, and a terrifying cloud of dust thousands of feet high and 300 miles long that swept over the people of Melbourne.

6. For 40 minutes the dust was difficult to breathe through.

7. When the storm passed, it left 11,000 tons of topsoil on the city.

8. Within a week's time, raging brushfires nearly surrounded the people of Melbourne.

9. Warnings from fire-fighting officials urged the inhabitants of Macedon, a suburb of Melbourne, to flee.

10. On Ash Wednesday, high winds and a series of brushfires created a firestorm that in a few hours destroyed everything owned by the citizens of Macedon.

**1b(2) Learn to recognize objects and other kinds of complements.**

Not every sentence has a complement.

> The storm slowly weakened.

> The clouds quickly dispersed.

Sometimes a complement is possible even if none is stated.

> The public applauded.

> [A complement, though it is not stated, may be added because the verb, *applauded*, can also be used as a transitive verb: "The public applauded the rainbow's beauty."]

If the sentence has a complement, it can be found by following the subject and verb with "who," "whom," or "what."

> The monsoon was a spectacle.

> [The monsoon was what? *Spectacle* is the complement.]

> It covered Indonesia.

> [It covered what? *Indonesia* is the complement.]

> It circled the Indian Ocean in 1983.

> [It circled what? *Indian Ocean* is the complement.]

> The trip around the Indian Ocean ended by early spring of 1983.

> [There is no word to answer the "Who?" "Whom?" or "What?" Thus the sentence has no complement.]

*Function*     Following a *transitive* verb, a complement (or complements) is a word (or words) to which the action of the verb is transferred or passed along. Three types of complements may follow transitive verbs: *direct objects, indirect objects,* and *object complements.* The direct object is the most common type of complement following a transitive verb. Sometimes it is accompanied by an indirect object, which usually precedes it, or an object complement, which usually follows it.

DIRECT OBJECT          The Australian drought spawned huge dust storms.

> [The action of the verb is passed along to the direct object, *dust storms.*]

| | |
|---|---|
| INDIRECT OBJECT AND DIRECT OBJECT | The drought dealt Australian farmers the severest blow. |
| | [The action of the verb is passed along to both the indirect object, *farmers*, and the direct object, *blow*. An indirect object follows a verb like *give, send, bring, buy*, or *sell* and shows to whom or for whom the verb is doing something.] |
| DIRECT OBJECT AND OBJECT COMPLEMENT | Australians labeled the drought "the dry." |
| | [The object complement, *the dry*, is another name for the direct object, *drought*. An object complement follows a verb like *name, elect, make*, and *consider*.] |
| DIRECT OBJECT AND OBJECT COMPLEMENT | Months of drought made farming impossible. |
| | [Here the object complement, *impossible*, is an adjective that describes the direct object, *farming*.] |

**Note:** One test for a direct object is to make the active verb passive—that is, to add a form of *be* to the main verb. The word that is the object of the active verb then becomes the subject of the passive verb.

ACTIVE   The drought killed herds of livestock.

PASSIVE   Herds of livestock were killed by the drought.

[Note that *drought*, the subject of the active verb, now follows the passive verb.]

ACTIVE   A similar drought brought South Africa a new wave of disease and famine.

PASSIVE   South Africans were brought a new wave of disease and famine by a similar drought.

[*Drought*, the subject of the active verb, *brought*, follows the passive verb.]

A complement (or complements) following a linking verb (forms of *be* and verbs like *seem, feel, appear*, and *look*) points back to the subject of the sentence; it either describes the subject or renames it in some way. Such complements are called *subject complements*. A complement that renames the subject is either a noun or a pronoun; it is often referred to as a *predicate nominative* or *predicate noun*. A complement that describes the subject is an adjective; it is often referred to as a *predicate adjective*.

| | |
|---|---|
| PREDICATE NOMINATIVE | El Niño is a controlling influence in world weather. |

[The subject complement, *influence*, more or less renames the subject.]

| | |
|---|---|
| PREDICATE ADJECTIVE | El Niño seems unpredictable. |

[The subject complement, *unpredictable*, describes something about the subject, *El Niño*.]

*Position*    The complement is usually the third main part of the sentence, but it may appear first in a question or in an emphatic sentence. There is no complement in a sentence that begins with the expletive *there* or *it*.

USUAL ORDER    El Chichón is a volcano in Mexico.

QUESTION    What influence did El Chichón have on El Niño?

EMPHATIC    Awesome indeed was the eruption of El Chichón.

*Form*    The form of the noun complement, whether it is an object or a subject complement, is the same as the form of the subject. It can be distinguished from the subject only by its position in the sentence as the third main part of the basic formula.

SUBJECT    The *eruption* of El Chichón concealed El Niño from satellite sensors.

OBJECT    El Niño concealed the *eruption* of El Chichón from satellite sensors.

Pronoun subject complements have the same form as pronoun subjects: *I, he, she, we, they,* and *who.* However, many pronouns used as objects have distinct forms: *me, him, her, us, them,* and *whom.*

| | |
|---|---|
| SUBJECT COMPLEMENT | The meteorologist is he. |

[Compare "*He* is the meteorologist." The subject complement has the same form that the subject would have.]

| | |
|---|---|
| OBJECT | No one ignored her. |

[Compare "*She* ignored everyone." The object differs in form from the subject.]

Some pronouns, like nouns, have the same form whether they are subject complements or objects—for example, *you, it, each, some, many,* and *one.*

| | |
|---|---|
| SUBJECT COMPLEMENT | The last meteorologist to identify El Niño was *you.* |
| OBJECT | The others beat *you.* |

Adjectives have the same form whether they are subject complements or object complements.

SUBJECT COMPLEMENT   Jennifer was *lucky*.

OBJECT COMPLEMENT   Jennifer considered herself *lucky*.

# SUMMARY

**Function**   Asking the question "Who?" "Whom?" or "What?" of the subject and its verb reveals whether or not a sentence has a complement. Complements function either as objects—direct or indirect or object complements—that receive the action of transitive verbs ("She predicted *El Niño*.") or as subject complements that rename or describe the subjects of linking verbs ("The winner is *she*.").

**Position**   The complement is usually the third main part of the sentence ("Jennifer was *lucky*."), but in questions and emphatic sentences the complement may be stated first ("*Lucky* was Jennifer.").

**Form**   Nouns have the same form whether they are used as subjects, as objects, or as subject complements. Most personal pronouns have different forms as objects (*me, him, her, us, them, whom*) than they do as subject complements (*I, he, she, we, they, who*). Some pronouns have the same form whether they are used as objects or as subject complements (*you, it, each, one, some, many*, for example). Adjectives have the same form whether they are used as subject complements ("El Niño was *unpredictable*.") or as object complements ("The meteorologist called El Niño *unpredictable*.").

**1c Learn to recognize the parts of speech.**

Now that you have learned about the basic structure of a sentence, you are ready to begin working with all the elements that combine to give a sentence its meaning. The following chart lists the various functions words can perform in a sentence and the types of words that perform each function.

| *Function* | *Kinds of Words* |
|---|---|
| Naming | Nouns and Pronouns |
| Predicating (stating or asserting) | Verbs |
| Modifying | Adjectives and Adverbs |
| Connecting | Prepositions and Conjunctions |

The next chart summarizes the parts of speech that you will study in detail in the rest of this section (except for interjections).

| *Part of Speech* | *Uses in Sentences* | *Examples* |
|---|---|---|
| 1. Verbs | Indicators of action, occurrence, or state of being | Shane *wrote* the research paper. Anna *evaluated* the sources. They *are* students. |
| 2. Nouns | Subjects and objects | *Sarah* gave *Shane* the *photographs* of *El Chichón*. |
| 3. Pronouns | Substitutes for nouns | *He* will return *them* to *her* later. |
| 4. Adjectives | Modifiers of nouns and pronouns | The *detailed* charts are *careful, useful* guides. |
| 5. Adverbs | Modifiers of verbs, adjectives, other adverbs, or whole clauses | presented *clearly* a *very* interesting study *entirely too* long *Indeed,* we are ready. |

| Part of Speech | Uses in Sentences | Examples |
|---|---|---|
| 6. Prepositions | Words used before nouns and pronouns to relate them to other words in the sentence | *in* a hurry<br>*with* no thought *to* them |
| 7. Conjunctions | Connectors of words, phrases, or clauses; may be either coordinating or subordinating | monsoons *or* typhoons<br>before the floods *and* after them<br>*since* the beginning of spring |
| 8. Interjections | Expressions of emotion (unrelated grammatically to the rest of the sentence) | *Good grief!*<br>*Ouch!*<br>*Well,* we tried. |

## 1d Learn to recognize phrases and subordinate clauses.

A phrase is a series of related words (words grouped together) that lacks either a subject or a verb or both. You are already familiar with phrases that may function as the verb of a sentence—the main verb with one or more auxiliaries (*will be writing*) and the verb with a particle (*put up with* (**1a**)). Other phrases may function as the subject or object (**1d(1)** below) or as modifiers (**1d(2)**).

### 1d(1) Learn to recognize phrases and subordinate clauses used as subjects and objects.

The main types of word groups that function as subjects and as objects are verbal phrases and noun clauses.

*Verbal Phrases*    The verbal phrase is the kind of phrase that most frequently functions as a subject or object. The main part of the verbal phrase is the verbal itself—a word that shows action, occurrence, or a state of being as a verb does but that cannot function as the verb of a sentence because it lacks a subject.

> VERB    Scientists in Tahiti first *detected* El Niño in 1982.

> VERBALS    *detecting, to detect, having detected*

Notice that these verbals cannot substitute for the verb *detected* in a sentence.

> Scientists in Tahiti *detecting* El Niño in 1982    [fragment]
> Scientists in Tahiti *to detect* El Niño in 1982    [fragment]
> Scientists in Tahiti *having detected* El Niño in 1982    [fragment]

But such verbals, alone or with other words in verbal phrases, can function as subjects or objects just as individual nouns or pronouns can.

> NOUN    The *appearances* of El Niño have affected the world's climate.    [subject]

> VERBAL PHRASE    *Studying the appearances of El Niño* reveals its effect on world climate.    [subject]

> VERBAL PHRASE    *To study the appearances of El Niño* is a worthy task.    [subject]

> VERBAL PHRASE    *Having studied the appearances of El Niño* makes one more appreciative of the delicate balance between humans and nature.    [subject]

> NOUN    I enjoy the *study* of weather patterns.    [object]

> VERBAL PHRASE    I enjoy *studying weather patterns*.    [object]

> VERBAL PHRASE    I plan *to study weather patterns*.    [object]

> VERBAL PHRASE    I will never regret *having studied weather patterns*.    [object]

*Noun Clauses*    A clause is a series of related words (words grouped together) that has both a subject and a verb. One kind of clause, referred to as a *main clause* or *independent clause*, can stand alone as a sentence. The other, called a *subordinate clause* or *dependent clause,* may function as a noun—either a subject or object—or as a modifier in a sentence. (**1d(2)** discusses the use of phrases and subordinate clauses as modifiers. In fact, they are more commonly used as modifiers than as subjects or objects.) As nouns, subordinate clauses usually are introduced by one of these words: *who, whom, whose, which, that, whoever, whomever, what, whether, how, why,* or *where.* These introductory words are clause markers; they are printed in boldface in the following examples.

NOUN          Our *discovery* surprised us.   [subject]

NOUN CLAUSE      **What** *we discovered about trade winds* surprised us.   [subject]

NOUN          We reported our *discovery.*   [object]

NOUN CLAUSE      We reported **what** *we discovered about trade winds.*   [object]

NOUN CLAUSES     **Whoever** *studies trade winds* will learn **that** *shifting trade winds can destroy the economy of a huge portion of the world.*   [subject and object]

*Verbal Phrases and Noun Clauses as Subject Complements*      Verbal phrases and noun clauses can replace nouns and pronouns not only as subjects and objects but also as subject complements.

NOUN          His passion was *nature.*

VERBAL PHRASE   His passion was *studying nature.*

VERBAL PHRASE   His ambition was *to study nature.*

NOUN CLAUSE      His opinion was *that everyone should study nature.*

**Verbal Phrases and Noun Clauses as
Subjects, Direct Objects, and Subject Complements**       Exercise 1–8

NAME _____ SCORE _____

DIRECTIONS   Each of the following sentences contains one or more verbal phrases or noun clauses functioning as subject, direct object, or subject complement. First, underline such verbal phrases and/or noun clauses. Then write in the blank (1) *S* for a phrase or clause functioning as the subject of the sentence, (2) *DO* for a phrase or clause functioning as a direct object, or (3) *SC* for a phrase or clause functioning as a subject complement. If you write two or more things in the blank, use dashes between them. (Be sure to look for the main verb of the sentence before you try to identify the subject, direct object, and subject complement.)

EXAMPLE
What we hope to do is to monitor the next El Niño.       *S-SC*

1. That a Niño will occur in the next 10 years seems likely.       _____

2. Recording all the atmospheric and oceanic effects of El Niño
   will be very important.       _____

3. Scientists assume that all El Niños share a pattern of behavior.       _____

4. Before the 1982–83 experience, scientists thought that they understood the pattern.       _____

5. Some even believed that they understood the causes.       _____

6. The  primary cause seemed to be  a change in intensity of Pacific high and low barometric pressures.       _____

7. The positioning of a high pressure zone near Tahiti and of a
   low pressure zone near Indonesia usually creates westerly
   flowing trade winds.       _____

8. The constant trade winds continue to pile up a huge mound of
   warm water in the  western Pacific.       _____

9. A shift in the pressure centers seems to stop or to reverse the
   wind patterns.       _____

10. According to the theory, stopping or reversing the trade winds
    creates a huge wave of warm water.       _____

11. The wave begins to surge eastward across the Pacific.       _____

12. In 60 days what had been a mound of warm water in the western Pacific moves all the way across the ocean to the east. _____

13. What had been warm and inviting tropical water becomes a killer. _____

14. The warm wave begins to change the balance between humans and nature throughout the Pacific and Indian basins. _____

15. To study El Niño is to examine the fundamental relationships between humans and nature. _____

**1d(2) Learn to recognize words, phrases, and subordinate clauses used as modifiers.**

A modifier is a word or word cluster that describes, limits, or qualifies another, thus expanding the meaning of the sentence. Adjectives are the modifiers of nouns or pronouns; adverbs are the modifiers of verbs, adjectives, other adverbs, and sometimes whole sentences. The function of an adjective or an adverb can be fulfilled by a single word, a phrase, or a subordinate clause, as the following sentences demonstrate.

ADJECTIVES  *One* kind *of weather phenomenon that we usually can predict* is the summer monsoon.

[All three adjectival modifiers (a word, a prepositional phrase, and a subordinate clause, in that order) qualify the subject *kind*.]

ADVERBS  *On February 8, 1983,* tons of topsoil in a massive dust storm *unexpectedly* swept *into view* *while residents of Melbourne, Australia, stared in fear and disbelief.*

[All four adverbial modifiers (a prepositional phrase, a word, another prepositional phrase, and a subordinate clause, in that order) modify the verb *swept*.]

**Single-Word Modifiers**  Some authorities consider articles (*a, an,* and *the*), number words (*some, few, many,* and so on), and possessive pronouns (*my, its, your,* and so on) to be modifiers, while others call these words "noun determiners." They are both, and all three normally signal that a noun follows.

*The* dust storm made *its* visit memorable by leaving 11,000 tons of topsoil on *one* city.

Other single-word modifiers describe some quality of or set some kind of limitation on the words they refer to.

In 1983 a *rare* hurricane slammed *unexpectedly* into Hawaii, *six tropical* cyclones struck Polynesia, and *severe* drought *drastically* reduced crop production in South Africa.

Except when they are used as subject complements, adjective modifiers, by their very nature, are almost always found near the nouns or pronouns that they refer to. In emphatic word order, an adjective modifier may follow the noun or pronoun that it qualifies, but in usual word order the adjective precedes the word that it modifies.

USUAL ORDER    The *persistent, uninterrupted* drought caused famine and spread disease.

EMPHATIC    The drought, *persistent* and *uninterrupted,* caused famine and spread disease.

Adverb modifiers usually are not so clearly tied to the words that they modify and may move around more freely in the sentence as long as their location does not cause awkward or difficult reading.

*Undeniably,* the research was worthwhile.
The research, *undeniably,* was worthwhile.
The research was *undeniably* worthwhile.
The research was worthwhile, *undeniably.*

**Phrases as Modifiers**   A phrase, as you may remember, is a word cluster that lacks either a subject or a verb or both. The two types of phrases that function as modifiers are verbal phrases and prepositional phrases.

*Verbal Phrases*   The key word in the verbal phrase is the verbal itself (see **1d(1)**). Participles, which usually end in *ing, ed,* or *en* and are often preceded by *having,* can function only as adjective modifiers.

PARTICIPLES    *Having spent* years *preparing* for the moment, Anderson immediately recognized the beginning of the hurricane.

The participial phrase, which consists of the participle and sometimes a modifier and an object that are part of the participle's word cluster, is frequently used to expand the basic formula of a sentence. The use of a participial phrase often avoids a series of short, choppy sentences.

SHORT, CHOPPY    The hurricane was *slowly disintegrating.* It flattened 1,500 houses on Tahiti.

PARTICIPIAL
PHRASE    *Slowly disintegrating,* the hurricane flattened 1,500 houses on Tahiti.

OR

The hurricane, *slowly disintegrating,* flattened 1,500 houses on Tahiti.

An infinitive phrase may function as a modifier too. Unlike a participial phrase, however, it may be used as either an adjective or an adverb.

ADJECTIVAL   The tendency *to produce hurricanes in unexpected areas* made the last El Niño even more destructive.   [The infinitive phrase modifies the subject, *tendency.*]

ADVERBIAL   Not every El Niño is able *to produce hurricanes.*   [The infinitive phrase modifies the predicate adjective (subject complement) *able.*]

Sometimes the verbal has its own subject. It is then called an absolute phrase because it does not modify a single word in the sentence but rather the entire sentence (see also **12d**). Although an absolute phrase is not a sentence, it does have a greater degree of independence from the sentence than an ordinary verbal phrase does.

PARTICIPIAL   *Threatening the destruction of entire villages,* the hurricane paused
PHRASE   just offshore.   [The verbal *threatening* modifies the subject, *hurricane,* and should stand near it in the sentence.]

ABSOLUTE   *Their lives threatened by hurricanes,* the residents of small islands
PHRASE   fled to the mainland.   [The verbal, *threatened,* has its own subject, *lives;* thus the meaning of the phrase is clear wherever it is placed in the sentence.]

Like a participial phrase, an absolute phrase can be used effectively to combine short, choppy sentences.

SHORT, CHOPPY   The lives of many residents of small islands were threatened by El Niño's hurricanes. They refused to return home.

ABSOLUTE   *Their lives having been threatened by El Niño's hurricanes,* many
PHRASE   residents of small islands refused to return home.


*Prepositional Phrases*   A prepositional phrase begins with a preposition—a word like *in, of, to,* or *with*—and ends with an object, either a noun or a pronoun. The preposition is the word that connects the whole phrase to one of the main parts of the sentence, to another modifier, or to the object of another prepositional phrase. (A prepositional phrase often rides piggyback on a preceding prepositional phrase.)

1

The hurricanes curtailed the influx *of cash-bearing tourists,* and Tahitians had far

2                              3

too little money *for repairs.* Yet Tahiti, protected *by its mountains,* suffered less

4                       5

than the Tuamotus, a scattering *of low-lying atolls with no natural defenses*

6

*against the giant waves.*


[The first prepositional phrase (adjectival) explains the object complement, *influx;* the second one (adjectival) modifies the direct object, *money;* the third (adverbial) modifies the participle, *protected;* the fourth and fifth (adjectival) modify the gerund appositive, *scattering;* the sixth (adjectival) modifies the object of the preceding prepositional phrase, *defenses.*]

Often, as in the case of *with no natural defenses,* the prepositional phrase does not immediately follow the word it modifies. When you see a preposition (such as *with*), you know that an object ("with no natural *defenses*") and perhaps a modifier of the object ("with *no natural* defenses") follow.

There are so few prepositions that you can easily memorize a list of the most common ones (see the Appendix). But the prepositions that we do have, we use again and again. We write few sentences that do not include at least one prepositional phrase. Notice how incomplete the meaning of the following sentence would be without the prepositional phrases that qualify the meaning of the words that they modify.

Giant waves clawed *at church eaves,* and the islanders tied their boats *to the strong-*

*est coconut palms.*

[Without the prepositional phrase, the sentence reads "Giant waves clawed, and the islanders tied their boats."]

# Word and Phrase Modifiers:
# Adjectives and Adverbs

## Exercise 1-9

NAME _____ SCORE _____

DIRECTIONS   In each of the following sentences, the word in italics is qualified by one or more single-word and/or phrase modifiers. First underline these modifiers; then draw an arrow from each one to the italicized word. Do not underline or draw an arrow from the articles—*a*, *an*, and *the*. Write *adj* in the blank if the modifier or modifiers are functioning as adjectives and *adv* if the modifier or modifiers are functioning as adverbs. Notice how the modifiers make the italicized words more exact in meaning.

EXAMPLES

A U.S. Department of Agriculture *biologist* examining honey bee

cadavers detected ominous specks on the bees' thorax.                    *adj*

The minute internal discolorations *were examined* under a micro-

scope.                                                                    *adv*

1. They were honey bee tracheal mites, which *attach* themselves

   inside the breathing tube of young bees.                              _____

2. The mites *kill* the bees by sapping their respiration and

   sucking their life fluids.                                            _____

3. In Florida a routine inspection turned up another disturbing

   *sign* on some young orange tree cuttings.                            _____

4. An incurable *disease* called citrus canker had attacked the

   cuttings.                                                             _____

5. The canker *destroys* crops by blemishing fruit, stripping off

   leaves, and weakening the tree.                                       _____

6. The bee *colonies* were quickly gassed and the citrus burned.        _____

7. Biologists began a crucial search for *responses* to both

   outbreaks.                                                            _____

8. They initiated massive and costly *fumigation* of honey bee
   hives. _____

9. An attack of citrus canker *can* only *be stopped* by burning. _____

10. In recent years USDA researchers have turned their efforts
    toward discovering *methods* of biocontrol of these and other
    pests. _____

11. Researchers now know that pests develop *resistance* to even
    the most specific poisons. _____

12. USDA researchers *have altered* their approach to pest control
    by importing hundreds of pests' natural enemies as biocontrol
    agents. _____

13. These importations have saved *tens* of millions of dollars in
    crops and chemical sprays. _____

14. The cereal leaf beetle, the alfalfa weevil, and the alfalfa
    blotch leaf miner *have been controlled* by parasites and
    predators from Italy, France, and other parts of Europe. _____

15. Even the stubborn Colorado potato beetle and the Mexican
    bean beetle *have* lately *been showing* signs of succumbing. _____

**Subordinate Clauses as Modifiers** In **1d(1)** you studied one kind of subordinate clause—the noun clause, which can function as a subject or an object. (A subordinate clause contains both a subject and a verb but, unlike a main clause, cannot stand by itself as a sentence because of the subordinator that introduces it.) Other kinds of subordinate clauses—the adjective clause and the adverb clause—act as modifiers.

*Adjective Clauses* Adjective clauses are introduced by a subordinator such as *who, whom, that, which,* or *whose*—often referred to as *relative pronouns.* A relative pronoun relates the rest of the words in its clause to a word in the main clause, and, as a pronoun, also serves some noun function in its own clause, often as the subject. (Remember that a clause, unlike a phrase, has both a subject and a verb.)

Dr. Bengt Danielsson, *who* is a resident of Tahiti and a leading Pacific anthropol-

ogist, predicts the loss of the small islands' traditional cultures.

[The relative pronoun *who* relates the subordinate clause to the subject of the main clause, *Dr. Bengt Danielsson,* and also serves as subject of the verb, *is,* in its own clause.]

An adjective clause follows the noun or pronoun that it modifies. It cannot be moved elsewhere without confusing either the meaning or the structure of the sentence.

| | |
|---|---|
| CORRECT PLACEMENT | The people *who were displaced from their islands* often chose not to return. |
| INCORRECT PLACEMENT | The people often chose not to return *who were displaced from their islands.* |

Sometimes the relative pronoun is omitted when the clause is short and no misreading could result.

| | |
|---|---|
| WITH SUBORDINATOR | A transistor radio is the one item *that* islanders consider indispensable. |
| WITHOUT SUBORDINATOR | A transistor radio is the one item islanders consider indispensable. |

*Adverb Clauses* An adverb clause is introduced by a subordinator such as *since, when, if, because, although,* or *so that* (see the Appendix for a list of the most commonly used subordinators). Like the adjective clause, the adverb clause adds another subject and verb (and sometimes other elements) to the sentence. But unlike the relative pronoun that introduces the adjective clause, the subordinator of an adverb clause does not function as a main part of its own clause. The adverb clause usually modifies the verb of the main clause, but it may also modify an adjective or adverb in the main clause.

*Because* *some islanders did not return home when the hurricane ended*, their tra-

ditional cultures probably are doomed.

[The subordinator *because* introduces the first adverb clause, which modifies the verb, *are;* the second clause, introduced by *when* modifies the verb of the first adverb clause, *did return.*]

After El Niño, traditional island life was not as attractive to some islanders *as it*

*once must have been.*

[The subordinator *as* introduces the adverb clause, which modifies the adjective *attractive.*]

Unlike an adjective clause, an adverb clause often can move around freely in the sentence without changing the meaning or confusing the structure of the sentence. (See also Section **25**.)

*When scientists arrived on Christmas Island in 1982,* the resident population of 17 million seabirds had disappeared.

The resident population of 17 million seabirds had disappeared *when scientists arrived on Christmas Island in 1982.*

## Subordinate Clause Modifiers:
## Adjectives and Adverbs

Exercise 1–10

NAME_____SCORE_____

DIRECTIONS   Write *adj* in the blank if the italicized subordinate clause is an adjective modifier and *adv* if it is an adverb modifier. (To help make sure of your classification, try moving the italicized clause to different places in its sentence and notice whether the new arrangement affects the meaning or the structure of the sentence. If the movement of the clause affects the meaning or ruins the structure of the sentence, you know that it is an adjective clause.)

EXAMPLE
The greatest loss of foods to pests occurs *after the foods are placed in*

   *storage.*                                            *adv*

1. *As they grow* crops and livestock are protected from pests.   _____

2. Scientists rely on a campaign *that costs half a billion dollars a year* to protect them from pests.   _____

3. *Although these massive expenditures save U.S. farmers thirty dollars for every one dollar invested,* the biocontrol industry is not winning an unconditional victory over pests.   _____

4. Private companies and the government have been slow to fund research and development in biocontrol *because the greatest losses of food occur after harvest.*   _____

5. Fortunately, researchers have begun to develop methods of biocontrol *that are economical.*   _____

6. In one experimental program government biologists imported insects *that preyed on other insects.*   _____

7. For example, foreign parasites now help control the gypsy moth *which has been a difficult pest to control.*   _____

8. *Although it is no larger than a pinhead,* the Columbia wasp helps control Colorado potato beetles.   _____

9. *When it lays its eggs among the beetle's eggs,* it ensures that its own offspring will have food—and that the beetle's eggs will never hatch.   _____

*43*

10. Biologists carefully choose natural enemies of pests *that will not become pests themselves.*            _____

11. Farmers *who use natural enemies to control pests* must have patience.            _____

12. Natural enemies do not provide the immediate control *that farmers want.*            _____

13. *If the Mediterranean fruit fly appears,* methods of natural control are particularly slow.            _____

14. In Florida biologists released some 240 million Hawaiian Medflies *that had been sterilized with cobalt-60 radiation.*            _____

15. Biologists hoped that fertile females would exhaust their one-to-two month life span trying to mate with sterile males *before they could lay eggs capable of hatching.*            _____

16. *Because biologists do not believe this method can eradicate the Medfly,* they are looking for other forms of control.            _____

17. Biologists seem most worried about pests *that have not yet arrived in the United States.*            _____

18. The treatment *which has the most promise against new pests* involves using bacteria and viruses.            _____

19. Chemical fungicides soon lose this effectiveness *because they generate resistance.*            _____

20. *Because certain bacterial-spore sprays also kill fungi, are harmless to animals, and do not generate resistance,* they promise to be the fungicides of the future.            _____

**1e Learn to use main clauses and subordinate clauses in various types of sentences.**

Sometimes a writer has two or more related ideas to set forth. Depending on the relationship of the ideas and on the desired emphasis, the writer may express the ideas in separate sentences or combine them in one of several ways.

**Types of Sentences**   There are four types of sentences: *simple, compound, complex,* and *compound-complex.* Which of these types a given sentence is depends on the number of main and subordinate clauses it includes.

*Simple Sentences*      The simple sentence consists of only one main clause and no subordinate clauses. A simple sentence is often short but not necessarily so: one or more of the basic sentence parts—the subject, verb, or complement—may be compound and many single-word and phrase modifiers may be attached to the main clause.

SIMPLE   The primary diet of seabirds is fish.

SIMPLE   *Attempting to follow the schools of fish being driven away by El Niño's*

   *warm waters,* the seabirds abandoned Christmas Island.

   [The main clause, "The seabirds abandoned Christmas Island," has been expanded by two verbal phrases "*Attempting . . .*" and "*being . . .*"]

SIMPLE   *One year later a few* noddies, frigates, tropic birds, and boobies had

   returned *to the island* and had begun nesting.

   [The subject and verb are compound; *one year later* and *to the island* modify the verb *had returned; a few* modifies the compound subject.]

*Compound Sentences*      A compound sentence consists of two or more main clauses (but no subordinate clauses) connected by a coordinating conjunction (*and, but, or, nor, for, so, yet*) or by a conjunctive adverb (such as *thus* or *therefore*) or other transitional expression (such as *as a matter of fact*). (A semicolon may substitute for the coordinating conjunction; see Section **14.**) In a compound sentence the connecting word (in boldface below) acts like the fulcrum of a seesaw, balancing grammatically equivalent structures. Note that coordinating conjunctions have a fixed position in the second main clause; many conjunctive adverbs and transitional expressions, however, may either begin the second clause or take another position in it.

COMPOUND   Scientists do not know the fate of the seabirds, **but** they are cautiously

   optimistic about reviving the population.

   [The first main clause is balanced by the grammatically equivalent second main clause. The coordinate conjunction *but* joins the clauses.]

COMPOUND    Sooty terns raise only one chick at a time; **therefore,** their population increases slowly.

[The conjunctive adverb *therefore* balances the first main clause against the grammatically equivalent second main clause.]

***Complex Sentences***    A complex sentence consists of one main clause and one or more subordinate clauses. The subordinate clause in a complex sentence may function as the subject, a complement, a modifier, or the object of a preposition. As is true of the compound sentence, the complex sentence has more than one subject and verb; however, at least one of the subject-verb pairs is introduced by a subordinator such as *that, what, whoever, who, when,* or *if* (in boldface below) which makes its clause dependent on the main clause.

COMPLEX    **When** scientists examined the Pacific coral reefs, they discovered vast areas of dead reef.

[The subordinate clause functions as an adverbial modifier.]

COMPLEX    Scientists soon realized **that** El Niño's 88°F water had killed the coral reefs.

[The subordinate clause functions as the direct object.]

COMPLEX    The explanation of **what** killed the coral reefs focuses on the polyps **that** build and maintain the reefs.

[The first subordinate clause functions as the object of the preposition *of;* the second functions as an adjectival modifier.]

***Compound-Complex Sentences***    A compound-complex sentence consists of two or more main clauses and at least one subordinate clause. Thus it has three or more separate sets of subjects, verbs, and sometimes complements.

COMPLEX-COMPOUND    The polyps contain an algae *that protects them from the sun's ultraviolet rays,* but *when warming waters killed the algae,* the unprotected polyps died from exposure to the sun.

[The subordinate clauses (in italics) introduced by the subordinators *that* and *when* (in boldface) function as adjectival and adverbial modifiers, respectively.]

## Compound Subjects and Verbs
## and Compound Sentences

Exercise 1–11

NAME _____ SCORE _____

DIRECTIONS   Underline the simple subject or subjects in each of the following main clauses once and the verb or verbs twice. If the sentence is a compound sentence, insert an inverted caret (**V**) between the two main clauses. (Notice that the main clauses are correctly joined by a comma plus a coordinating conjunction, by a semicolon, or by a semicolon plus a conjunctive adverb or transitional phrase.) In the blank write *sub* if the subject is compound, *verb* if the verb is compound, and *cs* if the sentence is compound.

EXAMPLE

The bacterium BT is harmless to mammals, birds, and beneficial in-

sects but is deadly to a galaxy of worms and caterpillar pests.                    *verb*

Viral insecticides are also promising, and four have recently been reg-

istered.                                                                              *cs*

1. Viral insecticides are eaten, multiply inside the pest, and mi-

   grate lethally to other organs.                                                   _____

2. The insect dies, but the virus survives to await another victim.                 _____

3. Bacteria and viruses, however, are tricky weapons against

   pests.                                                                            _____

4. Chemical insecticides work faster, and they work within a

   broader range of temperatures and lighting conditions.                           _____

5. Insects can eat bacteria and viruses and still survive another

   five to ten days.                                                                 _____

6. Viruses and bacteria must be grown through twelve genera-

   tions prior to use in the field.                                                  _____

7. The laboratory cultivation refines the viruses and bacteria and

   makes them easier to control.                                                     _____

8. In other societies gardeners collect dead insects, grind them up,

   and spray them on fruits and vegetables.                                         _____

9. Lethal bacteria are alive in the carcasses, and the spray simply

   concentrates them to the gardener's advantage.                                    _____

10. These traditional approaches to pest control are effective and are illustrations of the desire to control pests without unnecessarily harming the environment. _____

**Subjects and Verbs in Main and Subordinate Clauses: Complex Sentences**

Exercise 1–12

NAME _____ SCORE _____

DIRECTIONS  Each sentence below contains one main clause and one subordinate clause—each clause, of course, with its own subject and verb. Underline the subjects once and the verbs twice. In the blank, write the subordinator that introduces the subordinate clause. (Remember that a relative pronoun subordinator—for instance, *who, whom, that, which*—often serves as the subject or complement of its own clause. Remember also that an entire subordinate clause may serve as the subject or complement of a main clause.)

EXAMPLES

Because pond <u>water</u> <u><u>contains</u></u> many kinds of bacteria, <u>it</u> can be a useful insecticide.          *Because*

If <u>you</u> <u><u>look</u></u> during the right season, <u>you</u> <u><u>can find</u></u> millions of viruses on the cabbages at the local supermarket.          *If*

1. The viruses usually only inconvenience the people who ingest them. _____

2. In concentrated amounts, however, they can kill insects that eat them. _____

3. The trick is to concentrate them when and where they are needed. _____

4. In 1900, a French entomologist hypothesized that the female great peacock moth might use "a kind of wireless telegraphy" to attract suitors. _____

5. Sixty years later, while they were working with female silkworms, a team of German scientists isolated the first insect sex pheromone. _____

6. The sex pheromone chemical is the "wireless telegraphy" which females use to attract males. _____

7. Although the female gives off infinitesimal amounts of the pheromone, the potent chemical can attract a male fifty yards or more away. _____

49

8. Researchers report that they have identified and banked the sex pheromone for virtually every leading insect pest in the world. _____

9. After they understand an insect's particular system of using the pheromone, researchers hope to use it to control insect behavior. _____

10. Scientists now do not understand what process enables males to identify and respond to the pheromone. _____

## Subordinate (Dependent) Clauses:
## Functions in Sentences

Exercise 1–13

NAME _____ SCORE _____

DIRECTIONS    Classify each italicized subordinate clause in the following sentences as a subject (S), a complement (C), or a modifier (M). As you do the exercise, notice the subordinator that introduces the clauses.

EXAMPLE
Fire-ant hills in Texas have been virtually wiped out by a man-made

chemical *that regulates insect development.*                          *M*

1. *Because fire-ant hills are entrenched in 230 million acres in nine southern states,* the success in Texas is modest.          _____

2. Researchers, however, believe *that their success with fire ants will be repeated with other insects.*          _____

3. The man-made substance *which retards fire ants' development* affects only fire ants.          _____

4. *When it is introduced into the environment,* it is completely safe for all living creatures except fire ants.          _____

5. *That they may be able to attack other insects with similar artificial weapons* gives researchers great hope.          _____

6. Researchers know exactly *what they want.*          _____

7. They want weapons *over which they have total control.*          _____

8. Researchers also use artificial and natural pheromones to train dogs *who then sniff out potentially damaging insects.*          _____

9. This has been a particularly effective tactic *when it has been used to discover pests in stored food.*          _____

10. A novel application of pheromones has been to attract not pests but predators *which prey on the pests.*          _____

11. Farmers and gardeners know *that the spined soldier bug will eat practically any insect.*          _____

12. Luring this predator with pheromones is a mixed blessing *because the bug is voracious and nonselective.*          _____

13. However, most farmers think *its benefits outweigh its draw-backs.*

————————

14. *After it has done its job,* the soldier bug poses no other problem to the environment.

————————

15. It hibernates all winter, lays eggs, and returns the next spring and summer *when it is most needed.*

————————

16. *Whoever devises a commercial mixture for attracting an assortment of natural predators* will be assured of commercial success.

————————

17. Research into insect brain function has generated a new class of antibiotics *that kill parasites but not their hosts.*

————————

18. The result is a weapon against dangerously embedded parasites, such as animal heartworm, *that is safe, incredibly fast-working, and powerful.*

————————

19. We can see the benefits of such a chemical *if we contrast it with the infamous DDT.*

————————

20. DDT has an effect on insect brains similar to that of the new antibiotics, but *when it is loosed on the environment,* it attacks the brains of mammals as well.

————————

## 2

**In general, write complete sentences.**

Once you become aware of the parts of the sentence (Section **1**), you will sense the difference between a complete sentence and an incomplete one, a fragment. Although fragments are usually not a clear way to communicate with your reader, they may be effective, and even necessary, in a few sentences, particularly in answering questions, stating exclamations, and recording dialogue.

QUESTION AND FRAGMENT ANSWER What policy governs the National Park Service management of parks? *The policy of natural management, of not interfering with the workings of nature.*

SENTENCE AND FRAGMENT EXCLAMATION An infestation of pinkeye temporarily blinded and caused the deaths of 107 bighorn sheep in Yellowstone National Park. *How terrible!*

DIALOGUE A park official explained, "The fundamental question is what role humans should play in a natural environment. The park service must decide how much human activity a park's ecosystem can absorb. At present the ecosystem is nearly overwhelmed by visitors. Over a million a year!"

Fragments are used in dialogue simply to record people's speech patterns. The fragment used in answering a question or in stating an exclamation allows an idea to be communicated without repeating most of the preceding sentence.

Effective sentence fragments, like those used in answering questions, stating exclamations, and recording dialogue, are written intentionally. The very shortness of most fragments calls attention to them; thus they are used for emphasis. Ineffective fragments, however, are rarely written intentionally. Rather they are written because the writer could not sense the difference between a sentence part and a complete sentence.

**2a Learn to sense the difference between a phrase, especially a verbal phrase, and a sentence.**

Any sentence becomes a fragment when the verb is replaced by a verbal.

SENTENCE Antibiotics *are* an effective treatment of pinkeye.

VERBAL PHRASES Antibiotics *being* an effective treatment of pinkeye.
Antibiotics *having been* an effective treatment of pinkeye.

Sometimes a prepositional phrase is incorrectly punctuated as a sentence, usually because the phrase is either very long or is introduced by words like *for example* or *such as.*

| | |
|---|---|
| SENTENCE | Park rangers could have tranquilized the sheep and treated them with medication for pinkeye. |
| PREPOSITIONAL PHRASE | *For* example, *with* antibiotics and eye ointment. *In* the mountains *with* eyes swollen shut *by* pinkeye. |

An appositive is a word or word group following a noun or pronoun that defines or restates the noun or pronoun. An appositive cannot stand alone as a sentence.

| | |
|---|---|
| SENTENCE | The park service labels such treatment "unnatural." |
| APPOSITIVE | An example of man's unnecessary intrusion on nature. |

Another common fragment is caused by the separation of the two parts of a compound predicate.

| | |
|---|---|
| SENTENCE | The disease culled the least resistant animals from the herd. |
| PREDICATE | And *left* stronger animals to pass on their disease resistance to their progeny. |

## 2b  Learn to sense the difference between a subordinate clause and a sentence.

Any sentence can be made a fragment by inserting a subordinator before or after the subject. (See the list of subordinators in the Appendix.)

| | |
|---|---|
| SENTENCE | The park service makes no official differentiation between "good" and "bad" in nature. |
| SUBORDINATE CLAUSE | *Because* the park service makes no official differentiation between "good" and "bad" in nature. |

## 2c  Learn the best way to correct a fragment.

An obvious way to correct a fragment is to supply the missing part, to make the fragment into a sentence. But most fragments are best corrected by reconnecting them to the sentences they belong with. Examine the following paragraph, in which the word groups that are likely to be incorrectly written as fragments are printed in italics.

> *When elk and deer die of starvation in the winter*, they provide critical spring forage for the grizzly bear and other carnivores. *By not interfering in the deaths of animals*, the park service allows the complex processes of the ecosystem to continue uninterrupted *and encourages nature's ability to keep its resources in balance*.

**Sentences and Fragments**                                    Exercise 2–3

NAME _____ SCORE _____

DIRECTIONS   In the following paragraphs are ten fragments of various types—prepositional and verbal phrases, subordinate clauses, appositives, and parts of compound predicates. First, circle the numbers that stand in front of fragments; then revise the fragments by attaching them to the sentences they belong with. (See **12b** and **12d** if you need help with punctuation.)

[1]In the early part of the century. [2]Wolves and cougars were considered an embodiment of evil. [3]Because of their violent methods of killing and because they took game that human hunters wanted. [4]By the 1930s the wolf had been exterminated, and the cougar population was severely depleted in the Yellowstone ecosystem. [5]Human manipulation of the environment has continued. [6]In the 1960s Yellowstone Park rangers killed thousands of elk. [7]Because the elk had overpopulated the range. [8]Grizzlies, when they interfere with humans in the park, are still trapped. [9]And moved, and sometimes shot. [10]This human interference may have severe long-term implications. [11]Perhaps nothing less than the restructuring of the gene pool. [12]Some biologists believe that such culling out of bears with aggressive tendencies may result in a weaker breeding stock. [13]That lacks the necessary and natural aggression.

[14]The wolves are still absent from Yellowstone Park. [15]Which points up one of the flaws in the department's philosophy of natural management. [16]Several critical parts of the ecosystem are missing. [17]The wolf, for example, was integral to the Yellowstone ecosystem. [18]Both because it preyed largely on weak and sick animals. [19]And because it kept down the deer and elk populations. [20]Helping to prevent such things as a massive winter die-off because of populations grown beyond the carrying capacity of their winter range.

## Fragments: Effective and Ineffective                    Exercise 2–4

NAME _____ SCORE _____

DIRECTIONS   The following paragraphs include three effective fragments and ten ineffective fragments, incomplete sentences that the writer did not plan. Circle the number
that stands in front of each fragment. Then revise the ineffective fragments either by re-
writing them as complete sentences or by connecting them to the sentences they belong
with. (See **12b** or **12d** if you need help with punctuation.) Place an X by the number of
each effective fragment.

¹Although it covers 2.2 million acres. ²Larger than the combined areas of
Rhode Island and Delaware. ³Yellowstone Park makes up less than half of the
Yellowstone ecosystem. ⁴Only two parks, Denali and Olympic, have reasonably
complete ecosystems. ⁵Because most parks embody only a portion of their ecosystems. ⁶The wildlife have needs outside the park boundaries. ⁷Each winter, the elk,
deer, sheep, and bison moving from summer pastures to the lower elevation and
more moderate climate of a winter range. ⁸There the wind sweeping much of the
snow off and leaving a snow crust that can be pawed through. ⁹But now the winter range is not always accessible. ¹⁰Because private ranchers control much of it.
¹¹For example, the 16,000 elk in the northern herd winter on neighboring
ranches. ¹²Destroying the haystacks and forage the ranchers have set aside for
their livestock.

¹³The 2,000 bison in Yellowstone Park present special problems. ¹⁴Unimpressed
by boundaries and oblivious to fences, they often wander into nearby towns.
¹⁵What an unforgettable memory for a winter tourist! ¹⁶Volkswagen-sized beasts
grazing unconcernedly on the grassy road medians as cars rush by. ¹⁷Park rangers
try to drive the bison into the park. ¹⁸Where some may starve because food is so

difficult to obtain. [19]Stubborn animals are shot. [20]Their meat, perhaps, to be auctioned off.

[21]The  bison also are carriers of brucellosis. [22]A disease to which they are immune but which causes domestic livestock to abort. [23]Angry ranchers think of the bison as serious threats to their way of life. [24]And as threats made more difficult to accept because the park officials refuse to treat the bison for a disease that is naturally caused.

## 3

**Learn the standard ways to link two closely related main clauses.**

In Section **1** you studied the two main ways to expand a sentence—subordination and coordination. Subordination often requires the use of a comma or commas for the subordinated addition to the main clause. (See also **12b** and **12d**.)

Coordination, too, requires a comma when two main clauses are connected by a coordinating conjunction—*and, but, or, nor, for, so,* and *yet.*

> The reproductive rate of grizzly bears is tied directly to the amount of available food**,** *but* park authorities are fiercely opposed to feeding the bears.

If the coordinating conjunction is removed, the two main clauses may still be connected; however, the standard mark of punctuation between the two clauses then becomes the semicolon.

> The reproductive rate of grizzly bears is tied directly to the amount of available food**;** park authorities are fiercely opposed to feeding the bears.

Even if another type of connective—a conjunctive adverb like *then, therefore,* or *however*—is inserted between the main clauses, a semicolon is still the standard mark of punctuation to be used after the first main clause.

> The reproductive rate of grizzly bears is tied directly to the amount of available food**;** *however,* park authorities are fiercely opposed to feeding the bears.

If a comma is used between two main clauses not connected by a coordinating conjunction, the sentence contains a *comma splice.* In other words, the comma has been made to perform a function that standard usage has not given it.

> COMMA SPLICE   The reproductive rate of grizzly bears is tied directly to the amount of available food, park authorities are fiercely opposed to feeding the bears.

> COMMA SPLICE   The reproductive rate of grizzly bears is tied directly to the amount of available food, however, park authorities are fiercely opposed to feeding the bears.

Some writers feel they can avoid comma splices by omitting all commas from their writing. And they are correct. But in so doing they violate standard practices of punctuation even further. Instead of writing comma-splice sentences, they write *fused* (or run-together) sentences. And fused sentences are even more ineffective than comma-splice sentences because they are more difficult to understand at first reading.

> FUSED SENTENCE   In Yellowstone Park garbage dumps were a chief source of food for grizzlies park authorities closed those dumps in 1968.

**3a The standard punctuation of two main clauses not connected by a coordinating conjunction is the semicolon.**

In 1967 two young women were killed in Yellowstone Park by bears who were accustomed to feeding on garbage; the tragedy hastened the process of closing garbage dumps in the park. [The semicolon acts like the fulcrum of a seesaw, with the idea in one main clause balanced by the idea in the other.]

There are two other ways to avoid a comma splice or fused sentence.

TWO SENTENCES     In 1967 two young women were killed in Yellowstone Park by bears who were accustomed to feeding on garbage. The tragedy hastened the process of closing garbage dumps in the park. [Placing the two ideas in separate sentences emphasizes them equally.]

SUBORDINATION     Because two women were killed in 1967 in Yellowstone Park by bears who were accustomed to feeding on garbage, the process of closing garbage dumps in the park was hastened. [Subordinating one of the ideas establishes a cause and effect relationship.]

**3b The standard punctuation of two main clauses connected by a conjunctive adverb or a transitional phrase is the semicolon.**

Most biologists agree that Yellowstone Park can support a population of thirty to seventy grizzlies; *however,* a few biologists sharply disagree.
They argue that the park could support many more grizzlies; *in fact,* they argue that the park service should feed the grizzlies in order to expand the population.

Notice that a conjunctive adverb or a transitional phrase may also be placed in the middle of a main clause and that the standard marks of punctuation are then commas.

The park's philosophy of natural management, *however,* required eliminating the dumps.
A few biologists believe, *in fact,* that the garbage dumps had become a part of the bears' ecosystem.

You may need to consult or even memorize the list of commonly used conjunctive adverbs and transitional phrases in the Appendix.

**3c The standard mark of punctuation for a divided quotation made up of two main clauses is the semicolon or an end mark (a period, question mark, or exclamation point).**

"Natural management is idealistic and impossible," said the biologist; "by causing the garbage dumps to be eliminated, it may even have harmed the grizzly population."
"Natural management is idealistic and impossible," said the biologist. "By causing the garbage dumps to be eliminated, it may even have harmed the grizzly population."

## Comma Splices and Fused Sentences

Exercise 3–1

NAME _____ SCORE _____

DIRECTIONS   In each of the following sentences insert an inverted caret (**V**) between main clauses. Then indicate in the first blank at the right whether the sentence is correctly punctuated according to standard practice (*C*), contains a comma splice (*CS*), or is fused (*F*). Correct each error by the method you consider best, showing in the second blank whether you have used subordination (sub.), a period (**.**), a semicolon (**;**), or a comma plus a coordinating conjunction (conj.). Use each type of punctuation at least once.

EXAMPLE

Although ^ some biologists wanted the Yellowstone Park service

to eliminate the garbage dumps ˅ gradually the park

service chose to close them all immediately in 1968.      *F*      *sub*

1. Bears who were displaced by the closing of the dumps began wandering into campgrounds and developed areas, officials relocated, transported, or, when necessary, killed them outright.      _____   _____

2. By about 1973, the need to do so declined a natural population of bears that could live on the ordinary fare of roots, berries, and ground squirrels had developed.      _____   _____

3. What did achieving this natural balance cost, how many bears were killed?      _____   _____

4. The park service claims it had to kill 37 grizzlies; some critics put the count at 189.      _____   _____

5. The number killed is significant some biologists believe that the killing led to the present decline in numbers of grizzlies in Yellowstone Park.      _____   _____

6. Killing many bears and withdrawing an important food source affected the entire population some biologists believe the present small population will be unable to recover.      _____   _____

7. Before the garbage dumps were closed, the average litter size was 2.2 cubs after the dumps were closed, the average litter size dropped to 1.9 cubs. _____ _____

8. Proponents of natural management say the decrease is unimportant, critics, however, argue that it is. _____ _____

9. An already small population of grizzlies needs a strong reproductive rate because the decline each year steadily decreases the breeding population for later years. _____ _____

10. The breeding population ultimately becomes too small to keep the total population at a steady number when that happens, the population is doomed. _____ _____

**Comma Splices and Fused Sentences**                    Exercise 3-2

NAME _____  SCORE _____

DIRECTIONS    In each of the following sentences insert an inverted caret (**V**) between main clauses. Then indicate in the blank whether the sentence contains a comma splice (*CS*) or is fused (*F*). Correct each comma splice or fused sentence by using one of the four possible methods: subordination, an end mark (two sentences), a semicolon, or a comma plus a coordinating conjunction. (Be prepared to discuss the effect each of the methods has on the ideas in the two clauses: to emphasize one or both ideas, to balance one idea with another, to establish a relationship between the ideas.) Use each method twice, on two different sentences.

EXAMPLE
Natural management has been heralded as the ultimate concept in

wildlife management, <sup>V</sup> however, in recent years it has received in-

creased criticism.                                              _CS_

*natural management has been heralded as...;*
*however, in recent years... criticism.*

1. The National Park Service adopted the concept of natural management, it wanted to create parks that were as free as possible from human intervention.                    _____

2. "The goal is to create parks that illustrate primitive America," explained one biologist "if we do not interfere, the ecosystem will sustain itself naturally."                    _____

3. Reaching its goals has been difficult for the park service, the forces of the second half of the twentieth century press on parks from every side. _____

4. Despite the pressures, the park service steadfastly clings to its management philosophy, for example, it continues to reject suggestions that it should feed the grizzly population in Yellowstone Park. _____

5. The park service believes that the grizzly population is decreasing because of poachers, also it blames the destruction of grizzly habitat for the decreases. _____

6. The park service considered garbage dumps as unacceptable intrusions by humans on the grizzly population, indeed, the service eliminated the dumps in order to protect, not to damage, the grizzlies. _____

# 4

## Master the uses and forms of adjectives and adverbs.

Both adjectives and adverbs function as modifiers; that is, they make the meaning of the words they refer to more exact. In the examples below, notice that the meaning becomes clearer and more detailed as modifiers are added.

> The naturalist photographed the trumpeter swan.
> The *amateur* naturalist photographed the *rare* trumpeter swan.
> The *completely camouflaged amateur* naturalist *slowly* photographed the *rare and once endangered* trumpeter swan.

The adjectives—*camouflaged, amateur, rare, endangered*—modify the noun subject, *naturalist,* and the noun complement, *trumpeter swan.* Typically, adjectives modify nouns and sometimes pronouns. The adverbs—*completely* and *once*—modify the adjectives *camouflaged* and *endangered* and the verb *photographed.* Typically, adverbs modify verbs and modifiers (both adjectives and adverbs).

A modern dictionary will show you the current usage of adjectives and adverb modifiers. But here are a few guidelines.

### 4a Use adverbs to modify verbs, adjectives, and other adverbs.

> Trumpeter swans have *always* been an inspiring sight. [*Always* modifies the verb, *have been.*]
> The world's largest swan is *pure* white and *often* weighs 30 to 35 pounds. [*Pure* modifies the adjective modifier, *white; often* modifies the verb, *weighs.*]
> *Surprisingly often* an endangered species manages to recover from near extinction. [*Often* modifies the verb, *manages; surprisingly* modifies the adverb modifier, *often.*]

### 4b Distinguish between adjectives used as complements and adverbs used to modify verbs. (See also 1c.)

Adjectives, like nouns, are used as complements after linking verbs like *be, appear, become, feel, look, seem, smell,* and *taste.* Such adjective complements refer to the subjects of their clauses.

> Although locating trumpeter swans is *difficult,* naturalists are *determined* to count
>
> the population.
>
> [*Difficult* refers to the subject of the subordinate clause, *locating; determined* refers to the subject of the main clause, *naturalists.*]

They believe that they are *successful* because they use airplanes to survey the nesting

sites.

[*Successful* refers to the subject of the subordinate clause, *they.*]

*Successful* are their methods.

[For emphasis, the complement, *successful,* comes before but still refers to the subject, *methods.*]

A sensory verb like *feel, taste,* or *look* is followed by an adverb instead of an adjective when the modifier refers to the verb.

> The biologist looked *gloomily* out the window, his efforts to count the swans having been thwarted by heavy clouds. [Compare "The biologist looked gloomy," in which *gloomy,* an adjective complement, modifies the subject, *biologist.*]

A linking verb followed by an adjective complement may also be modified by one or more adverbs, coming either before or after.

> The biologist *suddenly* looked gloomy *yesterday.* [Both adverbs modify *looked.*]

## 4c Use the appropriate forms of adjectives and adverbs for the comparative and the superlative.

Many adjectives and adverbs change form to indicate degree. The comparative degree (a comparison of two things) is usually formed by adding *er* to the modifier or by putting *more* or *less* before the modifier. The superlative degree (a comparison of three or more things) is formed by adding *est* to the modifier or by putting the word *most* or *least* before the modifier. Some desk dictionaries show the *er* and *est* endings for those adjectives and adverbs that form their comparative and superlative degrees in this way (for example, *old, older, oldest*). Most dictionaries show the changes for highly irregular modifiers (for example, *good, better, best*). As a rule of thumb, most one-syllable adjectives and most two-syllable adjectives ending in a vowel sound (*tidy, narrow*) form the comparative with *er* and the superlative with *est.* Most adjectives of two or more syllables and most adverbs form the comparative by adding the word *more* (*less*) and the superlative by adding the word *most* (*least*).

> NONSTANDARD  Counting the population of swans from the air was *more easier* than slogging through swamps. [The *er* shows the comparative degree; *more* is superfluous.]
>
> STANDARD  Counting the population of swans from the air was *easier* than slogging through swamps.

NONSTANDARD  It was the *better* prepared of all the U.S. Fish and Wildlife Service's attempts to save an endangered species.  [*Better* is used to compare only two things.]

STANDARD  It was the *best* prepared of all the U.S. Fish and Wildlife Service's attempts to save an endangered species.

**Note:**  Not all adjectives and adverbs have a form for the comparative and superlative degrees. Most adjectives made from nouns— like *governmental*, for example—have no other forms. (One does not say that something is "more governmental" than something else or that something is the "most governmental" of all.) Other modifiers, like *perfect* and *unique,* are in themselves an expression of the superlative degree.

## 4d  Avoid the awkward substitution of a noun form for an adjective.

We correctly use many nouns as modifiers of other nouns—*soap* opera, *book* club, *swan* song—because there are no suitable adjective forms available. But when adjective forms are available, you should avoid awkward noun substitutes.

AWKWARD  *Education* television presented a special on the trumpeter swan.

BETTER  *Educational* television presented a special on the trumpeter swan.

## 4e  Avoid the double negative.

The term *double negative* refers to the use of two negatives to express a single negation.

NONSTANDARD  He did *not* have *no* memory of the swans.  [double negative: *not* and *no*]

STANDARD  He did *not* have a memory of the swans.  [single negative: *not*]
OR
He had *no* memory of the swans.  [single negative: *no*]

Another redundant construction occurs when a negative such as *not, nothing,* or *without* is combined with *hardly, barely,* or *scarcely.*

NONSTANDARD  He *couldn't hardly* stop talking about the return of the swans.

STANDARD  He could hardly stop talking about the return of the swans.

NONSTANDARD  The park was established *without scarcely* any opposition.

STANDARD  The park was established with scarcely any opposition.

## Adjectives and Adverbs                    Exercise 4–2

NAME _____ SCORE _____

DIRECTIONS   While preserving the meaning, rewrite each of the following sentences, changing the italicized adjective to an adverb and the italicized noun to a verb or an adjective, as in the example below. (You will have to make a few other changes in the sentence in addition to changing the italicized words.)

EXAMPLE
The swan sounded a *threatening honk* as the fox approached his nest.

*The swan honked threateningly as the fox approached his nest.*

1. The swan, called a "cob," took *confident steps* to the edge of the nest.

2. Immediately the swan's threatening behavior made a *strong impression* on the fox.

3. To confuse the swan was obviously the fox's *main intention.*

4. Instead of attacking the swan, the fox lay down and demonstrated an *unexpected passivity.*

## 5

**Master the case forms of pronouns to show their functions in sentences.**

The form that a noun or pronoun has in a sentence indicates its function, or case: *subjective*, *objective*, or *possessive*. Nouns usually change their form for only one case—the possessive. (In Section **15** you will study the ways the apostrophe indicates that change.) Certain pronouns, however, change their form for each case, and you must be aware of the various forms if you want to use these pronouns correctly.

| SUBJECTIVE | OBJECTIVE | POSSESSIVE |
|---|---|---|
| I | me | my, mine |
| we | us | our OR ours |
| he, she | him, her | his, her, OR hers |
| you | you | your OR yours |
| they | them | their OR theirs |
| who OR whoever | whom OR whomever | whose |

**5a A pronoun has the same case form in a compound or an appositive construction as it would have if it were used alone.**

When you are using a single pronoun, you may have no difficulty choosing the right case.

    *I* watched the *National Geographic* special with *her.*

But when other pronouns or nouns are added, you may become confused about case and write, "Him and me watched the special with Sam and she." If you have a tendency to make such errors in case, think of the function each pronoun would have if it were used in a separate sentence.

    *He* watched the special.   [NOT *Him* watched the special.]
    *I* watched the special.   [NOT *Me* watched the special.]
    *I* watched the special with *her.*   [NOT *I* watched the special with *she.*]

Then you will be more likely to write the correct case forms:

    *He* and *I* watched the *National Geographic* special with Sam and *her.*

**5b The case of a pronoun depends on its use in its own clause.**

When a sentence has only one clause, the function of the pronoun may seem clear to you.

    *Who* is sponsoring the Save the Manatee Club?  [*Who* is the subject of the verb, *is sponsoring.*]

But when another clause is added, you must be careful to determine the pronoun's use in its own clause.

> I know *who* is sponsoring the Save the Manatee Club. [Although *who* introduces a clause that acts as the direct object of the verb *know*, in its own clause *who* is the subject of the verb *is sponsoring*.]

An implied rather than a stated clause often follows the subordinating conjunctions *than* or *as*.

> She did as well in the training *as* I. [The implied meaning is "as I did."]
> John knows you better *than* me. [The implied meaning is "than John knows me."]

## 5c In formal writing use *whom* for all objects. (See also 5b.)

> The biologist *whom* they named to head the project has resigned. [object of the verb *named*]
> The scientist to *whom* they assigned the project has resigned. [object of the preposition *to*]

## 5d In general, use the possessive case before a verbal used as a noun.

As you may remember from Section **1d**, a gerund is a verbal that ends in *ing* and is used as a noun. The possessive case is used before a gerund, which acts as a noun, but not before a participle, which also sometimes has an *ing* ending but acts as an adjective.

> Bob's parents got tired of *his* complaining that the manatees were destroying his fishing nets. [*Complaining* is a gerund and functions as the object of the preposition *of*.]
> That afternoon the warden found *him* working on a huge hole in one of his nets. [*Working* is a participle modifying *him*.]

## 5e Use the objective case for direct and indirect objects, for objects of prepositions, and for both subjects and objects of infinitives (*to* plus the verb).

> The other fishermen gave *me* instructions for repairing the net.
> Between *you* and *me*, I was too tired to remember *them*.
> As a result it was easy for *him* to make the repairs but impossible for *me*. ["To do it" is implied after "for me."]

## 5f Use the subjective case for subjects and for subject complements.

> *She* and *I* watched the manatees feeding in the canal.
> The owner of the land on this side of the canal is *he*. [You may find it more comfortable to avoid using the pronoun as a complement. If so, write, "He is the owner of the land on this side of the canal."]

**5g Add *self* to a pronoun (*himself, herself, itself, ourselves, themselves*) when a reflexive or an intensive pronoun is needed.**

A reflexive pronoun follows the verb and refers to the subject; an intensive pronoun emphasizes the noun or pronoun it refers to.

> I blamed *myself* for not seeing the manatee.  [*Myself* refers back to *I*.]
> I *myself* will take the blame for not seeing the manatee.  [*Myself* intensifies *I*.]

The pronoun ending in *self* is not used as a subject or an object unless it refers to the same person as the subject.

> The other fishermen asked me to represent them.  [NOT *myself* and *themselves*]
> He blamed *himself* for not being aware of the manatees in this area of the river.  [*Himself*, the object, refers to the same person as *he*, the subject.]

# 6

**Make a verb agree in number with its subject; make a pronoun agree in number with its antecedent.**

Subjects and verbs must have the same number: a singular subject requires a singular verb, and a plural subject requires a plural verb. (Remember that an *s* ending shows plural number for the subject but singular number for the verb.)

SINGULAR    The worker *uses* gill nets.

PLURAL    The workers *use* gill nets.

Similarly, a pronoun must agree in number with its antecedent, the noun or pronoun it refers to.

SINGULAR    The *fisherman* carefully mends *his* nets after *he* returns from *his* day of fishing.

PLURAL    The *fishermen* carefully mend *their* nets after *they* return from *their* day of fishing.

## 6a The verb agrees in number with its subject.

**(1) The verb must be matched with its subject, not with the object of a preposition or with some other word that comes between the subject and verb.**

Unfortunately the *combination* of fishermen and gill nets *has proved* fatal to many whales.    [*Combination*, not *gill nets*, is the subject.]

Many *whales*, in addition to food fish, *lose* their lives in gill nets.    [Most writers agree that nouns following expressions like "together with," "in addition to," and "along with" do not affect the number of the subject. Notice that the whole phrase is set off with commas.]

Subjects and verbs that end in *sk* or *st* must be carefully matched. Because of our tendency to leave out certain difficult sounds in speaking, many of us also fail in our writing to add a needed *s* to a verb or a subject ending in *sk* or *st*.

The *biologists study* the safest way to rescue the whale.
The *fisherman asks* for the biologist's help.

**(2) Subjects joined by *and* are usually plural.**

The *biologist* and her *assistant work* frantically to free the whale.

**Exception:**    If the two subjects refer to the same person or thing, or if *each* or *every* comes before the subject, the verb is singular.

The biologist and leader of the Whale Research Group *directs* the rescue efforts.
Every biologist and every fisherman *recognizes* the danger inherent in the rescue efforts.

**(3) Singular subjects joined by *or, nor, either . . . or,* and *neither . . . nor* usually take a singular verb.**

Neither a boat nor a net *is* likely to survive an encounter with a whale.

**Exception:** If one subject is singular and one plural, the verb is matched with the nearer subject, or the sentence is revised to avoid the agreement difficulty.

Neither the boat nor the nets *survive* the encounter with the whale.

OR

The nets *do* not *survive* the encounter with the whale, and neither *does* the boat.

**(4) When the subject follows the verb (as in sentences beginning with *there is* or *there are*), special care is needed to match up subject and verb.**

There *is* a *ring* of fish nets around the Labrador Sea.
There *are thousands* of fish nets in the Labrador Sea.
*Included* among the nets *are thousands* of expensive cod traps.

**(5) The number of a relative pronoun (*who, whom, which, that*) used as the subject of a clause is determined by the number of its antecedent.**

Attached to the cod traps are leader nets that *funnel* fish into the traps.

[*Nets*, the antecedent, is plural; therefore *that* is considered plural.]

Every fisherman who *uses* these traps must learn how to deploy the leader nets.

[*Fisherman*, the antecedent, is singular; therefore *who* is considered singular.]

**(6) Pronoun subjects like *each, one, anybody, everybody, either,* and *neither* usually take singular verbs.**

*Each* of the cod traps *costs* more than $10,000.
*Everybody* with an interest in whales also *wants* to protect fishermen from being harmed, both physically and financially, by the whales.

Pronoun subjects like *all, any, half, most, none,* and *some* may take either a singular or plural verb; the context determines the choice of the verb form.

*All* of the rescue team members *understand* the fishermen's problems with whales.
*All* of their interest *is* not just on behalf of the whales.

**(7) In general, use a singular verb with collective nouns regarded as a unit.**

*The number* of whales killed by nets *has decreased* in recent years.   [*The number* is usually regarded as a unit.]
A *number* of humpback whales *are killed* by nets each year.   [A *number* usually refers to individuals.]
The *team is* on the bus.
The *team are* in their dormitories.

**(8) The verb agrees with the subject, not the subject complement, but it is usually best to avoid disagreement of verb and subject complement by revising the sentence to eliminate the linking verb.**

AWKWARD    My usual *snack* at whale rescue attempts *is* sardines and Perrier. [The verb *is* correctly agrees with the subject *snack*, but the disagreement of verb and subject complement seems awkward to many writers.]

REVISED    At whale rescue attempts I usually snack on sardines and Perrier. [Replacing the linking verb with an action verb eliminates the problem of disagreement of verb and subject complement.]

**(9) Nouns like *news*, *civics*, and *measles*, even though they have the s ending, take singular verbs. Single titles, even if plural in form, are considered singular in number, as are words referred to as words.**

The dictionary is the best guide for determining if nouns like these, which have plural endings, take singular verbs.

*Economics* sometimes *determines* a fisherman's reaction to a whale caught in his net. [The dictionary describes *economics* as singular.]
*The Singing Whales* is an important book about humpback whales.
"Ethnobotanists" *is* often misspelled. Do you know what it means?

**6b A pronoun agrees in number and gender with its antecedent** (see also **27b**).

**(1) Use a singular pronoun to refer to such antecedents as *each*, *everyone*, *nobody*, *one*, *a person*, *a woman*, *a man*.**

*Each* of the women takes *her* turn viewing the whales.

Today writers make every effort to avoid sexism in the use of personal pronouns. Whereas writers once wrote, "Each of us should do his best," they now try to avoid using the masculine pronoun to refer to both men and women. To avoid sexism, some writers give both masculine and feminine pronoun references.

Each of us took *his* or *her* turn.
Each of us took *his/her* turn. [Compare "Each of us took *a* turn."]

Other writers prefer to use *one's* in place of his or her.

One should take *one's* turn.

Perhaps the easiest way to avoid sexism is to use plural pronouns and antecedents unless a feminine or a masculine pronoun is clearly called for.

All of them took *their* turns.
All of us took *our* turns.
            BUT
Each of the women took *her* turn.

**(2) A plural pronoun is used to refer to two or more antecedents joined by *and;* a singular pronoun is used to refer to two or more antecedents joined by *or* or *nor.***

> Bené *and* Loisteen have taken *their* turns at the observation tower.
> Neither Bené *nor* Loisteen wants *her* turn to end.

If it is necessary to have one singular and one plural antecedent, make the pronoun agree with the closer antecedent.

> Neither Bené nor her *friends* know when *their* turns will end.

Again, as with the verb (see **6a(3)**), it is sometimes best to rephrase to avoid the pronoun agreement difficulty.

> Bené does not know when *her* turn will end, nor do her friends know when theirs will end.

**(3) Use either a singular or a plural pronoun to refer to a collective noun like *team, staff,* or *group,* depending on whether the noun is considered a unit or a group of individuals.**

> The *staff* of the whale rescue center is planning *its* annual seminar for fisher-men.   [*Staff* is acting as a unit. Notice that both the pronoun and the verb must be the same number.]
> The *staff* are discussing *their* ideas for the seminar.   [The individuals on the staff are being referred to; thus both the pronoun and the verb are plural.]

When the collective noun is considered plural, as *staff* is in the preceding example, many writers prefer to use *staff members* rather than a noun that looks singular in number.

> The *staff members* agree about their responsibility to educate fishermen about freeing whales caught in nets.

The pronoun that refers to such antecedents as *all, most, half, none,* and *some* is usually plural, but in a few contexts it can be singular.

> *All* of them took *their* turns.
> *Most* of the viewers saw more than *they* ever had before.
> *Most* of their preparation proved *itself* worthwhile.

**Agreement of Subject and Verb**                          Exercise 6–2

NAME _____ SCORE _____

DIRECTIONS   In the following sentences the subjects and verbs are in agreement. Rewrite the sentences, making all italicized singular subjects and verbs plural and all italicized plural subjects and verbs singular. (You will need to drop or add an article—*a, an, the*—before the subject and sometimes change another word or two to make the sentence sound right.) When your answers have been checked, you may want to read the sentences aloud to accustom your ear to the forms that agree with each other.

EXAMPLE
In the 1980s different *kinds* of fish *became* more popular as luxury foods.

*In the 1980s a different kind of fish is becoming more popular as a luxury food.*

1. As a consequence, inshore *fishermen are* able to make money.

2. There *is* a huge *increase* in the number of nets now in the water.

3. Fishing *pressure* on inshore waters *is* increasing dramatically.

4. At the same time, a *whale finds* fewer of its natural foods in offshore waters.

5. For example, humpback *whales* usually *feed* on capelin.

6. But the *capelin is decreasing* in number.

7. Consequently, humpback *whales are moving* closer to shore to feed.

8. The *whales move* closer to shore and inevitably *encounter* the fishermen's nets.

9. *Conflicts* between the needs of the fishermen and the needs of the whale *are* inevitable.

10. The whale rescue *group is* trying to help whales and fishermen coexist and thus help keep the balance between humans and nature.

## 7

**Use the appropriate forms of verbs.**

You will remember from Section **1** that the verb is the most essential part of the basic formula for a sentence. Sentences may be written without subjects—though few are, of course. And sentences are frequently written without complements. But without a verb, there is no sentence. To use this essential part of the sentence correctly, you must know not only how to make the present tense of the verb agree with its subject in number (see Section **6**) but also how to choose the right tense of the verb to express the time you intend: present, past, future, present perfect, past perfect, or future perfect.

Verbs have three main tenses—present, past, and future—and three secondary tenses—present perfect, past perfect, and future perfect. A verb's ending (called its *inflection*) and/or the helping verb or verbs used with it determine the verb's tense.

| | |
|---|---|
| PRESENT | fly |
| PAST | flew |
| FUTURE | will fly |
| PRESENT PERFECT | has OR have flown |
| PAST PERFECT | had flown |
| FUTURE PERFECT | will have flown |

Actually, there are several ways to form a given tense in English. For the past tense, for example, you could write any of these forms:

She *flew* over the island.
She *was flying* over the island.   [continuing past time]
She *did fly* over the island.   [Emphatic: Notice that this one form of the past tense uses *did* plus the present form of the main verb, *fly*.]
She *used to fly* over the island.   [*Used to* (NOT *use to*) suggests an action that no longer occurs.]

Native speakers of English use most forms of a verb correctly without even thinking. But a few verbs and a few verb forms give many of us difficulty; this section concentrates on these forms and these verbs.

**7a Avoid misusing the principal parts of verbs and confusing similar verbs.** (See the Appendix for a list of the principal parts of some of the most common troublesome verbs.)

Most verbs are *regular* verbs; that is, they form their tenses in a predictable way. The *ed* or *d* ending is used for the past tense and perfect tenses, including the past participle form of a verbal. The *ing* ending is used to form the progressive and the present participle.

| | |
|---|---|
| PAST | She *counted* the nesting sites. |
| PRESENT PERFECT | She *has counted* the nesting sites. |
| PAST PERFECT | She *had counted* the nesting sites before dark. |
| FUTURE PERFECT | By this afternoon she *will have counted* the nesting sites. |
| PAST PARTICIPLE | *Having counted* the nesting sites, she returned home. |
| PROGRESSIVE | She *is counting* nesting sites during her flight. [also *was counting, has been counting, had been counting, will have been counting*] |
| PRESENT PARTICIPLE | *Counting* the nesting sites during her flight, she does not notice the rain storms. |

Most dictionaries do not list the principal parts of a regular verb like *count: count* (Present), *counted* (Past and Past Participle), and *counting* (Present Participle).

But if a verb is irregular—that is, if it forms its past tense in some way other than by adding an *ed* or *d*—the dictionary will usually list three or four principal parts.

> *race, raced, racing*  [Notice that only a *d* is added to form the past and past participle; therefore the principal parts may be listed in the dictionary.]
>
> *drive, drove, driven, driving*  [This verb has four listings in the dictionary because it changes form for the past and the past participle as well as the present participle.]

If a verb undergoes no change except for the *ing* ending of the present participle, the dictionary still lists three principal parts because the verb is not a regular verb.

> *burst, burst, bursting*

Be careful to distinguish between verbs with similar spellings like *sit/set, lie/lay,* and *rise/raise.* Remember that *sit, lie,* and *rise* cannot take objects while *set, lay,* and *raise* can.

object          object

Before she *sat* down, she *raised* the window shades and *laid* out her binoculars and

object

bird-watching guidebook.

The binoculars *were set* on a table that *sat* nearby.

Notice in the second example above that the word you expect to be the object of *set*—that is, *binoculars*—is made the subject of the sentence. Thus the subject of the sentence is not acting but is being acted upon. In such a case, the verb is said to be *passive*.

The verbs *set, lay,* and *raise* can be made passive, but the verbs *sit, lie,* and *rise* cannot be because they cannot take objects.

> The binoculars were *set* down.  [NOT *sat down*]
> The binoculars were *laid* down.  [NOT *lain down*]
> The window shade was *raised*.  [NOT *was risen*]

Of these six difficult verbs, the most troublesome combination is *lie/lay* because the past tense form of *lie* is *lay*.

> She *lays* out the binoculars and book and then *lies* down to rest.
> After she had *laid* out the binoculars and book, she *lay* down to rest.

Be careful to add the *d* or *ed* ending to the past and perfect tenses of verbs like *use* and to verbs that end in *k* or *t*.

> She has use*d* the binoculars only once.
> She ask*ed* her friend to help fill the bird feeder.

Be careful to spell correctly the principal parts of verbs like *occur, pay,* and *die* that double or change letters.

> occur, occu*rr*ed, occu*rr*ing
> pay, pa*id,* paying
> die, died, d*y*ing

**7b Make the tense forms of verbs and/or verbals relate logically in a sentence or discussion.**

*Verbs in Main and Subordinate Clauses*  When both the main-clause verb and the subordinate-clause verb refer to action occurring now or to action that could occur at any time, use the present tense for both verbs.

> When naturalists *count* nesting sites, they *are looking* for changes in the bird population.  [*Are looking*, the progressive form, denotes action that takes place in the past, present, and (probably) future.]

When both the main and the subordinate verbs refer to action that occurred at a definite time in the past, use the past tense for both verbs.

> When the eider ducks *were nesting*, they *were* easy prey for foxes.  [*Were nesting*, the past progressive form, suggests an action that took place in the past but on a continuing basis.]

When both the main and the subordinate verbs refer to action that continued for some time but was completed before now, use the present perfect tense for both verbs.

Naturalists *have cautioned* tourists about disturbing the eider ducks during nesting season because some ducks *have abandoned* their nests after being frightened.

Notice that the present tense can be used with the present perfect tense without causing a shift.

Some naturalists *have stopped* allowing any human intrusion during the nesting season because they *do* not *want* the ducks to be disturbed.

Some naturalists *do* not *allow* human intrusion during the nesting season because they *have seen* ducks abandoning their nests after being disturbed.

*Main Verbs and Verbals*    When the main verb's action occurs at the same time as the verbal's, use the present-tense form of the verbal.

Professor Jackson *continues* to study the nesting sites.
Professor Jackson *continued* to study the nesting sites.
*Continuing* to study the nesting sites, Professor Jackson *blames* human intrusion for the decreasing population.
*Continuing* to study the nesting sites, Professor Jackson *blamed* human intrusion for the decreasing population.

On the few occasions when the action of the verbal occurs before the action of the main verb, use the present-perfect tense form of the verbal.

Professor Jackson *would like to have studied* the nesting sites for two years. [Compare "Professor Jackson *wishes she had studied* the nesting sites for two years."]

*Having failed* to receive further government funding, Professor Jackson was forced to end her studies.   [The failure to receive obviously occurred before Jackson ended her studies.]

*Compound Constructions*    Be sure that verb tenses in compound predicates are consistent.

Professor Jackson *failed* to complete her studies of the nesting sites but *collected* very valuable information on the nesting behavior of eider ducks.

### 7c In writing, use the subjunctive mood in the few expressions in which it is still appropriate.

Although the subjunctive mood has been largely displaced by the usual form of the present tense (the *indicative* mood), the subjunctive is still used in a few instances: (1) to express a condition contrary to fact, (2) to state a wish, (3) to indicate clauses of demand, recommendation, or request.

If she *were invited*, Professor Jackson would return to study the nesting sites.
She wishes that she *were* scheduled to return.
The possibility that she will be asked to return requires that she *be prepared* to leave at a moment's notice.

# Verb Forms

Exercise 7–1

NAME _____ SCORE _____

DIRECTIONS   Use your dictionary to look up the principal parts of the verbs listed below. If the verb is a regular verb—that is, adds an *ed* for the past and the past participle and an *ing* for the present participle—write *regular* in the blank. But if the verb is not predictable in its tense forms, write *irregular* in the blank and fill in the two or three other parts that your dictionary lists after the present tense form.

EXAMPLES

buy   *bought buying*   _____*irregular*_____

talk   _____*regular*_____

1. see   _____

2. fish   _____

3. grow   _____

4. write   _____

5. drown   _____

6. send   _____

7. fly   _____

8. pay   _____

9. break   _____

10. choose   _____

11. lead   _____

12. kiss   _____

13. prepare   _____

14. occur   _____

15. take   _____

*VERB FORMS*

16. fill            _____

17. pass           _____

18. permit        _____

19. think         _____

20. carry         _____

21. start         _____

22. surpass     _____

23. hit            _____

24. sail           _____

25. shake        _____

**Troublesome Verbs**                            Exercise 7–2

NAME _____ SCORE _____

DIRECTIONS   In the following sentences cross out the incorrect form or forms of the verb in parentheses and write the correct form in the blank.

EXAMPLE
Eider ducks are cautious, gentle creatures whose feathers

(produce, ~~produced~~) eiderdown.                  *produce*

1. Eiders will nest anywhere they (are, were) protected.                                        _____

2. Vigur, a mile-square island in Iceland's West Fjords, (maintains, maintained) a large eider population.                                  _____

3. The ducks usually (nested, nest) on the same site each season.                                _____

4. An eider creates its nest from the soft feathers, the down, that it (pulls, pulled) from its breast.          _____

5. Vigur's human residents have (achieve, achieved) an admirable balance with nature by collecting the down without harming the ducks.            _____

6. For years, the residents (collect, have collected) the down from returning birds.               _____

7. One resident explains, "If the eiders (hatched, hatch) their eggs successfully one year, they return the next year."                          _____

8. These farmers (succeeded, succeed) because they protect the life cycle of the duck.             _____

9. Other farmers (demonstrated, demonstrate) little sensitivity to the continuing existence of eiders and drive the ducks away as they collect the down.                                     _____

10. Human traffic (poses, posed) the worst threat to eiders.                                        _____

11. Rules that were set down years ago by the residents of Vigur now (helped, help) to protect the eiders.   _____

12. The first rule (prohibited, prohibits) early morning walks.   _____

13. If humans (take, took) early morning walks, they will interrupt the duck's morning baths.   _____

14. Ducks who (are, were) interrupted in their baths might not return to their nests to keep their eggs warm.   _____

15. Eiders never (leave, left) their nests except to take morning baths.   _____

16. The hens (fasted, fast) throughout the four-week incubation period.   _____

17. They (sit, sat, set) patiently on their nests and allow farmers to remove down from the nests.   _____

18. The second rule (was, is) never to backtrack on a hike because backtracking scares ducks off their nests a second time.   _____

19. The last rule (required, requires) humans to watch where they are stepping.   _____

20. Female ducks (are, were) wonderfully camouflaged, and a carelessly placed foot may land on a duck and injure it.   _____

# Verb Forms

NAME _____ SCORE _____

DIRECTIONS   In the following sentences cross out the incorrect form or forms of the verb in parentheses and write the correct form in the blank.

EXAMPLE
I would like (~~to be~~, to have been) a student of the late Hu Jin-Chu, the field naturalist who was China's foremost authority on the giant panda.

*to have been*

1. A million years ago the giant panda (ranges, ranged) widely across China and into what now is Burma.

_____

2. As the climate became drier and people (begin, began) to encroach on its living space, it gradually retreated to the edge of the Tibetan highlands.

_____

3. By historical times the Chinese (realize, realized) that the species was rare.

_____

4. But not until 1975 and 1976 did they (came, come) to the panda's aid.

_____

5. In 1975 and 1976 the Chinese realized that the bamboo that is the staple food for pandas (is, was) dying off.

_____

6. In Sichuan province, which (supported, supports) a large panda population, at least 150 pandas died from starvation.

_____

7. Alarmed, the Chinese (organize, organized) a detailed census; the results suggested that only 1,000 pandas might still be alive.

_____

8. It soon (becomes, became) apparent that the problem was caused by a curious feature of the bamboo itself.

_____

9. Bamboo can reproduce vegetatively; that is, new plants can grow from the roots of other plants. But it only (flowers, flowered) and produces seeds once in its life.    _____

10. After a bamboo plant flowers and (produced, produces) seeds, it dies.    _____

11. The Chinese (learn, learned) that the life cycle of bamboo is very long—about a century in the case of umbrella bamboo.    _____

12. Then, some internal clock (makes, made) all the plants in a given species, young and old, flower and die at the same time.    _____

13. Pandas (eat, ate) about twenty species of bamboo that grow in Sichuan.    _____

14. Large numbers of pandas (die, died) in that area of Sichuan that also experienced a massive die-off of umbrella bamboo.    _____

15. When the Chinese (realize, realized) that the natural growth pattern of bamboo was responsible for the pandas' starvation, they were left knowing that the disaster could recur at any time.    _____

# MANUSCRIPT FORM                                    ms 8

## 8

**Follow acceptable form in writing your paper.**

Your instructor may indicate the exact form needed for preparing your papers. Usually an instructor's guidelines include the points discussed in this section.

### 8a Use proper materials.

If you handwrite your papers, use wide-lined, $8\frac{1}{2}$ × 11-inch theme paper (not torn from a spiral notebook). Write in blue or black ink on one side of the paper only.

If you type your papers, use regular white $8\frac{1}{2}$ × 11-inch typing paper (not onion skin). Use a black ribbon, doublespace between lines, and type on one side of the paper only.

### 8b Arrange the writing on the page in an orderly way.

*Margins and Indention*    Theme paper usually has the margins marked for you. But with unlined paper, leave about $1\frac{1}{2}$ inches at the left margin and at the top of each page after the first one; leave 1 inch at the right margin and at the bottom of each page. Indent the first line of each paragraph about 1 inch, but leave no long gap at the end of any line except the last one in a paragraph.

*Paging*    Use Arabic numbers (2, 3, and so on) in the upper right-hand corner to mark all pages.

*Title*    On the first page, center your title about $1\frac{1}{2}$ inches from the top or on the first ruled line. Do not use either quotation marks or underlining with your title. Capitalize the first word of the title and all other words except articles, prepositions, coordinating conjunctions, and the *to* in infinitives; then begin the first paragraph of your paper on the third line. Leave one blank line between your title and the first paragraph. (Your instructor may ask you to make a title page. If so, you may or may not rewrite the title on the first page of the paper.)

*Identification*    Instructors vary in what information they require and where they want this information placed. The identification will probably include your name, your course title and number, the instructor's name, and the date.

*Punctuation*    Never begin a line of your paper with a comma, a colon, a semicolon, or an end mark of punctuation; never end a line with the first of a pair of brackets, parentheses, or quotation marks.

*Poetry*    If you quote four or more lines of poetry, indent the lines about 1 inch from the left margin and arrange them as in the original. Long prose quotations (more than four lines) should also be indented. (See also **16a**.)

### 8c  Write clearly and neatly.

Write so that your instructor can read your paper easily. Most instructors will accept a composition that has a few words crossed out with substitutions written neatly above, but if your changes are so plentiful that your paper looks messy or is difficult to read, you should recopy the page.

### 8d  Divide words at the ends of lines according to standard practice.

The best way to determine where to divide a word that comes at the end of a line is to check a dictionary for the syllable markings (usually indicated by dots). In general, though, remember these guidelines: never divide a single-syllable word; do not carry over to the next line a syllable like "ed" or one letter of a word; divide a hyphenated word only at the hyphen. Keep in mind that an uneven right margin is expected and that too many divisions at the ends of lines make a paper difficult to read.

### 8e  Proofread your papers carefully.

Always leave a few minutes at the end of an in-class writing assignment for proofreading. Few people write good papers without revising their first drafts. When you need to make a change, draw a straight horizontal line through the part to be deleted, insert a caret (∧) at the point where the addition is to be made, and write the new material above the line. When writing out-of-class papers, try to set your first draft aside for several hours or even for a day so that you can proofread it with a fresh mind.

## 9 / 10

**Use capitals and italics in accordance with current practices.**

A recently published dictionary is the best guide to current standards for capitals, italics, abbreviations, and numbers. There are a few general rules to follow for these problems in mechanics (Sections **9**, **10**, and **11**), but whenever you
are in doubt about how to handle a particular word, you should consult an up-
to-date dictionary.

**9a Capitalize words referring to specific persons, personifications, places,
things, times, organizations, peoples and their languages, religions and their
adherents, holy books, holy days, and words denoting the Supreme Being. Capitalize words derived from proper names and words used as essential parts of
proper names.**

| | |
|---|---|
| PERSONS | Shakespeare, Buddha, Mr. White |
| PERSONIFICATION | John Doe, Uncle Sam, Mother Nature |
| PLACES | Puerto Rico; La Grange, Georgia; Western Avenue; the West (referred to as an area) |
| THINGS | the Statue of Liberty, the Bible, History III, the First World War |
| TIMES | Wednesday, July 4; Thanksgiving; the Age of Enlightenment |
| ORGANIZATIONS | the Peace Corps, the Rotary Club, Phi Beta Kappa |
| RACES AND LANGUAGES | Oriental, English, Latin |
| RELIGIONS AND THEIR ADHERENTS | Islam, Christianity, Judaism, Moslem, Christian, Jew |
| HOLY BOOKS AND HOLY DAYS | Koran, the Bible, Torah, Ramadan, Advent, Passover |
| WORDS DENOTING THE SUPREME BEING | Allah, God, Jehovah |
| WORDS DERIVED FROM PROPER NAMES | Swedish, New Yorker, Anglican |
| ESSENTIAL PARTS OF PROPER NAMES | the Bill of Rights, the Battle of the Bulge, the New River |

**9b In general, capitalize a person's title if it immediately precedes the person's name but not a title that follows the name.**

In the last election, Representative Carl Lockman faced Sam Stewart, former governor, in the race for senator.

Note that usage varies with regard to capitalization of titles of high rank when not followed by a proper name (Senator OR senator). Titles of family members are capitalized only when they are written in combination with a name (Uncle Ben) or when they are used in place of a name (I asked Father for a loan.).

**9c Capitalize the first and last words of a title or subtitle and all other key words within it.**

Professor Moore suggested that I read two articles: "What's a Panda's Thumb?" and "Evolution of the Panda's Thumb."

***Caution:*** Articles—*a, an, the*—and prepositions, coordinating conjunctions, and the *to* in infinitives are not capitalized in a title or subtitle unless they are the first or last words.

**9d Capitalize the pronoun *I* and the interjection *O.***

**9e Capitalize the first word of each sentence, including a quoted sentence.**

Naturalists think that giant pandas may be doomed to extinction.

OR

She said, "Pandas may be doomed to extinction."
"How sad!" exclaimed a student.

**9f Avoid capitals for words that name classes rather than specific persons, places, or things.**

The doctor held a conference at a convention center in the downtown section of our town.

Also avoid the common tendency to capitalize seasons, directions, and general courses of study.

This spring I am going to study botany at a southern university.

**10 To show italics, underline the titles of books, films, plays, works of art, magazines, newspapers, and long poems; the names of ships and airplanes; foreign words; and words, letters, and figures spoken of as such.**

You will immediately think of the word *elegant* when you see Guy Coheleach's paintings of the great cats: *The Chase*, showing a cheetah streaking after a Thomson's gazelle; *Clouded Siesta*, showing a clouded leopard asleep in a tree; and *Manchurian Chase*, showing Siberian tigers cavorting in the snow. All three paintings are reproduced in the text *Modern Wildlife Artists* and in the video-cassette *Painting the Great Cats*.

**Caution:** Do not underline the title of your own essay or overuse italics for emphasis.

## Capitals and Italics

Exercise 9/10–1

NAME _____ SCORE _____

DIRECTIONS    Words in one of each of the following groups should be capitalized and/ or italicized (underlined). Identify the group that needs capitalization and/or italics by writing either *a* or *b* in the blank at the right. Then make the necessary revision for the appropriate group of words.

EXAMPLE
(a) a class at our college                                              _____

(b) 𝒢eology 203 at 𝓂arymount 𝒞ollege                    _____*b*_____

1. (a) responded, "you will see me again"

   (b) responded that you will see me again              _____

2. (a) a course in history

   (b) a course in spanish                                          _____

3. (a) visited another country during the holiday

   (b) visited canada during the christmas holiday      _____

4. (a) reading the last of the mohicans by james fenimore cooper

   (b) reading a novel about pioneer times                _____

5. (a) boarded the queen mary for its last crossing of the atlantic

   (b) boarded an ocean liner for its last transoceanic voyage      _____

6. (a) a story in a weekly magazine about the death of a popular

   rock singer

   (b) "singing is better than any dope," a story in newsweek

   about the death of janis joplin                            _____

7. (a) representative gornto visiting arizona

   (b) the representative from our state                     _____

8. (a) admired the painting by the artist

   (b) admired guernica by picasso _____

9. (a) the pronunciation of the word party as "pah-ty" in the south

   (b) the pronunciation of words in a southern state _____

10. (a) a famous war in history

    (b) the war of 1812 _____

11. (a) went to see a well-known play during our annual trip to a neighboring city

    (b) went to see hello dolly! during our annual trip to new york _____

12. (a) the president of our country will be inaugurated on tuesday, january 20.

    (b) the president of a popular club at our college _____

13. (a) keats' courting of death in la belle dame sans merci

    (b) the many poems that personify human qualities _____

14. (a) economics 200 to be offered in the spring

    (b) a course in economics to be offered in the spring _____

15. (a) the grandmother who joined a charitable organization

    (b) my swedish grandmother who joined the salvation army _____

## 11

**Learn when to use abbreviations, acronyms, and numbers.**

In specialized kinds of writing—such as tables, indexes, and footnotes—abbreviations, acronyms, and figures are appropriate, but in ordinary writing abbreviations are used sparingly, figures are used only for numbers that would require three or more words to write out, and most acronyms should be spelled out the first time they are used.

**11a  Before proper names, use the abbreviations *Mr., Mrs., Dr.,* and *St.* (for *Saint*) as appropriate. Use such designations as *Jr., Sr., II,* and *Ph.D.* after a proper name.**

> *Ms.* Gates invited *Dr.* Fleming to tell the story of *St.* Jude.

**11b  Spell out names of states, countries, continents, months, days of the week, and units of measurements.**

> When Mary was born on *July* 8 at the hospital in La Ceiba, *Honduras*, she weighed seven *pounds*, three *ounces*, but seven days later, at home in New Orleans, *Louisiana*, she weighed nine *pounds*.

**11c  Spell out *Street, Road, Park, River, Company,* and similar words when used as part of proper names.**

> From Byron *Avenue* in Riverview *Park* you can see the Stones *River* and the Stones River *battlefield*.

**11d  Spell out the words *volume, chapter,* and *page* and the names of courses of study.**

> The notes on *biology* are taken from *chapter* 3, *page* 7.   [*Ch.* 3, *p.* 7 would be acceptable in a footnote.]

**11e  Spell out the meaning of any acronym that may not be familiar to your reader when you use it for the first time.**

> The National Wildlife Federation (NWF) funded the study of giant pandas. Support from the NWF gives us reason to believe that we may save the pandas from extinction.
>
> OR
>
> The NWF (National Wildlife Federation) funded the study of giant pandas.

**11f Spell out numbers that require only one or two words, but use figures for other numbers.**

> After *twenty-two* years of gourmet cooking, he had gone from a size *thirty-two* to a size *forty*.
> Our home covers *1,600* square feet.

Note the ways figures are used in the following instances:

    (1) the hour of the day: 4:00 P.M. (p.m.) OR four o'clock in the afternoon
    (2) dates: *May 6, 1977*
    (3) addresses: *55* North Broadway
    (4) identification numbers: Channel *4*, Interstate *40*
    (5) pages or divisions of a book: page *40*, chapter *6*
    (6) decimals and percentages: *.57* inches, *10* percent
    (7) a series of numbers: a room *25* feet long, *18* feet wide, and *10* feet high; The vote was *50* to *6* in favor, with *7* abstentions.
    (8) large round numbers: two million light-years
    (9) at the beginning of a sentence: One hundred fifty people filed applications.

**11g Recognize the meanings of several common Latin expressions, which are usually spelled out in English in formal writing but may be abbreviated in ordinary writing.**

> i.e. [that is], e.g. [for example], viz. [namely]
> cf. [compare], etc. [and so forth], vs. OR v. [versus]

**Caution:** Never write *and etc.*, and use the word *etc.* itself sparingly. In general, naming another item is more effective.

> This course covers rhetoric, punctuation, grammar, mechanics, and spelling. [Naming another item, *spelling*, is more effective than writing *etc.*]

## Abbreviations and Numbers

Exercise 11-1

NAME _____ SCORE _____

DIRECTIONS   Rewrite each of the following items using an abbreviation or a figure if the abbreviation or figure would be appropriate in ordinary writing. If not, simply rewrite the item as it stands.

EXAMPLES
three o'clock in the afternoon

*3:00 p.m.*

on Tuesday afternoon

*on Tuesday afternoon*

1. on page fifteen of chapter three

2. fourteen thousand dollars

3. Jim Nunnery, the doctor on our street

4. the Raiders versus the Cowboys

5. Eighty percent of those registered voted.

6. debate about the Equal Rights Amendment

7. life in California in nineteen seventy-seven

8. the economics class in Peck Hall

9. one hundred pounds

10. on the twenty-first of January

11. Riverview Park off Thompson Lane

12. Susan Collier, our senator

13. Shane Colvin, a certified public accountant

14. between the United States and Canada

15. a lot that is one hundred feet long and ninety-five feet wide with seventy-five feet of road frontage

# THE COMMA ,/12

## 12

**Let your sentence sense guide you in the use of the comma.**

In speaking, you make the meaning of a sentence clearer or easier to follow by pauses and by changes in voice pitch. When you read the following sentence aloud, notice that you pause twice (and that your voice also drops in pitch) to make the sentence easier for a listener to follow:

> Rain forests, among the most complex ecosystems on Earth, are in danger of being eliminated.

In writing, of course, you use punctuation marks, not voice pitch, to make your sentences easier to follow. And you decide where to put the punctuation marks on the basis of your sentence sense (Section **1**).

Remember that the word order in an ordinary sentence follows this pattern:

SUBJECT–VERB–COMPLEMENT.
Rain forests are complex.

Often when you write a sentence that varies in some way from this pattern you will use a comma or commas. If you add something before the subject, you often follow the introductory addition with a comma.

Addition, S–V–C.
However, rain forests are complex.

**Note:** A dash may sometimes be used in the same way as a comma. See Section **17**.

If you interrupt the sentence pattern, you often use two commas:

S, addition, V–C.
Rain forests, however, are complex.

S–V, addition, C.
Rain forests are, however, complex.

If you add a word or group of words to the end of the sentence pattern, you often use a comma:

S–V–C, addition.
Rain forests are complex, however.

Of all the marks of punctuation, the most frequently used is the comma. Commas have four main uses.

**a** to follow a main clause that is linked to another main clause by a coordinate conjunction (*and, but, or, nor, for, so,* or *yet*);
**b** to follow certain introductory elements;

**c** to separate items in a series, including coordinate (equal in rank) adjectives;
**d** to set off nonrestrictive, parenthetical, and miscellaneous elements.

**12a  A comma follows a main clause that is linked to another main clause by a coordinating conjunction: *and, but, or, nor, for, so,* or *yet.***

Main clauses can stand alone as simple sentences. When they do, they may even be introduced by a conjunction (see **30b(3)**).

> Biologists believe that the world's rain forests are disappearing. But they are looking for ways to save the forests.

When the two main clauses are linked by a coordinating conjunction, a compound sentence results.

> PATTERN   MAIN CLAUSE**,** coordinating conjunction MAIN CLAUSE.

> Biologists believe that the world's rain forests are disappearing, but they are looking for ways to save them.

The semicolon may also be used when the two main clauses that are linked by a coordinating conjunction contain other commas.

> The botanist Robert Dressler discovered a plant that anchors itself to the branches of rain forest trees, catches falling debris, and then turns the debris into humus**;** so, logically, he named it the "trashbasket plant."

Notice in the following examples that a comma is used before a coordinating conjunction only when the conjunction links two main clauses.

| | |
|---|---|
| TWO VERB PHRASES | A rain forest contains layers of incredibly complex biological interactions and offers biologists the material for years of study. |
| TWO SUBORDINATE CLAUSES | Because the ecosystems are so complex and because study conditions are so harsh**,** biologists need years to complete their studies. |
| TWO MAIN CLAUSES | The discovery of new biological phenomena is a frequent occurrence**,** so most biologists eagerly seize an opportunity to study a rain forest. |

## Commas between Main Clauses                    Exercise 12–1

NAME _____ SCORE _____

DIRECTIONS    In the following sentences, insert an inverted caret (**V**) wherever two main elements are joined. Then insert either a comma or a semicolon after the first main clause. Write the mark that you have added in the blank at the right as well. If a sentence does not have two main clauses, write *C* in the blank to show that the sentence is correct and needs no punctuation mark.

EXAMPLES

The Amazon is the largest single geographical feature of the South

American continent, and it is both a river and a giant river valley.     _____,_____

A massive tropical rain forest covers what is usually called the Ama-

zon jungle.                                                              ___C___

1. The Amazon River and the rain forest together form Amazonia the river and its tributaries drain the forest.     _____

2. The jungle covers an area of about 2.5 million square miles it is roughly the size of the United States west of the Mississippi.     _____

3. The largest portions of the jungle are in Brazil and Peru but it includes parts of eight South American countries.     _____

4. Half the land area of Brazil and Peru is tropical rain forest fortunately, both countries realize that protecting the forest is critical.     _____

5. If it were a country, Amazonia would be the ninth largest in the world.     _____

6. The Amazon River starts in the Peruvian Andes and 4,007 miles later it enters the Atlantic Ocean.     _____

7. Hundreds of small streams in the Andes pour into the Amazon and they provide its initial strength during its flow through Peru.     _____

8. It quickly becomes a mile-wide river and by the time it passes through Brazil, it is more than three miles wide.     _____

9. After it leaves the Peruvian Andes, the river runs in an enormous shallow bowl that covers most of central South America. _____

10. If it were stripped of trees, this flat basin might look like the Great Plains of the United States or the Sahara of Africa. _____

11. The river cuts a deep trough through the bowl on its final 2,000-mile course to the Atlantic but it drops only one hundred feet. _____

12. The many large tributaries that force their way into the channel provide the river's immense power without the tributaries the river would come to a halt. _____

13. The statistics that describe the Amazon are astonishing for example, it pushes an estimated 160 million tons of silt a year along the flooded plain. _____

14. The statistics are so remarkable that they seem to belong in the *Guinness Book of World Records* but statistics from equally reliable sources also tend to contradict each other. _____

15. For example, Brazilians claim that the Amazon is fifty miles longer than the Nile River Peruvians, however, find it to be fifty miles shorter than the Nile, making it the second largest river in the world. _____

**12b A comma usually follows adverb clauses that precede main clauses. A comma often follows introductory phrases (especially adverb phrases) and transitional expressions. A comma follows an introductory interjection or an introductory *yes* or *no*.**

The introductory element, which offers a variation from subject-first word order (see also Section **30**), is usually followed by a comma.

PATTERN    Introductory element, MAIN CLAUSE.

> Because rain forests are among the basic life-support systems of the Earth, we must preserve them.

**(1)  When an adverb clause precedes the main clause, it is usually followed by a comma.**

> *Although biologists realize the crucial importance of rain forests,* they have been unable to stop deforestation.

There is usually no comma before the adverb clause when it follows the main clause:

> Countries in the tropics often have to choose between preserving the forests and meeting the needs of the people *when their populations outstrip their resources.*

But if the adverb clause at the end begins with *although* a comma is normally used.

> Deforestation is a profitable enterprise, *although in the long run it destroys the forest and the land.*

Some writers omit the comma after the introductory adverb clause when the clause is very short or when it has the same subject as the main clause, but there is nothing wrong with including the comma.

> *When the land is cleared* it immediately begins to erode.
> OR
> *When the land is cleared,* it immediately begins to erode.

**(2)  A comma usually follows an introductory verbal phrase and may follow an introductory prepositional phrase.**

> *Falling all year,* the tropical rains quickly wash the land away.   [introductory verbal phrase]
> *In a single year,* an area the size of Great Britain is destroyed.   [introductory prepositional phrase]

The comma is often omitted after prepositional phrases if no misreading could result.

> *In 1970* Brazil began to sponsor studies of the rain forests.
> *By funding the research efforts,* Brazil hopes to save its most precious resources.   [The comma prevents misreading.]

**(3) A comma follows an introductory transitional expression, an interjection, and some-
times a single word modifier.**

*To be exact,* the Amazon is the largest single geographical feature on the South
American continent.

*Yes,* the Amazon is a river and a rain forest.

*Together,* river and forest form Amazonia—what the world calls the Amazon.

*Certainly* humans would benefit from learning to control this massive natural re-
source.　[Writers may or may not use a comma after an introductory word like
*yet, thus,* or *certainly* depending on how closely they feel the word is related to
the rest of the sentence. If they see the word as functioning primarily for transition, they use a comma; if they see it primarily as an adverb, closely related to
the verb, they do not use a comma.]

## Commas after Introductory Elements                    Exercise 12-2

NAME _____  SCORE _____

DIRECTIONS    After each introductory element, either write a zero (0) to indicate that no comma is needed or add a coma. Also write the zero or the comma and the last word of the introductory phrase or clause in the blank.

EXAMPLES

In 1817 the French explorer Claude François mapped the major trib-

utaries of the Amazon.                                                         _____0_____

Geographically, the basin sits between two of the oldest rock forma-

tions on Earth.                                                               _____,_____

1. Discharging 3.4 million gallons of water a minute into the Atlantic the river stains the sea brown with silt for 150 miles.          _____

2. Fourteen times the discharge of the Mississippi the daily flow
   is enough to supply New York City with water for nine years.           _____

3. Several hundred feet deep at some points the Amazon is called
   the Rio Mar.                                                            _____

4. Flowing ponderously to the sea the river frequently floods
   areas more than one hundred miles across for months at a
   time.                                                                   _____

5. After oceangoing freighters enter the river they can travel
   2,300 miles upstream to the port of Iquitos, Peru.                     _____

6. Containing one-fifth of the world's fresh water the Amazon
   basin is drained by two hundred major tributaries.                     _____

7. In fact seventeen of the major tributaries are more than one
   thousand miles long.                                                    _____

8. Comparing the tributaries to the Mississippi we can visualize
   their size.                                                             _____

9. Comparing the tributaries to the Mississippi helps us visualize
   their size.                                                             _____

*127*

10. Ten of the tributaries discharge more water than the Mississippi. _____

11. Changing the area around it dramatically the Amazon flows between two of the oldest rock formations on Earth. _____

12. Having been worn down to rippled plateaus the rock formations on each side of the basin were prominent mountain ranges about 600 million years ago. _____

13. Nearly two miles deep a layer of sediment covers the basin between the plateaus. _____

14. During a particularly bad flood season the basin resembles an inland sea. _____

15. According to scientific theories it probably once was an inland sea. _____

**12c Commas are used between items in a series and between coordinate adjectives. A series is a succession of three or more parallel elements.**

**(1) Use commas between three or more items in a series.**

PATTERN   1, 2, and 3 . . .
OR   1, 2, 3 . . .

>                 **1**        **2**        **3**
> The Amazon includes parts of Brazil, Peru, and Colombia.

>                                  **1**
> The Amazon intrigues scientists because it contains over a million species of plants
>
>     **2**                                     **3**
> and animals, it is home to primitive tribes of hunter–gatherers, and it contains
>
> a vast mineral wealth.

> The jungle is estimated to spread for 2.5 million square miles and includes parts of
>      **1**       **2**    **3**        **4**      **5**     **6**       **7**
> eight countries: Brazil, Peru, Colombia, Ecuador, Bolivia, Venezuela, Surinam,
> **8**
> and Guayana.

The comma before the *and* may be omitted only if there is no difficulty reading the series or if the two items should be regarded as one unit.

>                                      **1 2**   **3**
> Tribal villages are indicated on your map by the numbers 5, 7, and 9.   [Without
>
> the last comma the series remains clear: "Tribal villages are indicated on your
>
> map by the numbers 5, 7 and 9."]

>                                 **1**      **2**       **3**
> For easy identification the villages are marked with numbers, letters, and blue and
>
> white circles.   [*Blue and white* refers as a unit to *circles;* thus there is no comma
>
> before the last *and.*]

All the commas are normally omitted when a coordinating conjunction is used between each item in the series.

>         **1**         **2**            **3**
> Some people misread or misinterpret or even refuse to believe the directions on the
>
> map.

Semicolons may be used between the items in the series if the items themselves contain commas or if the items are main clauses. (See also **12a**.)

> Scientists believe deforestation has serious global consequences: first, it alters the regional climate, most noticeably by causing a decrease in rainfall; second, it erodes the landscape, causing topsoil to wash into the sea; third, it contributes to the global greenhouse effect, eventually raising the average temperature around the world.

**Caution:** Remember that no comma is used when only two items are linked by a conjunction.

> *Gold* and *precious stones* enticed many early explorers of the Amazon.

**(2) Use commas between coordinate adjectives that are not linked by a coordinating conjunction.**

If the adjectives are coordinate, you can reverse their order or insert *and* or *or* between them without loss of sense.

> The *humid,* intensely *hot* forest transformed explorations into *exhausting, dangerous* ventures.

> The intensely *hot* and *humid* forest transformed explorations into *dangerous* and *exhausting* ventures.

**Caution:** Adjectives that are not coordinate take no commas between them.

> The *large rain* forest affects the climate of the entire region. [You would not say "large *and* rain forest . . ."]

> COORDINATE ADJECTIVES *small, dying* tree [You can say "*dying, small* tree" or "*small and dying* tree."]

> ADJECTIVES THAT ARE NOT COORDINATE *large deciduous* tree and *largest evergreen* forest [You would not say "*large and deciduous* tree" or "*evergreen largest* forest."]

## Commas between Items in a Series
## and between Coordinate Adjectives

Exercise 12-3

NAME _____ SCORE _____

DIRECTIONS    In each sentence, identify each series that needs commas by writing *1, 2, 3,* and so on above the items and in the blank on the right; identify coordinate adjectives by writing *a, b,* and *c* above the adjectives and in the blank. Insert commas or semicolons where they belong in the sentence and also in the blank to show the punctuation of the pattern. Write *C* in the blank if a sentence has no items in a series or no coordinate adjectives that need punctuation.

EXAMPLES

The rain forest continues to grow and spread its boundaries at a slow, inexorable rate.            *a, b*

Intuition, common sense, and experience tell us that it will not spread forever.            *1, 2, 3*

1. The wet stable climate has produced a huge variety of plant life.            _____

2. One-half of the remaining forest on Earth grows in the vast fertile and fragile Amazon basin.            _____

3. A comprehensive current catalog of animal and plant life is available.            _____

4. The catalog lists nearly a million species of plants and animals: 2,500 species of snakes 2,000 of fish 1,500 of birds and 50,000 of higher plants.            _____

5. Until the last decade, human beings were one of the rarest animal species.            _____

6. For perhaps 12,000 years the land was occupied by isolated primitive peaceful tribes of hunter–gatherers.            _____

7. These nomadic secretive tribes migrated from the Andes into the Amazon valley.            _____

8. They may have numbered three or four million people when Europeans arrived in the valley took control and began eliminating them.            _____

9. By the early 1600s, French Dutch English and Portuguese had settled around the mouth of the Amazon.     ———————

10. When the Portuguese finally took control of the region in 1639, the Indian population had been decimated by violence disease and forced migration.     ———————

11. The whites intended to plunder the land, not colonize it, because it contained exportable natural resources.     ———————

12. The Westerners' encounters with the river spawned a series of colorful essentially true myths about the Amazon's effects on human beings.     ———————

**12d Commas are used to set off (1) nonrestrictive clauses and phrases, (2) parenthetical elements such as transitional expressions, and (3) items in dates and addresses.**

A parenthetical or nonrestrictive addition that comes before the basic sentence pattern is followed by a comma.

> *One of the most informative books on the Amazon basin,* The Amazon and Time traces the evolution of the basin.

If the parenthetical or nonrestrictive addition comes after the basic sentence, a comma precedes it.

> The Amazon and Time explains how scientists study the history of the basin, *particularly the first 100 million years of its existence.*

The most common position of the parenthetical or nonrestrictive addition is in the middle of the sentence, where one comma precedes it and another comma follows it.

> In one of his essays, *"The Inland Sea,"* Fred Colvin discusses the first 10 million years.
>
> He claims that several forces, *including the formation of the Andes mountains,* helped create the inland sea.

**(1) Nonrestrictive clauses and phrases are set off by commas. Restrictive clauses and phrases are not set off.** (See also **13a**.)

A restrictive clause or phrase limits the meaning of the word it refers to.

> The magazine *that "The Inland Sea" is taken from* is called *Natural History*. [The *that* clause limits the meaning of the word *magazine*. Note that the relative pronoun *that* always introduces a restrictive clause.]
>
> Anyone *reading this magazine* is impressed with the informative articles. [The verbal phrase *reading this magazine* limits the meaning of the word *anyone*.]

A nonrestrictive clause or phrase does not limit the meaning of the word it refers to; rather, it adds information about a word that is already clearly limited in meaning. The nonrestrictive clause or phrase is set off with commas.

> "The Inland Sea," *taken from the magazine Natural History,* provides a comprehensive report on the development of the Amazon basin. [The verbal phrase *taken from the magazine Natural History* adds further information about the subject "The Inland Sea."]
>
> Fred Colvin, *who is a history professor and freelance science writer,* presents very technical information in a way that even an uninformed reader will understand. [The *who* clause adds information about *Fred Colvin*.]

Of course, not all adjective clauses and phrases are as obviously restrictive or nonrestrictive as the ones used in the above examples. Many times you can determine whether a clause or phrase is restrictive or nonrestrictive only by referring to the preceding sentence or sentences.

Before Europeans arrived in the Amazonian basin, primitive tribes roamed the forests. They probably originated in the Andes and migrated into the basin looking for food. The tribes, whom scientists describe as "hunter–gatherers," never developed sophisticated cultures or social structures.   [Without the first two sentences, the *whom* clause would be restrictive, or necessary to limit the meaning of *tribes*.]

Sometimes, depending on the writer's intended meaning, a clause or phrase may be either restrictive or nonrestrictive. Notice the difference in meaning between the two sentences below, which differ only in punctuation.

The European explorers *who expected to find treasure in the Amazonian basin* treated native tribes very harshly.   [Without commas before *who* and after *basin*, the sentence suggests that not all European explorers expected to find treasure.]
The European explorers, *who expected to find treasure in the Amazonian basin*, treated native tribes very harshly.   [With commas before *who* and after *basin*, the sentence suggests that all European explorers expected to find treasure.]

**(2) Parenthetical elements, nonrestrictive appositives, absolute and contrasted elements, and words in direct address are set off by commas.**

Parenthetical elements include a variety of constructions that introduce supplementary information to a sentence or that make up transitions between sentences.

We read several essays, *such as "Forests Without Protectors" and "Our Lost Wildlife,"* about the Amazon.   [In this sentence, *such as* introduces a nonrestrictive phrase. In a sentence like "An essay such as "Our Lost Wildlife" describes the cost of our destruction of the rain forests," *such as* introduces a restrictive phrase. Note also that when a comma is used with *such as*, the comma comes before *such*, with no comma after *as*.]
"When you examine the statistics," *Professor Colvin reports*, "you are dismayed at how much wildlife already is extinct."   [An expression such as *Professor Colvin reports* (*says*, *claims*, *replies*, and so on) is considered parenthetical. See **16a(2)** for further information on the placement of commas in dialogue.]
Professor Elizabeth Brown, *as well as other biologists*, believes that at least one species of plant or animal is lost each day.   [Expressions like *as well as*, *in addition to*, and *along with* usually introduce parenthetical matter.]
*In fact*, Professor Brown has an extensive list of species that are threatened with extinction.   [A transitional expression such as *in fact* is always considered parenthetical.]
According to Professor Brown, the lemur, *although it lives in very remote terrain*, is threatened with extinction.   [Parenthetical matter may be stated in a subordinate clause.]

Appositives are usually set off by commas, though on a few occasions they are restrictive.

The controversial essay *"The Lure of El Dorado"* explains that political ambitions are destroying the Amazon basin.   [The title of the essay is a restrictive appositive needed to identify which essay is being referred to; thus it is not set off with commas.]

"The Lure of El Dorado," *a controversial essay,* explains that political ambitions are destroying the Amazon basin.    [The appositive is nonrestrictive; thus it is set off with commas.]

Absolute phrases are verbal phrases that are preceded by their subjects. They affect the meaning of the entire sentence in which they appear (not just a single word, phrase, or clause). Absolute phrases are always set off by commas.

According to Cynthia Rudolph, one justification alone should save the forests, *humanity's relationship to other living creatures effectively countering its greed.* [The verbal *countering* has its own subject, *relationship.*]

Contrasted elements are always set off by commas.

Rudolph believes that the desire for knowledge, not for wealth or power, should inspire humans to save the forests.

Words in direct address do just what you would expect them to do: they address someone or something directly. They are always set off by commas.

"Do not fall prey, *South America,* to a false practicality," Rudolph seems to be saying in "The Lure of El Dorado."

**(3) Geographical names and items in dates and addresses (except for zip codes) are set off by commas.**

Send your applications by May 17, 1987, to Box 5393, Murfreesboro, Tennessee   37130.

Dates are sometimes written and punctuated differently in official documents and reports.

On Friday, 19 June 1987, the finalists checked into the hotel.

When only the month and the year are given, no comma is necessary:

May 1987

**12e A comma is occasionally used to prevent misreading even when it is not called for by any of the principles already discussed.**

CONFUSING    Those of you who wish to write for further details.

CLEAR       Those of you who wish to, write for further details.

## Commas to Set Off Nonrestrictive Clauses
## and Phrases and Parenthetical Elements  Exercise 12-4

NAME _____ SCORE _____

DIRECTIONS   In the following sentences, set off each nonrestrictive or parenthetical addition with a comma or commas. Then in the blank write (1) a dash followed by a comma (—,) if the nonrestrictive or parenthetical addition begins the sentence, (2) a comma followed by a dash (,—) if the nonrestrictive or parenthetical addition ends the sentence, (3) a dash enclosed within commas (,—,) if the nonrestrictive or parenthetical addition comes within the sentence, or (4) *C* if there is no nonrestrictive or parenthetical addition to set off.

EXAMPLE
Most visitors to the Amazon, however rugged they may be, find themselves overwhelmed by the environment.    ,—,

1. Disappointed by his first encounter with the region Alfred Russell Wallace remarked, "The weather was not so hot, the people were not so peculiar, the vegetation was not so striking as the glowing picture I had conjured up in my imagination."    _____

2. Travel tales beloved by the Victorian audiences usually were robust adventure stories.    _____

3. Wallace's account which was written in 1848 did little to satisfy its audiences as an adventure tale.    _____

4. Wallace a famous adventure-writer of his day specialized in exotic travelogs.    _____

5. Teddy Roosevelt one of the first writers of robust adventure stories was also one of the first to visit the Amazon.    _____

6. Actually Roosevelt's *Through the Brazilian Wilderness* published in 1914 is one of the tamest and most scholarly works of the genre.    _____

7. He was of course the personification of robustness.    _____

8. Bursting with the joy of life he tramped through the forest shooting everything in sight.    _____

9. Certainly he wouldn't have taken the trip if there had been no danger involved. _____

10. "South America," he wrote, "makes up for its lack relatively of large man-eating carnivores by the extraordinary ferocity or bloodthirstiness of certain small creatures." _____

11. His description of one of these creatures the piranha fish is a model of exuberant writing. _____

12. "The head of the piranha with its short muzzle, malignant eyes, and gaping jaws embodies evil ferocity." _____

13. Roosevelt continued on his journey a truly arduous one by anyone's standards. _____

14. Telling of battles with vampire bats and with ants that ate his clothes he reveled in the physically demanding trek. _____

15. Encountering a jaguar near a river crossing he dropped it with a single shot. _____

16. He also discovered a river which his Brazilian guides thoughtfully named after him. _____

## All Uses of the Comma

NAME _____ SCORE _____

DIRECTIONS    Decide whether each comma used in the following sentences (a) separates main clauses, (b) sets off an introductory addition, (c) separates items in a series or coordinate adjectives, or (d) sets off a parenthetical or nonrestrictive addition. Write *a, b, c,* or *d* above each comma and in the blank to the right of the sentence.

EXAMPLE

*d*

Roosevelt continued on his journey, a truly arduous one by anyone's

standards.                                                                                          *d*

1. Roosevelt's stories recounted battles with vampire bats, with termites that ate his pith helmet, and with clouds of mosquitoes and gnats.                                                                      _____

2. Dubbing the land the "last frontier," he made a plea for developing it.                                                                            _____

3. He argued that this tenantless wilderness, a rich and fertile land, should not lie idle.                                                      _____

4. Roosevelt believed that the Amazon valley could become a home for the people of the poor, overpopulated countries of the world.                                                                             _____

5. Inspired at least in part by Roosevelt's adventures and stories, other men sought fame such as his.                                      _____

6. Such adventurers dominated the literature of the Amazon from the 1920s to the 1950s, and all of them described the area in exaggerated terms.                                                      _____

7. The "green hell," the "green unknown," or the "green death" were favorite descriptions of the Amazon area.                        _____

8. Using titles like *Lost World of the Amazon* or *Wilderness of Fools*, all claimed their stories were true.                          _____

9. Jorgen Bisch's *Across the River of Death* has a dramatic, over-wrought beginning: "Tomorrow we set off into the Green Hell

of the Mato Grosso territories . . . into which many have penetrated but from which so few have returned." _____

10. The giant, ubiquitous anaconda appears in all the stories. _____

11. An anaconda approached Bisch, hissing and showing its teeth. _____

12. "If it gets its teeth into you, you will never come out of the struggle alive." _____

13. Algot Lange, displaying the same sense of anticipation, described in his *In the Amazon Jungle* another encounter with an anaconda. _____

14. He called his anaconda the "awful, dreaded master of the swamps." _____

15. The snake was dispatched with a pistol, stretched out at his feet, and carefully measured. _____

16. Lange lost the snake's skin, which he reported as 56 feet long, before he returned home. _____

17. Recent accounts of the Amazon, while relatively scarce, are definitely more grim. _____

18. There is a sense of alarm in the writing, but the alarm is not over a half-imagined encounter with a snake. _____

19. Primarily produced by scientists, today's literature centers on the fear that human beings are destroying one of the greatest natural resources on Earth. _____

20. Typical titles are "Extinction and Conservation of Plant Species in the Amazon," "Endangered Animals of Peru," and "The Development of Rain Forests." _____

## All Uses of the Comma                                    Exercise 12–6

NAME _____ SCORE _____

DIRECTIONS    In the following sentences insert all necessary commas. Then write *a, b, c,* or *d* above each comma and in the blank to the right of the sentence to indicate that the comma (a) separates main clauses, (b) sets off an introductory addition, (c) separates items in a series or coordinate adjectives, or (d) sets off a parenthetical or nonrestrictive addition.

EXAMPLE

Warwick Ken*d*a Brazilian scientist*d*predicted in the mid-1970s that the

Brazilian forests would be gone by the end of the century.            *d*

1. According to recent research by the New York Botanical Garden's Amazon project 25 percent of the forest is already gone. _____

2. Other scientists estimate that twenty million acres a year are being cleared and they believe that up to a third of the forest already is gone. _____

3. Robert Goodland who is an ecologist and business executive has been an outspoken advocate of preserving the forests. _____

4. Goodland and botanist Howard Irwin have written a book *Amazon Jungle: Green Hell to Red Desert.* _____

5. Irwin and Goodland offer frightening dire predictions about the forests. _____

6. They emphasize what may be the sad fatal irony of the Amazon. _____

7. Although the tropical forest is lush it does not replenish itself after it is cut down. _____

8. The fertile soil supports huge trees yet it sometimes is only one inch thick. _____

9. Cutting the trees causes the thin soil to erode to bake in the sun and to become a brick-hard surface hostile to life. _____

10. The Amazon which contains half the remaining forest on Earth is a very fragile place. _____

11. Although the Amazon suggests a place of unlimited fertility we should think of it as a desert covered with trees. _____

12. Goodland predicts a serious disruption in Brazil's rainfall patterns and he says this will lead to a drastic change in Brazil's climate. _____

13. That disruption as he points out could extend to world weather patterns. _____

14. The Amazon is immense and it has the same effects on world weather as oceans do. _____

15. Tampering with it will have serious long-lasting consequences. _____

**All Uses of the Comma**                    Exercise 12-7

NAME _____ SCORE _____

DIRECTIONS   Write a sentence to illustrate each of the items listed.

EXAMPLE
an absolute element

1. a complete date

2. a nonrestrictive clause

3. a contrasted element

4. a restrictive phrase

5. a transitional expression

6. items in a series

7. a parenthetical element introduced by *such as*

8. two main clauses linked by a coordinating conjunction

9. an introductory verbal phrase

10. a complete address, including zip code

# 13

**Superfluous or misplaced commas make sentences difficult to read.**

The comma is the most frequently used punctuation mark. It is also the most frequently misused punctuation mark. While trying to master the correct use of the comma, many people tend to overuse it and to misplace it in sentence patterns, especially if they rely too much on the pause test for placement. Some short-winded writers, who pause after every third or fourth word, fill their sentences with commas that make the writing difficult to follow. In the example below, the circled commas should not be included.

> CONFUSING   The most alarming consequence (,) of destroying the Amazon jungle (,) is that we are losing living things forever (,) when we cut down the trees.

Actually, this sentence requires no internal punctuation at all, for the clauses and phrases that have been added to the basic sentence pattern are all restrictive; they are necessary to define or to limit the meaning of the words they modify.

> CORRECT   The most alarming consequence of destroying the Amazon jungle is that we are losing living things forever when we cut down the trees.

Section **13** is included as a caution against overuse and misplacement of commas. **The circled commas throughout the examples in this section should be omitted.**

**13a  Do not use a comma to separate the subject from its verb or the verb from its complement.**

Remember that commas are used to set off nonrestrictive or parenthetical additions. Do not use them to separate the parts of the basic (Subject–Verb–Complement) sentence.

> Making people understand the permanence of the loss (,) is the hardest task facing ecologists.   [The subject, *making*, should not be separated by a comma from its verb.]
> Most ecologists agree (,) that many living creatures are being destroyed before they are discovered.   [The verb, *agree*, should not be separated by a comma from its complement, the *that* clause.]

**13b  Do not use a comma after a coordinating conjunction; do not use a comma before a coordinating conjunction when only a word, phrase, or subordinate clause (rather than a main clause) follows the conjunction.** (See also **12a**.)

Indians living in the Amazon depend on it for existence, but (,) they are being ignored by the advancing horde of developers.   [The comma comes before, not after, the coordinating conjunction.]

Developers in the Amazon have been blind to the destruction of the forest (,) and to the plight of the Indians.   [compound prepositional phrases—no comma before *and*]

**13c  Do not use commas to set off words or short phrases (especially introductory ones) that are not parenthetical or that are very slightly so.**

In the forest (,) the Indians find all they need to live.

Research (,) for ecologists (,) often means living in the forest for weeks.

**13d  Do not use commas to set off restrictive clauses, phrases, or appositives.** (See also **12d**.)

The book (,) *Amazon* (,) explains the clash between those who would preserve the Amazon basin and those who would develop it.   [No commas are needed because the title *Amazon* is a restrictive appositive needed to define or limit *book*.]

Readers (,) hoping to find a total condemnation of the developers (,) will be disappointed with *Amazon*.   [No commas are needed because the verbal phrase is a restrictive addition needed to define or limit *readers*.]

The authors of *Amazon* became fascinated by the dreams and ambitions (,) that motivated the developers.   [No comma is needed because the *that* clause is necessary to define or limit *dreams and ambitions*.]

**13e  Do not use a comma before the first or after the last item in a series.**

Journals such as (,) *Natural History, Nature,* and *National Geographic* (,) publish the most recent scientific research on the Amazon basin.

Note the addition of the following two subsections.

**13f  In general, do not use a comma before an adverb clause at the end of a sentence.** (See also **12b**.)

The authors of *Amazon* are fascinated by the region (,) because it is one of the last frontiers on Earth.   [If the *because* clause came at the beginning of the sentence as an introductory addition, it would be followed by a comma.]

**13g  Do not use a comma between adjectives that are not coordinate.** (See also **12c**.)

The fragile (,) natural balance of the Amazon basin is easily disturbed by the actions of ambitious people.

## Superfluous Commas                         Exercise 13–1

NAME _____ SCORE _____

DIRECTIONS    Each of the following sentences is correctly punctuated. Explain why a comma is not added to each sentence at the place or places indicated in the question by listing the rule of caution (see **13a–13g**) that applies.

EXAMPLE
The National Weather Service twice daily launches approximately

200 weather-observing devices called "radiosondes."

Why is *twice daily* not set off by commas?                    *13d*

1. The radiosondes are carried aloft by balloons to altitudes of twenty miles and are released to measure winds, tempera-ture, and humidity.

    Why is there no comma after *miles*?                    _____

2. The National Weather Service gathers the data that it needs to predict weather changes and climate patterns.

    Why is there no comma after *data*?                    _____

3. The radiosondes float down on parachutes when the balloons burst.

    Why is there no comma after *parachutes*?                    _____

4. Hikers, hunters, and fishermen recover most of the radio-sondes.

    Why is there no comma after *recover*?                    _____

5. Each radiosonde carries an identification plate that tells the finder to contact the National Weather Service.

    Why is there no comma after *plate*?                    _____

6. In some states serious young students look for radiosondes as a hobby.

    Why is there no comma after *serious*?                    _____

7. "We have rebuilt 670,000 radiosondes in the past 40 years and have saved a total of $10 million," says the director of the National Weather Service.

   Why is there no comma after *years*?    _____

8. Until recently about 18,000 radiosondes were recovered each year.

   Why is there no comma after *recently*?    _____

9. But, for unknown reasons, several thousand fewer radio-sondes have been returned each year.

   Why is there no comma after *thousand*?    _____

10. Recovering, rebuilding, and reusing the radiosondes save the National Weather Service a great deal of money.

    Why is there no comma after *reusing*?    _____

11. What would you do if you encountered a grizzly?

    Why is there no comma after *do*?    _____

12. Most people scream, run, and hide in their tents.

    Why is there no comma after *hide*?    _____

13. The biologist C. T. Duke recommends another response.

    Why is *C. T. Duke* not set off by commas?    _____

14. Duke has developed a spray that appears to deter even a charging grizzly.

    Why is there no comma after *spray*?    _____

15. The deterrent is capsicum, the active ingredient in red pepper, and spraying a bear in the face with capsicum seems to take its mind off everything except running away.

    Why is there no comma after *and*?    _____

## 14

**Use the semicolon between parts of equal grammatical rank: (a) between two main clauses not joined by a coordinating conjunction and (b) between coordinate elements that already contain commas.**

A semicolon indicates that one part of a coordinate construction is finished. The semicolon acts like the fulcrum of a seesaw, balancing parts of equal grammatical rank.

> The Big Cypress Swamp stretches along the western bank of the Everglades and sprawls to the Gulf of Mexico; roughly the size of Delaware, it is part of the same unique south Florida wetlands system as the Everglades.   [two main clauses with no coordinating conjunction]
>
> Fifty years ago the Big Cypress, virtually untouched by humans, was filled with immense stands of bald cypress trees, many of them more than a hundred feet tall, eight feet thick, and six hundred years old; huge populations of alligators, most of whom had never seen a human; forbidding thickets and oppressive heat; biting insects; masses of snakes.   [items in a series, some of which contain commas]

**14a Use the semicolon to separate two main clauses not joined by a coordinating conjunction or two main clauses that contain commas and are also joined by a coordinating conjunction.**

PATTERN   MAIN CLAUSE; MAIN CLAUSE.

> Then, in the 1920's, engineers cut the Tamiami Trail through the swamps to carry travelers between south Florida's two coasts; in the 1940's most of the mammoth cypress were girdled, downed, and dragged out by the timbermen.   [two main clauses with no coordinating conjunction]
>
> In the 1950's and 1960's land developers began to drain the swamp, build roads, and make the land marketable; and by the 1970's the Big Cypress was well on its way to destruction.   [The first clause contains commas, so a semicolon must be used before the coordinating conjunction *and*.]

**Caution:** In a divided quotation, be especially careful to use a semicolon between the two main clauses of a sentence when they are not connected by a coordinating conjunction.

> "Land fever set in," recalled a National Park employee; "this was everybody's chance to make a fortune."

Remember that a conjunctive adverb, like *however*, or a transitional expression, like *for example* (see Section **1**), is not the same as a coordinating conjunction—*and*, *but*, *or*, *nor*, *for*, *so*, or *yet*. Thus, when a conjunctive adverb or a transitional expression is used to link two main clauses, a semicolon must come before it.

> Water flowing out of Big Cypress nourishes the western half of Everglades National Park; *therefore*, draining Big Cypress immediately endangered Everglades.

## 14b  Use the semicolon to separate a series of equal elements which themselves contain commas.

> Ecologists immediately began to argue that development of Big Cypress endangered the Everglades; that Big Cypress contained an aquifer that would be vital to the rapidly growing population of south Florida; and that, in fact, further development would disturb the ecology of the entire south Florida peninsula.
>
> When ecologists spoke to a group of Florida residents, they urged them to ask crucial questions—what will happen to the Everglades if Big Cypress is drained; can south Florida find another source of water for its growing population; and do we wish to bequeath to our children a Florida without the Everglades and Big Cypress?

## 14c  Use the semicolon between parts of equal rank only, not between a clause and a phrase or a subordinate clause and main clause.

> By the mid-1970's public opinion shifted in favor of protecting Big Cypress, primarily because the developers already had severely damaged the swamp with canals and roads and because a drought and fire in 1971 had demonstrated how easily the dry swamps could be destroyed.   [The subordinate clauses, introduced by *because*, are not equal in rank to the main clause; thus a semicolon would be inappropriate.]

# Semicolons

NAME _____ SCORE _____

DIRECTIONS    In the following sentences insert an inverted caret (**V**) between main clauses and add semicolons as needed. In the blank, copy the semicolon and the word or transitional expression immediately following, along with the comma if there is one. Write *C* in the blank if the sentence is correctly punctuated. (Not all sentences have two main clauses).

EXAMPLE
In 1974 Congress handed conservationists a landmark
triumph;it approved the purchase of more than half a
million acres in the heart of Big Cypress.                    ___;  it___

1. The purchase will be funded by federal and state money funding will come from federal and state grants.    _____

2. Investors bought much of the land years ago as an investment in "sunny Florida" now they are eager to sell their acres of swamp.    _____

3. In the mid-nineteenth century this part of Big Cypress was the haunt of Seminole and Miccosukee tribes because they could live in the swamp, they successfully eluded the U.S. Army.    _____

4. Water is the blood of Big Cypress low water levels threaten all its life.    _____

5. In the 1960s developers built more than 140 miles of canals in Big Cypress that severely lowered the water levels in fact, each year the canals drain 150 billion gallons of fresh water out of the swamp into the Gulf of Mexico.    _____

6. The drainage caused droughts, forced animals to leave the swamps in search of water, and endangered delicate flora, such as the rare ghost orchid

portions of Big Cypress began to resemble a desert, one resident remarked.

_____

7. Big Cypress is a natural attraction for wildlife therefore, the National Audubon Society has established a sanctuary, the Corkscrew Swamp Wildlife Sanctuary, within Big Cypress.

_____

8. Big Cypress featured alligators, flocks of wondrous birds, snakes, and unspoiled glades before it was touched by human beings now its centerpiece is Florida's only unlogged stand of giant cypress.

_____

9. Before Corkscrew was established, the wood storks had nearly disappeared from Big Cypress in recent springs the trees are filled with fledgling wood storks.

_____

10. Wood storks will range over an area fifty miles in diameter to find food the swamp had been so drained, however, that even in an area that large the storks could not find food.

_____

11. After the population of over 100,000 wood storks declined to less than 13,000 biologists found that the population could not recover.

_____

12. Corkscrew sanctuary is helping to restore the population by encouraging the small number there to remain and breed pumping water to the sanctuary helps keep it a swampy, inviting habitat year round.

_____

## Commas and Semicolons

Exercise 14-2

NAME _____ SCORE _____

DIRECTIONS   In the following sentences insert either a semicolon or a comma as needed within the sentence and also in the blank. If the sentence is correct as is, write *C* in the blank.

EXAMPLE

During the last twenty years, the United States has experienced a timber shortage;however, a system called "high yield" forestry has increased timber production.   ___;___

1. The recent concept in forestry is called "high yield" forestry by using the high-yield system companies can almost double their production.   _____

2. Foresters first clear-cut and burn over or scarify the land in neat rows they then plant seedlings.   _____

3. Periodic thinning helps tree growth and repellents discourage deer from browsing.   _____

4. A Douglas fir usually takes ninety years to mature in the high-yield system it would mature in forty years.   _____

5. Industry executives also envision growing new kinds of forests great plantations of trees planted in rows like corn and carefully cultivated and harvested by machines.   _____

6. Because they are more efficient for cultivation and logging pine-only plantations often replace mixed hardwood–softwood forests.   _____

7. Conservationists often do not approve of pine-only plantations in fact, they argue, such plantations are poor animal habitats.   _____

8. "Pine trees are susceptible to disease," explains a biologist "however, newly developed strains are hardier."   _____

9. Foresters search for trees that have superior characteristics and could be developed into new strains of trees.   _____

10. When they find outstanding trees they often give them names such as "Hercules" or "Mae West." _____

11. After sharpshooters use special bullets to shoot off high limbs, biologists collect the branch tips graft them onto young nursery stock and plant them in seed orchards. _____

12. Within a remarkably few years the grafted trees begin to yield seeds and the seeds are collected, planted in nursery beds, and cultivated for a year. _____

13. "We find a 10 to 20 percent improvement in growth," reports a forester "plus a 10 percent gain in mill production because of easier handling and better quality." _____

14. Biologists now are trying to breed trees for special uses for example, they are developing trees with very thin-walled cells for making paper. _____

15. Trees with thick-walled cells will be used for sturdier materials for example, to make boxes. _____

16. Ironically, the answer to the nation's timber shortage may lie with small lot owners not with large corporations. _____

17. More than 40 percent of the nation's timber grows on 296 million acres of private wood lots mainly west of the Mississippi. _____

18. Proper management could double the yield from these lands however, most owners simply sell off when they need the money. _____

19. The Forest Service believes that if small lot owners receive technical and financial support from government and industry and if timber prices rise the small lot owners will want to improve management of their timber. _____

20. If timber production on small lots does not increase significantly the nation may have to begin importing increased quantities of timber. _____

# 15

**Use the apostrophe (a) to indicate the possessive case—except for personal pronouns, (b) to mark omissions in contracted words and numerals, and (c) to form certain plurals.**

The apostrophe, in most of its uses, indicates that something has been omitted.

> don't  [do *not*]
> they're  [they *are*]
> children's books  [books *of* or *for* children]
> the artist's painting  [painting *of* or *by* the artist]

### 15a  Use the apostrophe to indicate the possessive case.

In general, a noun or a pronoun does not come immediately before another noun or pronoun: we do not write "children books" or "artist painting." When we do need to use a noun or pronoun before another noun or pronoun, we make the first one possessive by using an apostrophe. In a sense, we say that the first noun or pronoun owns the second one.

> parent's duty  [duty of one parent]
> parents' duty  [duty of two or more parents]
> everyone's duty  [duty of everyone]
> crater's edge  [edge of the crater]
> craters' edges  [edges of the craters]

**(1)  Add the apostrophe and an s ('s) to a noun or indefinite pronoun to indicate the singular possessive case.** (See the list of indefinite pronouns in the Appendix.)

> Teddy Roosevelt's picture hung on the teacher's wall.
> One's questions often go unanswered.

*Option:*  To form the possessive case of a singular noun that ends in *s*, add either the apostrophe and *s* or only the apostrophe.

> Tunis' geography  OR  Tunis's geography
> Columbus' ship  OR  Columbus's ship

**(2)  Add the apostrophe (') to all plural nouns that end in s to indicate the plural possessive case. Add the apostrophe and an s ('s) to all plural nouns not ending in s to indicate the plural possessive case.**

Always form the plural of the noun first. Then, if the plural noun ends in *s*, add only the apostrophe to show the possessive case.

> photographer  [singular]  photographers  [plural]
> dignitary  [singular]  dignitaries  [plural]
> The photographers' pictures hung in several dignitaries' offices.

If the plural noun does not end in *s*, add the apostrophe and an *s* to show the possessive case.

> man [singular] men [plural]
> woman [singular] women [plural]
> Men's and women's roles as biologists are interchangeable.

**(3) Add the apostrophe and an s to the last word of compounds or word groups.**

> my father-in-law's car
> someone else's turn
> the secretary of state's position

**(4) Add the apostrophe and an s to each name to indicate individual ownership, but to only the final name to indicate joint ownership.**

> John's and Andrew's schools were studying Australia. [John and Andrew attend different schools.]
> John and Andrew's school was playing in the tournament. [John and Andrew attend the same school.]

**15b Use the apostrophe to indicate omissions in contracted words and numerals.**

Be careful to place the apostrophe exactly where the omission occurs.

> The class of '92 [1992] can't [cannot] decide what to include in the time capsule that's [that is] to be blasted out of the solar system.

**15c Use the apostrophe and an s to form the plural of lowercase letters. If needed to prevent confusion, the apostrophe and an s can be used to form the plural of figures, symbols, abbreviations, and words referred to as words, but frequently only an s is added.**

> final *k*'s
> the 1970's OR the 1970s
> V.F.W.'s OR V.F.W.s
> *and*'s OR *ands*

**15d The apostrophe is not needed for possessive pronouns—*his, hers, its, ours, yours, theirs,* and *whose*—or for plural nouns not in the possessive case.**

> *Whose* messages are these—*yours* or *theirs*?
> *Her* family regularly held *its* reunion with the *Joneses.* [Joneses is plural but not possessive.]

**Apostrophes**                                    Exercise 15–1

NAME _____ SCORE _____

DIRECTIONS   Add all apostrophes needed in the following sentences. In the blank enter each word, number, or letter to which you have added an apostrophe. Be careful not to add needless apostrophes. If a sentence is correct, write *C* in the blank.

> EXAMPLE
> There's no apostrophe after the *s* in the word group "hu-
>
> manities major."                          *There's*

1. In the book *Great River* Philip Scarpinos subject is the upper Mississippi River in the first half of the twentieth century.                          _____

2. He concentrates on the urban-industrial portion of the river between the Twin Cities (at the head of commercial navigation) and St. Louis (near the Mississippis junction with the Missouri).    _____

3. Scarpino emphasizes two of the river landscapes most important features: a dam and a wildlife refuge.                                          _____

4. Iowas Keokuk Hydroelectric Project, completed in 1983, was the first large dam on the Mississippi and remains the river's only hydroelectric facility.   _____

5. The wetlands were declared one of the nations protected areas and were protected within the Upper Mississippi River Wildlife and Fish Refuge starting in 1924.                          _____

6. The authors story begins with the dam and wildlife refuge and then covers the larger issues of regional economic development, environment degradation, and the meaning of conservation before 1950.                                      _____

7. Between 1890 and 1950 the history of the great river reflects the clash of diverse and ultimately conflicting uses promoted by businessmens clubs, commercial fishermen, and the U.S. Army Corps of Engineers. _____

8. The interests of wildlife biologists, metropolitan water districts, and citizen groups further complicated the handling of the river. _____

9. The river history is best seen, then, in terms of interest-group politics. _____

10. Only slowly did people appreciate the consequences of river development—humanitys restless attempts to harness and to change the river. _____

11. But Scarpinos book also has its positive view of the river. _____

12. Its equally true that citizen groups mobilized to counter the actions of the special-interest groups. _____

13. The Izaak Walton League of America, a collection of urban sportsmen who organized in 1922 to preserve the American outdoors, spearheaded the effort to protect the river valleys wetlands. _____

14. The federal governments response was to create, in 1924, the Upper Mississippi River Wildlife and Fish Refuge to preserve wetlands from drainage along a 300-mile stretch of the river from Minnesota to Illinois. _____

15. Scarpino argues that the Leagues campaign represented a significant and successful application of the tactics that had been pioneered by the Sierra Club. _____

**Apostrophes**                                    Exercise 15-2

NAME _____ SCORE _____

DIRECTIONS   Rewrite the following word groups as a noun or a pronoun modified by another noun or pronoun in the possessive case.

EXAMPLES
A responsibility of everybody

*everybody's responsibility*

the responsibilities of the United Nations

*the United Nations' responsibilities*

1. the history of the Forest Service

2. the history of the United States

3. the results of the experiments

4. a poem by Marge Piercy

5. the extinction of dinosaurs

6. a party given by Mr. and Mrs. Jones

7. the escape of the satellite from orbit

8. the interests of the baby

9. an address by the governor of Texas

10. the role of the women

11. a telescope shared by Craig and Scott

12. a reunion at the Pearsons

13. decisions made by one

14. the design of the airport

15. the temple of Zeus

16. the riddle of the Sphinx

17. the column of the editor-in-chief

18. the cars of Carlson and Anna

19. the picture of Charles

20. the flippers of the whale

## 16

**Learn to use quotation marks to set off all direct quotations, titles of short works, and words used in a special sense, and to place other marks of punctuation in proper relation to quotation marks.**

When you use quotation marks, you let your reader know that you are quoting directly (that is, you are stating in the exact words) what someone has written, said, or thought.

> "Will you return this book to the library for me?" the note asked.
> "I'll be glad to," I told my friend when I saw her. But I thought to myself, "I think I'll check it out in my name and read it this weekend."

**16a Use quotation marks for direct quotations and in all dialogue. Set off long quotations by indention.**

**(1) Use double quotation marks (" ") before and after all direct (but not indirect) quotations; use a single quotation mark (' ') before and after a quotation within a quotation.**

| | |
|---|---|
| INDIRECT QUOTATION | He asked me if I wanted to visit Golden Gate Park. |
| INDIRECT QUOTATION | I told him that we could drive there this afternoon.   [*That* frequently introduces an indirect quotation.] |
| DIRECT QUOTATION | He asked me, "Do you want to visit Golden Gate Park?" |
| DIRECT QUOTATION | The brochure for Golden Gate Park recommends the aquariums as "windows into the lives of marine life."   [A phrase from the brochure is quoted.] |
| QUOTATION WITHIN A QUOTATION | Diana asked, "Did you hear the attendant say 'Stay back' when the children leaned over the tank of sharks?" |

**(2) In quoting dialogue (conversation), a new paragraph begins each time the speaker changes.**

> Five-year old Michael proudly announced to his brother, "I had a dream last night. I rode up and down on the escalator one thousand times with Mama and Daddy."
> "Did I ride the escalator with you?" asked four-year-old Bobby hopefully.
> "Nope. You weren't in the dream," the older boy responded smugly.
> "Well, tonight I'm going to dream about eating five thousand chocolate ice-cream cones," Bobby blurted out, "and you won't get any because you won't be in the dream!"

**Note:**   Commas set off expressions like *he said* that introduce, interrupt, or follow direct quotations.

The guide cautioned, "Be careful, please, while we are in the construction area."
"Be careful, please," the guide cautioned, "while we are in the construction area."
"Be careful, please, while we are in the construction area," the guide cautioned.

If the quoted speech is a question or an exclamation, a question mark or exclamation point—instead of a comma—follows the quoted passage.

"Do not touch!" the guide scolded a child. "Each of the glass panels is numbered and must be placed in the aquarium in sequence."

**Caution:** Remember that a divided quotation made up of two main clauses or two complete sentences must be punctuated with a semicolon or an end mark.

"Each panel is shaped to fit the contour of the round aquarium," the guide explained; "the numbers on the panels tell workers exactly where the panels are to be placed."

OR

"Each panel is shaped to fit the contour of the round aquarium," the guide explained. "The numbers on the panels tell workers exactly where the panels are to be placed."

**(3) Prose quotations that would require four or more lines of typing and poetry that would require four or more lines are indented from the rest of the text.**

**Prose** When you quote one paragraph or less, all lines of a long quotation (more than four lines) are indented ten spaces from the left margin and are double-spaced. When you quote two or more paragraphs, indent the first line of each complete paragraph thirteen spaces rather than the usual ten. Use quotation marks only if they appear in the original. (If the quotation is run in with the text, remember that it should begin and end with a double quotation mark.)

In Caroline Gordon's Aleck Maury: Sportsman, Mr. Maury has just found a new stream to fish. He sits on a log, opens his book of flies, and tries to decide which fly is worthy of being fished in such beautiful water.

> I sat down on a log, got out my fly book and solemnly weighed the possibilities. I used the method of exclusion. All the flies went promptly back into the book except three: a Royal Coachman, a Black Gnat, and Old Speck. (Cecil Morrison had taught me to tie the original Old Speck in my faraway youth. I reckon she took five hundred pounds of fish before she petered out on me. I have her made-to-order these days, red and white Guinea feathers tied on a No. 1 hook.) All the time I was looking over these flies I knew it was a work of supererogation. Old Speck was the only one worthy of the virgin stream. (99)

**Poetry** Fewer than four lines of poetry may be run into the text. If run in, the quoted material should begin and end with a double quotation mark. Use quotation marks within the quotation only if they appear in the original.

The eighteenth-century English writer John Gay was among the first writers to argue for fishing for trout with artificial flies and not with live bait. He pledged that "Around the steel no tortur'd worm shall twine, / No blood of living insect stain my line." [Use a slash to mark the end of a line when poetry is run into the text. Leave one letter space before and after each slash.]

OR

The eighteenth-century English writer John Gay was among the first writers to argue for fishing for trout with artificial flies and not with live bait. He pledged that

> Around the steel no tortur'd worm shall twine,
> No blood of living insect stain my line;
> Let me, less cruel, cast feather'd hook,
> With pliant rod athwart the pebbled brook,
> Silent along the mazy margin stray,
> And with fur-wrought fly delude the prey.

**16b Use quotation marks for minor titles—of short works such as television shows, short stories, essays, short poems, one-act plays, songs, articles from periodicals—and for subdivisions of books.**

As part of the documentation for her paper on Yeats' poem "The Fisherman," Alice used an essay titled "Art and Aristocracy" from the book *W. B. Yeats: His Poetry and Thought* by A. G. Stock.

One episode, "The American Sportsman," discussed the paintings of Winslow Homer as portrayals of the development of outdoor sports in America. I was particularly impressed by Homer's *Duckboat and Sea Oats*, which is set on the Atlantic coast.

**16c Use quotation marks to enclose words used in a special sense.**

The term "research paper" is broadly applied to anything from a three-source, five-page paper to a one-hundred-source, book-length doctoral dissertation. [*Research paper* may be either italicized or enclosed in quotation marks: see Section **10**.]

**Note:** Avoid the tendency some writers have of using quotation marks throughout a paper to call attention to what they consider clever phrasings. Often what they think are clever phrases are really only trite expressions, slang, or colloquialisms that could be better phrased. (See also **20c**.)

INEFFECTIVE    The municipal water-treatment plant is "up to" its old, "strange" ways again; the discharge is "knocking off" fish in "bunches."

BETTER    The municipal water treatment plant is once again dumping toxic effluent; the discharge into the Stones River is killing huge schools of fish.

**16d Do not overuse quotation marks.**

Quotation marks are not used for titles that head compositions. Quotation marks also are not used to enclose a cliché or to mark a *yes* or *no* in indirect discourse.

Yes, he did accuse her of beating around the bush.

NOT

"Yes," he did accuse her of "beating around the bush."

## 16e Follow the conventions of American printers in deciding whether various marks of punctuation belong inside or outside the quotation marks.

### (1) The period and the comma are usually placed inside the quotation marks.

"Well," he said, "I'm ready for the samples."

**Exception:** If you are citing a page reference for a quotation within the text, place the comma or the period after the page citation—and thus after the quotation marks.

When Livvie let go of old Solomon's watch, she released herself to life, and "all at once there began outside the full song of a bird" (77).

### (2) The semicolon and the colon are placed outside the quotation marks.

He read the instructions printed in the booklet titled "Lines and Lures": "Use 6 lb. to 15 lb. test line and 1/8 oz. to 3/8 oz. lures."
Another booklet was titled "Reels"; it suggested using "a medium weight spinning reel with at least a 5:1 retrieve ratio."

### (3) The dash, the question mark, and the exclamation point are placed inside the quotation marks when they apply to the quoted matter and outside the quotation marks when they apply to the whole sentence.

"What's up?" the assistant asked.    [The question mark applies to the quoted matter.]
Did you notice the container marked "This side up"?    [The question mark applies to the whole sentence.]
At what point did he say "Why are you telling me this?"    [a question within a question—one question mark inside the quotation marks]

**Quotation Marks**                                   Exercise 16–1

NAME _____ SCORE _____

DIRECTIONS   In the sentences below, insert all needed quotation marks. Then enter the quotation marks and the first and last word of each quoted part in the blanks. Be sure to include the other marks of punctuation used with the quotation marks in their proper position—either inside or outside the quotation marks. Do not enclose an indirect quotation. Write *C* in the blank if a sentence is correct without quotation marks.

EXAMPLE
The sentences in this exercise are based on the article
"The Land of the River" by Douglass Lee.                    *"The – River"*

1. We had ten feet of water where you're standing. I came in a boat the day after and just tree tops stuck out, he said.                              _____

2. I looked at his orange grove and then asked, Since you are likely to be flooded again, why did you replant?                                             _____

3. This is black clay, the best of the soil from all the way to Canada, he replied. It's hell to work, but it's great for citrus.                              _____

4. When he said the best of the soil from all the way to Canada, he was thinking of the soil brought to the delta by the Mississippi.                  _____

5. The river slows as it reaches the sea, and this great Father of Waters releases the soil and silt that it has gathered over all or parts of thirty-one states.   _____

6. The sediment becomes the delta, a strip of plain along the Louisiana coast that one romantic farmer described as deliriously fertile.              _____

7. Unfortunately the river has a habit of changing its course and abandoning its delta. As one biologist explained it, The river last changed course in the fourteenth century and began forming the modern delta, the Balize. _____

8. Now this fragile region is endangered again, he continued; the river is trying to change its course to follow the Atchafalaya River. _____

9. An abandoned delta, he said, soon erodes and practically disappears. _____

10. The Chandeleus Islands, a good example of an archipelago, are the remnants of the delta that preceded the Balize Delta. _____

# 17

Learn to use the end marks of punctuation—the period, the question mark, and the exclamation point—and the internal marks of punctuation—the colon, the dash, parentheses, brackets, the slash, and ellipses—in accordance with conventional practices.

The end marks of punctuation give most writers little difficulty except when they are used with direct quotations.

## 17a The period follows declarative and mildly imperative (command) sentences, indirect questions, and many abbreviations.

| | |
|---|---|
| DECLARATIVE SENTENCE | At least six times since the end of the last ice age, the Mississippi River has changed course dramatically. |
| MILDLY IMPERATIVE SENTENCE | Study the maps of the Mississippi delta. |
| INDIRECT QUOTATION | He was asked how the delta formed. |
| ABBREVIATION | Dr. Eugene Levy, who will give a lecture at 4:00 p.m., also has studied planet formation. |

## 17b The question mark follows direct (but not indirect) questions.

| | |
|---|---|
| DIRECT QUESTION | Would you like to know more about Dr. White's ideas? |
| QUOTED QUESTION | "Does Dr. White's theory of delta formation explain the delta's recent changes?" I wondered.   [No comma or period follows the question mark used at the end of a quoted passage.] |

Sometimes a declarative or imperative sentence can be made into a question by simply changing the period to a question mark.

Dr. White illustrated his theory?   [Compare "Did Dr. White illustrate his theory?" in which the verb must change to form a question.]

## 17c The exclamation point follows emphatic interjections and statements of strong emotion.

Dr. White explained that each change in course meant that the river had abandoned one delta and had begun building a new one. This cycle created most of the Louisiana coast. Remarkable!

"Bravo!" cried the audience when the rock group Erosion completed its performance.   [No comma or period follows the exclamation point used at the end of a quoted passage.]

Avoid using an exclamation point just to make your writing sound exciting or important.

> If not for a U.S. Army Corps of Engineers flood-control structure above Baton Rouge, the Mississippi would be changing course to follow the Atchafalaya River on a route to the sea 140 miles shorter than its present one.   [The content of the sentence, not an exclamation point at the end, communicates the writer's belief in the importance of the facts.]


## OTHER MARKS

Of the internal marks of punctuation (those that do not mark the end of a sentence), the semicolon (see Section **14**), the colon, and the dash are most closely related to the period because they bring the reader to a full stop—rather than to a pause as the comma does. Notice the difference between the way you read aloud a sentence that has a comma and one that has a colon, a dash, or a semicolon.

> The Atchafalaya River already siphons off 25 percent of the Mississippi water and has an upstart delta of its own, among the youngest in the world.   [a slight pause for the comma]
> Scientists now worry about erosion of the newest delta: the Balize, or "bird foot" Delta.   [a full stop for a colon]
> East of the Balize Delta are the Chandeleur Islands—remnant sandbars of the drowned St. Bernard Delta; about 1,800 years ago, the river abandoned the St. Bernard.   [a full stop for the dash and for the semicolon]

You have already studied the comma (Section **12**) and the semicolon (Section **14**). As you learn about the other commonly used marks of internal punctuation, you will become aware of the overlapping functions of some punctuation marks—that is, of the occasions when several different marks of punctuation are appropriate.

**17d The colon, following a main clause, formally introduces a word, a phrase, a clause, or a list. It is also used to separate figures in scriptural and time references and to introduce some quoted sentences.**

Following a main clause or sentence pattern, the colon and the dash often may be used interchangeably. The colon is a more formal mark of punctuation than the dash.

> A flight over the Chandeleur Islands reveals a lesson in sand: remote, beautiful, desolate, and isolated strips of sand, evidence of the eroded St. Bernard Delta.
> A broad sound separates the islands from the mainland marshes: the sand and water were living marsh not so many years ago.   [The dash is not generally used when a main clause is being introduced.]

The Balize Delta is a fertile producer of seafood and citrus: shrimp, oysters, satsumas, and oranges.   [A dash could also introduce this list.]

Dr. John Watson repeats the opinion of most scientists: "The Balize Delta is one of the most fertile areas in the world, but we must act quickly and carefully to preserve it."   [The dash is not used to introduce quotations.]

Except for this last example, in which a quotation is introduced following an expression like *he said* (in this case, *Watson repeats*), there is no reason to interrupt a sentence with a colon. Do not use a colon between a subject and verb or between a verb and its complement or object.

A river forms a delta as it nears the sea, the current slowing, sand, silt, and clay dropping, and the delta slowly rising on the shallow continental shelf.   [A colon after *sea* would interrupt the sentence pattern.]

A river forms a delta as it nears the sea: the current slows; sand, silt, and clay drop; and the delta slowly rises on the shallow continental shelf.   [The colon introduces a list of main clauses following a sentence pattern.]

The colon is also used between chapter and verse in scriptural passages and between hours and minutes in time references.

Exodus 5:24
6:15 P.M.

**17e   Like the colon, the dash may introduce a word, a phrase, a clause, or a list that follows a sentence pattern; unlike the colon, it may interrupt a sentence pattern to mark a sudden break in thought, to set off a parenthetical element for emphasis or clarity, or to set off an introductory list.**

When I visit the delta, I am more interested in the food—particularly the Cajun cooking—than in sightseeing.   [Dashes, or sometimes parentheses, are used to set off a sudden break in thought.]

Three Cajun dishes—blackened redfish, smothered okra, and crawfish gumbo—are my favorites.   [Colons are not used here because they would interrupt the sentence pattern. Commas are not used because the list itself contains commas. Parentheses could be used: see **17f**.]

Redfish (a marvelous gamefish), okra (that ubiquitous southern vegetable), and crawfish (the Cajun lobster)—all three become delicacies in the hands of a Cajun chef.   [The colon is not used here because it would interrupt the sentence pattern. Use the dash when an introductory list precedes the sentence pattern.]

Three foods that are quite ordinary in the hands of most cooks become delicacies when prepared by a Cajun chef—redfish, okra, and crawfish.   [The colon is also appropriate here to set off a list following the sentence pattern.]

**17f   Parentheses (1) set off supplementary or illustrative matter, (2) sometimes set off parenthetical matter, and (3) enclose figures or letters used for numbering, as in this rule.**

The primary use of the parentheses is to set off supplementary or illustrative material that is loosely joined to the sentence.

The Cajuns (Louisiana natives believed to be descended from French exiles from
Acadia) take great pride in their heritage. [The parentheses set off the definition; commas could also be used.]

Louisiana has produced many musicians and humorists who derive material from
their Cajun heritage (see definition on preceding page). [A lowercase letter begins the information in parentheses and a period follows the parentheses when
the material in parentheses forms a part of the sentence.]

**Parenthetical matter**   Three marks of punctuation are used to set off parenthetical matter. The most commonly used are commas, which cause the reader
only to pause and so keep the parenthetical matter closely related to the sentence. The least commonly used are parentheses, which minimize the importance of the parenthetical matter by setting it off distinctly from the sentence.
Dashes, the third mark used to enclose parenthetical matter, emphasize the parenthetical matter, since they cause the reader to stop at the beginning and end
of the matter. (Remember that dashes, or sometimes parentheses, are necessary
not for emphasis but for clarity when the parenthetical matter itself includes
commas.)

The Louisiana coast, as visitors soon learn, is home to people of many nationali-
ties.   [Commas would be used by most writers to set off this parenthetical matter.]

The Louisiana coast (as visitors soon learn) is home to people of many nationali-
ties.   [Parentheses minimize the importance of the parenthetical matter.]

The Louisiana coast—as visitors soon learn—is home to people of many national-
ities.   [Dashes emphasize the parenthetical matter.]

Many people from southeast Asia—Vietnam, Cambodia, Laos, and Thailand—set-
tle there because the delta country resembles their homelands. [Dashes are
needed for clarity to enclose the parenthetical matter that contains commas. Parentheses could also be used, but they would minimize the importance of the list
of places.]

**17g  Brackets set off editorial comments in quoted matter.**

When you need to explain something about a quotation, enclose your explanation within brackets to show that it is not part of the quoted matter.

Katherine Anne Porter uses a common metaphor to describe death: "She [Granny
Weatherall] stretched herself with a deep breath and blew out the light." [The
writer of the sentence added the name to explain the identity of *she*.]

**17h  The slash indicates options and shows the end of a line of poetry run in
with the text. (See also 16a(3).)**

An appreciation of life and/or love is apparent in Ezra Pound's lines "Sing we for
love and idleness, / Naught else is worth the having." [Note the space before
and after the slash in the poetry.]

**17i  Use ellipsis points (three spaced periods) to mark an omission from a quoted passage and to mark a reflective pause or hesitation.**

"Now a lot of these old muskrat trappers are true conservationists," the game warden claimed. "I've made friends for life here . . . and that's friends you can knock on their door at three o'clock in the morning, 20 miles from nowhere, and borrow gas."

The old man looked away, rocking gently, resting his head against the ladderback chair. "Well, maybe I have . . . maybe I haven't," he said, "I disremember."

—ROBERT HERRING

If ellipsis points are used to indicate that the end of a quoted sentence is being omitted, and if the part that is quoted forms a complete sentence itself, use the sentence period plus ellipsis points.

The shrimp catch . . . grew from an annual average of 41 million pounds in the 1930s to a second 91 million in 1982. . . .   —NATIONAL GEOGRAPHIC

## End Marks of Punctuation                    Exercise 17–1

NAME _____ SCORE _____

DIRECTIONS   Write a sentence to illustrate each of the following uses of an end mark of punctuation.

    EXAMPLE
    a quoted direct question

1. a mildly imperative sentence

2. a direct question

3. a sentence containing an abbreviation

4. an exclamation

5. a declarative sentence containing a direct quotation

6. an indirect quotation

7. a declarative sentence containing a quoted direct question

8. an indirect question

9. a declarative sentence containing a quoted exclamation

10. a quotation that includes the ellipsis mark

## Internal Marks of Punctuation                    Exercise 17–2

NAME _____ SCORE _____

DIRECTIONS    In the sentences below insert commas, semicolons, colons, dashes, parentheses, and brackets, as needed. Then enter in the blanks the marks you have added. If
more than one punctuation mark is possible, choose the one you think most writers
would use, but be prepared to discuss the effect of the other possible choice or choices.

EXAMPLE
The Corps of Engineers, the government agency trying to control the

river's flow, believes that it can prevent the river from abandoning

the present delta.                                           , ,

1. Many scientists recalling past attempts to chain the Mississippi
   shake their heads in dismay.                             _____

2. But the contest over the river's direction may already be lost
   because of one factor the significant changes humans have already made in the marshlands.                            _____

3. One official asserts that "We the Corps of Engineers are fighting a losing battle against the man-made levees."        _____

4. The primary method of controlling the river has been to build
   levees earthen embankments that protect roads and houses
   from flooding.                                           _____

5. Where roads go, so go the levees as the locals say but where
   the levees go, the marsh dies.                           _____

6. For example, levees almost completely seal off Plaquemines
   Parish 26,000 residents from the marsh.                  _____

7. But as they protect the residents the levees also prevent water
   from reaching and renewing the marshlands.               _____

8. The result is a dying marsh cut off from the necessary water.  _____

9. A senior official of the Louisiana Department of Wildlife and
   Fisheries LDWF put it succinctly These marshes are on a roller
   coaster.                                                 _____

10. Aerial mapping has shown an average loss of forty square miles of deltaic plain per year the rate of loss increases yearly.  _____

11. Levees damage marshes by denying them new layers of silt and fresh water equally damaging a cobweb of man-made canals hastens erosion.  _____

12. Some canals are dredged for boat traffic others for pipelines and rigs and still others purely for drainage.  _____

13. All dredging has the same effect ultimately it lets salt water into the river marshes, kills vegetation, and erodes marsh borders.  _____

14. A rising sea level some experts believe is hastening encroachment.  _____

15. To cap the situation the delta has reached the edge of the continental shelf where silt channeled by the levees drops straight out to sea.  _____

# SPELLING AND HYPHENATION sp 18

## 18

**Learn to spell and hyphenate in accordance with the usage shown in an up-to-date dictionary.**

Everyone notices the sign that invites you to eat at the "Resturant" or the one that offers "Wood for Sell." And, right or wrong, most people tend to brand both the owner and the maker of such a sign as uneducated. There is simply no other error in composition that is so universally recognized and deplored as the misspelled word. Because of the stigma of illiteracy that it carries, misspelling should be the first and most important concern of any poor speller.

If you are a poor speller, one who regularly misspells enough words to have your classwork or professional work graded down, you should begin a definite program for improving your spelling skills. There are many excellent spelling manuals available today that make use of the latest psychological studies to present words in a logical, easy-to-learn order.

You may also find the following procedures helpful.

**(1) Learn the rules of spelling presented in this section of the book.**

**(2) Proofread your papers carefully at least once for misspelled words only.**

As you write a rough draft, it is often difficult, and always distracting, to look up a great number of words, but you can put a check or some other identifying sign above those words you have any doubts about so that you can look up their spelling when you proofread.

If you have difficulty spotting misspelled words in your own composition, try to slow down your reading of the rough draft by pointing to each word with a pencil. Or even read your writing from right to left instead of the usual left to right to be sure that you see individual words rather than groups of words. You need, whenever possible, to make more than two drafts of your paper because you will be unlikely to see your errors in a rough draft that has many words and phrases crossed through or that has barely legible handwriting.

**(3) Keep a list of the words you tend to misspell.**

The words that you misspell on your writing assignments should be recorded in the Individual Spelling List at the end of the *Workbook*. Because most people have a tendency to repeatedly misspell certain words, you should review your own spelling list frequently to break your bad spelling habits.

A comparison of your spelling list with someone else's will usually show—surprisingly enough—only two or three words in common. The mastery of spelling is an individual matter, differing with each person. You get some benefit from mastering lists of frequently misspelled words, but your own Individual Spelling List is the all-important one for you to work with.

**(4) Write the words you misspell by syllables; then write the definitions of the words; finally, use the words in sentences.**

E NIG MAT IC    puzzling or baffling   [The poem was *enigmatic* until I learned the meanings of five key words that the poet used.]

AT TRIB UTE    as a noun, an object or quality which belongs to or represents someone or something   [The *attributes* of Santa Claus have been expanded over the years.]

On the following pages are rules that will help you to avoid misspelling many commonly used words. Following the explanation of each rule is an exercise to reinforce the rule in your mind.

## Misspelling Because of Mispronunciation — Exercise 18-1

NAME _____ SCORE _____

**18a To avoid omitting, adding, transposing, or changing a letter in a word, pronounce the word carefully according to the way the dictionary divides it into syllables.**

The places where common mistakes are made in pronunciation—and spelling—are indicated in boldface.

| | |
|---|---|
| OMISSIONS | candi**d**ate, every**t**hing, gover**n**ment |
| ADDITIONS | athlete, laun**d**ry, drowned |
| TRANSPOSITIONS | perform, children, tragedy |
| CHANGE | accurate, prejudice, separate |

DIRECTIONS   With the aid of your dictionary, write out each of the following words by syllables, indicate the position of the primary accent, and pronounce the word correctly and distinctly. In your pronunciation avoid any careless omission, addition, transposition, or change.

EXAMPLE
similar     *sim´·i·lar*

1. accidentally   _____

2. supposedly   _____

3. prisoner   _____

4. environment   _____

5. destruction   _____

6. escape   _____

7. circumstance   _____

8. surprise   _____

9. further   _____

10. candidate   _____

11. recognize   _____

12. temperament _____

13. asked _____

14. interpret _____

15. perhaps _____

16. prepare _____

17. partner _____

18. describe _____

19. especially _____

20. mischievous _____

21. family _____

22. prescription _____

23. used _____

24. hindrance _____

25. interest _____

26. athletic _____

27. hungry _____

28. library _____

29. represent _____

30. sophomore _____

## Confusion of Words Similar
## in Sound and/or Spelling

Exercise 18-2

NAME _____ SCORE _____

**18b Distinguish between words that have a similar sound and/or spelling, such as *lose-loose* and *to-too-two*.**

DIRECTIONS    In the following sentences, cross out the spelling or spellings in parentheses that do not fit the meaning, and write the correct spelling in the blank. Consult your dictionary freely.

EXAMPLE

Many experts believe that the future of the Mississippi

delta marshes depends (~~holey~~, ~~holy~~, wholly) on an in-

flux of fresh water.                                                  *wholly*

1. Of (course, coarse), stricter control of dredging is

    needed.                                                          _____

2. Many experts believe that (to, too, two) many ob-

    stacles block those people who would save the

    marshes.                                                         _____

3. They believe that local residents will not (except,

    accept) reductions in their use of the river.                   _____

4. If the reductions are not made, the (prophecy,

    prophesy) of doom will come true.                               _____

5. Even as some officials work to save the delta, oth-

    ers (propose, purpose) actions to destroy it.                   _____

6. For example, (there, their, they're) are plans to

    deepen the river channel at New Orleans by 40 to

    55 feet.                                                         _____

7. Although the added depth (maybe, may be) a way

    to increase boat traffic in the port, it also means

    that more water will flow out the channel, into the

    sea, away from the delta marshes.                               _____

8. During the drought and low water of 1980, a (wage, wedge) of ocean water slid upstream to hover near New Orleans' water intakes.                    _____

9. City officials nervously (waited, waded) out the crisis, hoping that salt water would not enter the city system.                    _____

10. Deepening the river channel will increase the likelihood that salt water will enter the system (thorough, through) the river intakes.                    _____

11. The Mississippi actually empties into the Gulf of Mexico through many smaller streams of water that branch (off, of) the central channel.                    _____

12. From the air the many branches resemble the roots of some huge tree as they crisscross the vast (tracks, tracts) of marsh.                    _____

13. The marsh lies between the branches of the river, and, as the flow of fresh water decreases, an (access, excess) of sea water kills marsh vegetation.                    _____

14. When the marsh vegetation dies, and before marine vegetation can (adapt, adopt) to the new area, the marshland erodes into the sea.                    _____

15. Soon the (hole, whole) marsh has disappeared.                    _____

# Adding Prefixes

Exercise 18-3

NAME _____ SCORE _____

**18c Add the prefix to the root word without doubling or dropping letters.** (The root is the base word to which the prefix or the suffix is added.)

| | | | | |
|---|---|---|---|---|
| un- | + | necessary | = | unnecessary |
| mis- | + | spell | = | misspell |
| dis- | + | agree | = | disagree |

DIRECTIONS   In the blank at the right enter the correct spelling of each word with the prefix added. Consult your dictionary freely. Some dictionaries hyphenate some of the following words. (See also **18g(3).**)

EXAMPLES

| | | | |
|---|---|---|---|
| mis- | + | quote | _*misquote*_ |
| pre- | + | eminent | _*preeminent*_ |
| 1. dis- | + | satisfied | _____ |
| 2. dis- | + | appear | _____ |
| 3. mis- | + | pronounce | _____ |
| 4. mis- | + | understand | _____ |
| 5. mis- | + | step | _____ |
| 6. un- | + | noticed | _____ |
| 7. un- | + | usual | _____ |
| 8. dis- | + | approve | _____ |
| 9. dis- | + | similar | _____ |
| 10. mis- | + | spent | _____ |
| 11. mis- | + | behave | _____ |
| 12. dis- | + | able | _____ |
| 13. mis- | + | interpret | _____ |

14. re- + take   _____

15. re- + evaluate   _____

# Adding Suffixes—Final *e*

NAME _____ SCORE _____

**18d(1) Drop the final *e* before a suffix beginning with a vowel but not before a suffix beginning with a consonant.**

| | | | | | | | | |
|---|---|---|---|---|---|---|---|---|
| bride | + | -al | = | bridal | fame | + | -ous | = famous |
| care | + | -ful | = | careful | entire | + | -ly | = entirely |

***Exceptions:*** *due, duly; awe, awful; hoe, hoeing; singe, singeing.* After *c* or *g* the final *e* is retained before suffixes beginning with *a* or *o: notice, noticeable; courage, courageous.*

DIRECTIONS   With the aid of your dictionary, write the correct spelling of each word with the suffix added. Write (*ex*) after each answer that is an exception to rule **18d(1)**.

EXAMPLES

argue      + -ing      *arguing*

dye        + -ing      *dyeing (ex)*

1. become      + -ing      _____

2. use         + -age      _____

3. hope        + -ing      _____

4. excite      + -able     _____

5. drive       + -ing      _____

6. outrage     + -ous      _____

7. like        + -ly       _____

8. write       + -ing      _____

9. advise      + -able     _____

10. arrange    + -ment     _____

11. value      + -able     _____

12. manage     + -ment     _____

13. advantage  + -ous      _____

14. judge    +   -ment    _____

15. extreme   +   -ly    _____

# Adding Suffixes—Doubling the Consonant     Exercise 18-5

NAME _____ SCORE _____

**18d(2) When the suffix begins with a vowel (*ing, ed, ence, ance, able*), double a final single consonant if it is preceded by a single vowel and is in an accented syllable.** (A word of one syllable, of course, is always accented.)

mop, mopped   [compare with *mope, moped*]
mop, mopping   [compare with *mope, moping*]
con•fer', con•fer'red   [final consonant in the accented syllable]
ben'e•fit, ben'e•fited   [final consonant not in the accented syllable]
need, needed   [final consonant not preceded by a single vowel]

DIRECTIONS   In the blank at the right enter the correct spelling of each word with the suffix added. Consult your dictionary freely.

EXAMPLE
control   +   -ed     *controlled*

1.  stop        +   -ing     *stopping*

2.  occur       +   -ing     _____

3.  pour        +   -ing     _____

4.  proceed     +   -ed      _____

5.  unforget    +   -able    _____

6.  begin       +   -ing     _____

7.  control     +   -able    _____

8.  transmit    +   -ing     _____

9.  equip       +   -ed      _____

10. meet        +   -ing     _____

11. prefer      +   -ed      _____

12. big         +   -est     _____

13. push        +   -ed      _____

14. fat      +   -er      _____

15. attach   +   -ed      _____

## Adding Suffixes—Final *y*                               Exercise 18–6

NAME _____ SCORE _____

**18d(3) Except before *ing*, final *y* preceded by a consonant is changed to *i* before a suffix.**

| | | | | | | | | |
|---|---|---|---|---|---|---|---|---|
| defy | + | -ance | = | defiance | happy | + | -ness | = happiness |
| modify | + | -er | = | modifier | modify | + | -ing | = modifying |

To make a noun plural or a verb singular, final *y* preceded by a consonant is changed to *i* and *es* is added. (See also **18f**).

| | | | | | | | | |
|---|---|---|---|---|---|---|---|---|
| duty | + | -es | = duties | deny | + | -es | = | denies |
| ally | + | -es | = allies | copy | + | -es | = | copies |

Final *y* preceded by a vowel is usually not changed before a suffix.

    annoy    +    -ed    =    annoyed        turkey    +    -s    =    turkeys

***Exceptions:*** *pay, paid; lay, laid; say, said; day, daily.*

DIRECTIONS    With the aid of your dictionary, enter the correct spelling of each word with the suffix added. Write (*ex*) after each word that is an exception to rule **18d(3)**.

EXAMPLES
| | | | |
|---|---|---|---|
| boundary | + | -es | *boundaries* |
| pay | + | -d | *paid (ex)* |
| 1. monkey | + | -s | _____ |
| 2. try | + | -es | _____ |
| 3. accompany | + | -es | _____ |
| 4. chimney | + | -s | _____ |
| 5. bury | + | -ed | _____ |
| 6. lay | + | -ed | _____ |
| 7. fallacy | + | -es | _____ |
| 8. hungry | + | -ly | _____ |
| 9. lonely | + | -ness | _____ |
| 10. donkey | + | -s | _____ |

# Forming the Plural

Exercise 18-7

NAME _____ SCORE _____

**18d(3) and 18d(5)** Form the plural of most nouns by (1) adding *s* to the singular form of the noun; (2) adding *es* to singular nouns ending in **s, ch, sh,** or **x;** or (3) changing the **y** to **i** and adding **es** if the noun ends in a **y** preceded by a consonant.

| | | |
|---|---|---|
| boy→boys | fox→foxes | mystery→mysteries |
| cupful→cupfuls | Harris→Harrises | beauty→beauties |
| Drehmel→Drehmels | genius→geniuses | reply→replies |

A few nouns change their form for the plural: *woman→women; child→children.* And a few nouns ending in *o* take the *es* plural: *potato→potatoes; hero→ heroes.* And a few nouns change an *f* to a *v* and add *s* or *es: calf→calves; knife→knives.*

DIRECTIONS   In the blank enter the plural form of each word. Consult your dictionary freely.

EXAMPLES
day  *days*

scratch  *scratches*

1. speech _____

2. box _____

3. industry _____

4. veto _____

5. wolf _____

6. Long _____

7. witch _____

8. scientist _____

9. address _____

10. city _____

11. question _____

12. ghetto _____

13. article _____

14. leaf _____

15. watch _____

16. man _____

17. professor _____

18. business _____

19. Jones _____

20. army _____

# Confusion of *ei* and *ie*

Exercise 18-8

NAME _____ SCORE _____

**18e When the sound is *ee* (as in *see*), write *ei* after *c* (*receipt, ceiling*), and *ie* after any other letter (*relieve, priest*); when the sound is other than *ee*, usually write *ei* (*eight, their, sleight*).**

*Exceptions:* either, neither, financier, leisure, seize, species, weird.

**Note:** This rule does not apply when *ei* or *ie* is not pronounced as one simple sound (*alien, audience, fiery*) or when *cie* stands for *shə* (*ancient, conscience, efficient*).

DIRECTIONS   With the aid of your dictionary, fill in the blanks in the following words by writing *ei* or *ie*. Write (*ex*) after any word that is an exception to rule **18e**.

EXAMPLES
dec___*ei*___ve

___*ei*___ther (*ex*)

1. rec_____ve

2. bel_____f

3. ch_____f

4. s_____ge

5. conc_____ted

6. y_____ld

7. gr_____f

8. l_____sure

9. misch_____f

10. sl_____gh

11. th_____f

12. gr_____ve

13. spec_____s

14. w_____ght

15. c_____ling

16. rel_____ve

17. h_____ght

18. f_____nd

19. n_____ther

20. f_____ld

# Hyphenated Words

Exercise 18-9

NAME _____ SCORE _____

**18f In general, use the hyphen (1) between two or more words serving as a single adjective before a noun, (2) with compound numbers from twenty-one to ninety-nine and with fractions, (3) with prefixes or suffixes for clarity, (4) with the prefixes *ex-*, *self-*, *all-*, and *great-* and the suffix *elect*, (5) between a prefix and a proper name, and (6) never after an adverb ending in *ly*.**

(1)  a *know-it-all* expression
(2)  *sixty-six, one-half*
(3)  *re-collect* the supplies (to distinguish from *recollect* an event)
(4)  *ex-wife, self-help, all-important, great-grandmother, mayor-elect*
(5)  *mid-July, un-American*
(6)  *highly respected* statesman

DIRECTIONS    Supply hyphens where they are needed in the following list. Not all items require hyphens.

EXAMPLES
a well-spent childhood

a childhood well spent

1.  a long distance call

2.  a four foot barricade

3.  a twenty five year old coach

4.  ex President Townes

5.  President elect Drehmel

6.  a high rise apartment

7.  a commonly used adjective

8.  chocolate covered cherries

9.  students who are career minded

10.  the all seeing eye of the camera

11.  a two thirds vote of the Senate

12.  Two thirds of the Senate approved.

13.  western style jeans

14.  the clumsily executed dance

15.  He is forty five.

16. She is my great aunt.

17. an all inclusive study

18. results that are long lasting

19. long lasting results

20. My small daughter is amazingly self sufficient.

21. The officer re searched the suspect.

22. a two part answer

23. The answer had two parts.

24. The up and down motion of the roller coaster made the girl ill.

25. The shop specializes in teen age fashions.

26. I feel all right today.

27. We are all ready to go.

28. a win at any cost attitude

29. in mid December

30. a walk in closet

## 19

**Learn the ways an up-to-date desk dictionary can guide you in the choice of words appropriate to your writing needs.**

An up-to-date desk dictionary is a necessary reference tool for today's student and professional person. (A desk dictionary is based on one of the unabridged dictionaries, like *Webster's Third New International*, usually found on a lectern in the library.) You have already seen how essential a current dictionary is for checking the spelling and hyphenation of words and for finding out when to abbreviate, capitalize, and italicize words. But an up-to-date dictionary serves still other purposes. For example, (1) it shows you how to pronounce a word like *harass*; (2) it lists the forms and possible uses of a verb like *sing*; (3) it explains what a given word means and gives example phrases and sentences which clarify the definition; (4) it gives the synonyms and antonyms of a word like *oppose*; (5) it gives information about a word's origin; and (6) it may provide usage labels for words like *poke, nowheres,* and *irregardless.* A desk dictionary may also supply you with miscellaneous information such as a brief history of the English language, the dates and identities of famous people, geographical facts, and lists of colleges and universities in the United States and Canada. A current desk dictionary, then, is one of the best investments you can make.

### 19a Learn to use an up-to-date dictionary intelligently.

Study the introductory matter to find out what your dictionary's guides to abbreviations and pronunciation are; to know what plural and tense forms your dictionary lists; to learn what attitude your dictionary takes toward usage labels (dictionaries vary in the kinds of labels they use, and some dictionaries label more words than others do); and to understand the order in which the meanings of words are listed—that is, in order of common usage or of historical development.

### 19b–19g Use words that have no usage labels unless the occasion demands otherwise.

Most words (and most meanings of words) in dictionaries are unlabeled; that is, they are appropriate on any occasion because they are in general use in the English-speaking world. But some words have labels that indicate they are used (1) by people in one section of the country (*Dialectal, Regional,* sometimes *Colloquial*); (2) by people who are often judged uneducated (*Nonstandard* and *Illiterate;* sometimes words in this category are not listed at all); (3) by people who use popular expressions that often do not remain long in the language (*Slang*); (4) in literature from past times (*Archaic, Obsolete, Obsolescent, Rare*);

or (5) by people in a specialized field of study (technical words like *pyrexia*, which a dictionary labels *Pathol.* to indicate that it is a term from pathology).

When the occasion demands the use of a word that is labeled—for example, an address to a medical convention might call for technical language or even jargon—the word may be judged appropriate because the audience will understand it. But in general speaking and writing, you should depend on the multitude of unlabeled words that most audiences or readers can be expected to understand.

LABELED WORDS     *Irregardless* of what my *screwy* friend advised, I was not *fixing to* drive my *pater's* new *set of wheels* in the demolition derby.

UNLABELED WORDS     *Regardless* of what my *crazy* friend advised, I was not *about*
(STANDARD)     *to* drive my *father's* new *automobile* in the demolition derby.

There is one class of words—labeled *Informal*, or sometimes *Colloquial*—that is commonly used and understood by most writers and speakers. These words are appropriate in speaking and in informal writing and are usually necessary in recording dialogue because most people speak less formally than they write. But, in general, you should avoid words labeled *Informal* or *Colloquial* in most of your college and professional writing.

INFORMAL     The student *lifted* the passage from a critic he was studying.

STANDARD OR     The student *plagiarized* the passage from a critic he was studying.
FORMAL

Except in dialogue, contractions are usually not appropriate in formal writing.

INFORMAL     *There's* hardly anyone who *doesn't* respond to a good play.

STANDARD OR     *There is* hardly anyone who *does not* respond to a good play.
FORMAL

## 19h Choose words and combinations of sounds that are appropriate to clear prose writing.

A poetic style is generally not appropriate in college essays or professional reports. Usually such writing seems wordy, vague, and even ridiculous.

FLOWERY     He was a *tower of power* in our community, a blazing *meteor in a prosperous enterprise.*

PLAIN BUT     He was a *powerful* man in our community, a *remarkably successful*
CLEAR     *businessman.*

**Using the Dictionary** Exercise 19–1

NAME _____ SCORE _____

The full title, the edition, and the date of publication of my dictionary are as follows: _____

_____

**1. Abbreviations** Where does the dictionary explain the abbreviations it uses?

_____

Write out the meaning of each of the abbreviations following these entries:

extend, *v.t.* _____

deray, *n., Obs.* _____

nohow, *adv., Dial.* _____

coracoid, *Anat., adj.* _____

**2. Spelling and Pronunciation** Using your dictionary, write out by syllables each of the words listed below, and place the accent where it belongs. With the aid of the diacritical marks, the phonetic respelling of the word (in parentheses or slashes immediately after the word), and the key at the bottom of the page or in the introductory matter, determine the preferred pronunciation (the first pronunciation given). Then pronounce each word correctly several times.

exquisite _____

harass _____

grimace _____

pianist _____

Write the plurals of the following words:

deer _____

index _____

criterion _____

datum _____

Rewrite each of the following words that needs a hyphen:

watercolor      _____

selfconscious    _____

extracurricular _____

**3. Derivations**    The derivation, or origin, of a word (given in brackets) often furnishes a literal meaning that helps you to remember the word. For each of the following words give (a) the source—the language from which it is derived, (b) the original word or words, and (c) the original meaning.

|  | *Source* | *Original word(s) and meaning* |
|---|---|---|
| nefarious | ____ | _____ |
| pseudonym | ____ | _____ |
| deprecate | ____ | _____ |

**4. Meanings**    Usually words develop several different meanings. How many meanings are listed in your dictionary for the following words?

discipline, *n.* ____     spend, *v.* ____     out, *adv.* ____

tortuous, *adj.* ____     in, *prep.* ____     magazine, *n.* ____

Does your dictionary list meanings in order of historical development or of common usage? _____

**5. Special Labels**    Words (or certain meanings of words) may have such precautionary or explanatory labels as *Archaic*, *Colloquial*, or *Nautical*. What label or special usage do you find for one meaning of each word below?

lush, *n.*     _____

your'n, *pro.*   _____

bust, *v.*     _____

ain't, *v.*     _____

hisself, *pro.*   _____

yare, *adj.*    _____

**Using the Dictionary**                    Exercise 19–1 (continued)

**6. Synonyms**   Even among words with essentially the same meaning, one word usually fits a given context more exactly than any other. To show precise shades of meaning, some dictionaries treat in special paragraphs certain groups of closely related words. What synonyms are specially differentiated in your dictionary for the following words?

consider, *v.* _____

sharp, *adj.* _____

**7. Capitalization**   Rewrite the words that may be capitalized.

history          _____

communism        _____

spartan          _____

pisces           _____

chauvinist       _____

german           _____

**8. Grammatical Information.**   Note that many words may serve as two or more parts of speech. List the parts of speech that each of the following words may be: *v., n., adj., adv., prep., conj., interj.*

check    _____

hold     _____

off      _____

number   _____

ring     _____

right    _____

Note the grammatical information supplied by your dictionary for verbs, adjectives, and pronouns.

List the principal parts of *lie:* _____

List the principal parts of *burst:* _____

List the principal parts of *cry:* _____

List the comparative and superlative degrees of the adjective *steady:* _____

_____

List the comparative and superlative degrees of the adjective *big:* _____

_____

Should *which* be used to refer to people? _____

What is the distinction between the relative pronouns *that* and *which?* _____

_____

_____

**9. Idiomatic Expressions** List two standard idiomatic expressions for each of the following words.

wait _____

track _____

die _____

**10. Miscellaneous Information** Answer the following questions by referring to your dictionary. Be prepared to tell in what part of the dictionary the information is located.

In what year was Thomas Edison born? _____

Where is Normandy located? _____

_____

What was Valhalla? _____

_____

Does your dictionary have a history of the English language? _____

Does your dictionary have a manual of style? _____

**Appropriate Usage**                                    Exercise 19–2

NAME _____ SCORE _____

DIRECTIONS   If the italicized word, with the meaning it has in its particular sentence, is labeled in your dictionary in any way, enter the label (such as *Informal* or *Slang*) in the blank. If the word is not labeled, write *Standard* in the blank. Discuss your answers in class to compare the usage labels of various dictionaries.

EXAMPLE
The scientists are *fooling around* with nature again.        *Informal*

1. Of course, we are accustomed to receiving some *mighty big* benefits from scientific research.        _____

2. But now some genetic engineers are promising a *totally radical* development.        _____

3. In northern California scientists are experimenting with frost-fighting bacteria that, *like*, protect potatoes from frost.        _____

4. Certain bacteria on plant leaves trigger the formation of frost. The bacteria *kind of* form a nucleus for ice crystallization.        _____

5. Scientists have discovered the gene in the bacteria that makes it an attractive ice nucleus. They *sort of* cut out the single gene and leave the remainder of the bacteria intact.        _____

6. When these modified bacteria are sprayed *everywhere* on the plants, they displace the ice-forming bacteria.        _____

7. The modified bacteria will lower the plant's freezing point and, scientists *reckon*, save billions of dollars worth of produce that ordinarily is lost to frost damage.        _____

8. Some scientists *ain't* so sure that genetic engineering is a good idea.        _____

9. Releasing organisms that may prove to have no enemies could create long-term *hassles*.   _____

10. *Being as* the gypsy moth has proved to be a costly foe, the need to act carefully is clear.   _____

11. However, organisms similar to the ice-resistant bacteria already *seem* to exist in nature.   _____

12. For that reason the Environmental Protection Agency has decided to permit this product of *tinkering* with nature to be used.   _____

**Appropriate Usage**                                    Exercise 19–3

NAME _____ SCORE _____

DIRECTIONS   In each sentence, choose the proper word or words from the pairs in parentheses. Cross out the incorrect word or words and write the correct one in the blank. Rely on your dictionary to help you choose the word with the correct meaning or the word that is appropriate in a formal essay.

EXAMPLE
Not long ago a weekly pulp magazine warned grocery

shoppers that genetic engineers have created "plant

people" who are walking around, eyes aglaze, (~~wad-~~

~~ing~~, waiting) to turn the tables on humans.          *waiting*

1.  And, in fact, Monsanto Company scientists in St. Louis recently did transfer a human (jean, gene) into a petunia.                                      _____

2.  The gene, which encodes a human pregnancy hormone, made the petunia plant cells produce (minute, minuet) quantities of that hormone.       _____

3.  The genes of all livings things are (composed, proposed) of the same four chemical bases.       _____

4.  This shared chemical base enables scientists to deliver a human gene into a plant cell, a process that (would of, would have) been thought impossible until recently.                                        _____

5.  In 1983 scientists began the gene transfer process by inserting a bacteria gene into a plant (sale, cell). _____

6.  By introducing foreign genes, scientists mean to (affect, effect) some property of the host cell.  _____

7.  Petunias, for example, often fall (pray, prey) to crown gall disease.                               _____

8. The (effect, affect) of transferring a human gene into a petunia cell was to enable the plant to produce antibodies against crown gall disease. _____

9. The effect was to (inoculate, immaculate) the plant. _____

10. With genetic engineering scientists try to increase yield, improve traits such as disease resistance or salt tolerance, and (partially, partly) modify plants to reduce the costs of growing them. _____

11. Traditional plant breeding has the same (inhibitions, ambitions). _____

12. We (marvel, marble), however, at the dramatic results from genetic engineering. _____

13. Scientists still do not have (lots of, much) information about which genes do what. _____

14. (Regrettably, regretfully) for plant biologists, more work has been done with animal genetic engineering than with plant genetic engineering. _____

15. Until the basic knowledge about genes increases, huge breakthroughs in the science are not (imminent, eminent). _____

## 20

### Choose words that are exact, idiomatic, and fresh.

Since the basic unit of communication is the word, you cannot write clearly and accurately unless you have built up a vocabulary of words to express the things you think and feel. Of the 500,000 entries in an unabridged dictionary, most college students can use no more than 15,000 in speaking and writing. Building a vocabulary, then, is a lifetime process. Usually the more people read, the more words they add to their recognition vocabularies. After they have seen the same words many times in different contexts, they add these words to their active vocabularies, the words they actually use in speaking and writing.

People who do not regularly read newspapers, magazines, and books often have few words to draw on whenever they speak or write. They may complain, "I know what I mean, but I can't put it into words." They may also say that some works by professional writers are "too hard to understand." The source of their difficulty in both writing and reading is an inadequate vocabulary.

You can begin now to increase your vocabulary by noticing the words you read in your course work and looking up definitions of all the words you are uncertain of. Sometimes reading a difficult paragraph aloud emphasizes the words you are not familiar with and, as a result, helps you understand why the paragraph is difficult for you.

While you are increasing your recognition vocabulary, you must take great care to make the best possible use of the words in your active vocabulary.

### 20a  Choose words that express your ideas exactly.

To express yourself exactly, you must choose words that have the denotations (the definitions found in dictionaries) and the connotations (the mental or emotional associations that go with the words) that you intend.

| | |
|---|---|
| PROBLEM WITH DENOTATION | The doctor decided that my persistent sneezing could be *contributed* to my allergy to ragweed. |
| CORRECT DENOTATION | The doctor decided that my persistent sneezing could be *attributed* to my allergy to ragweed. |
| PROBLEM WITH CONNOTATION | I took my best friend to my *domicile* for dinner. |
| CORRECT CONNOTATION | I took my best friend to my *home* for dinner. |

Remember that a wrong word is very noticeable when it results in a ridiculous sentence (see also **18b**).

WRONG WORD    I had fillet of *soul* for lunch.

CORRECT WORD    I had fillet of *sole* for lunch.

Whenever possible you should choose concrete rather than abstract words. Abstract words refer to ideas, whereas concrete words refer to definite objects. Abstract words are necessary to state generalizations, but it is the specific word, the specific detail, the specific example that engages the reader's attention. (See also Section **31**.)

GENERAL    Our canoe trip down the Caney Fork River was rewarding.

SPECIFIC    Our canoe trip down the Caney Fork River included hours of silent passage over clear waters, great fishing for rainbow trout, and sightings of many wild birds—even bald eagles.

GENERAL    Before the trip we learned about our canoe.

SPECIFIC    Before the trip we learned how to paddle the canoe, how to pack our gear in it, and what to do if the canoe were to tip over.

## 20b  Choose words that are idiomatic.

Idiomatic expressions are phrases that you use every day without thinking about their meaning: "I ran across an old friend" and "Angie played down the importance of money." Native English speakers use expressions like these naturally; but some idioms may seem unnatural, even ridiculous, to foreigners trying to learn our language.

Even native speakers sometimes have difficulty choosing the correct prepositions to make expressions idiomatic. For example, many would write "prior than" rather than the idiomatic "prior to." The dictionary is the best guide for helping you choose the preposition that should follow a word like *prior* to make an idiomatic expression.

UNIDIOMATIC    *According with* our plan, we beached the canoes once each hour for a brief rest.

IDIOMATIC    *According to* our plan, we beached the canoes once each hour for a brief rest.

## 20c  Choose fresh expressions rather than trite ones.

Many idiomatic expressions have been used so often that they have become trite—worn out and meaningless. At one time readers would have thought the expression "tried and true" was an exact and effective choice of words. But readers today have seen and heard the expression so often that they hardly notice it, except perhaps to be bored or amused by it. Clichés of this sort are common in most people's speech and may even occur at times in the work of professional writers, but they should generally be avoided because they no longer communicate ideas exactly. Beware also of political slogans, advertising jargon, and most slang expressions; they are often so overused for a brief period of time that they quickly become meaningless.

TRITE    Last but not least is the dedicated student who rises at the crack of dawn to hit the books.

EXACT    Last is the dedicated student who rises at 6:00 A.M. to study.

# Vocabulary Building                          Exercise 20-1

NAME ———————————————————————————————

DIRECTIONS   To see how becoming aware of words in your reading can lead to a better recognition vocabulary, try this experiment. Read aloud the first paragraph below, underlining the words whose meaning you are uncertain of; then look up the definitions and write them down; finally, reread the sentences in which these words appear. When you have finished with the first paragraph, go on to the second one. Notice how the words that gave you trouble in the first paragraph seem to stand out in the second paragraph, though sometimes as a different part of speech or in a different tense. If you cannot remember the definitions of the words, look again at your notes.

PARAGRAPH 1

Feelings about grizzlies are intense; often such feelings represent many complex elements which are difficult to reconcile. But all seem to agree that this endangered species is unequivocally a symbol of American wilderness. To be assured of a viable future, the huge bear needs land untouched by human beings, land that has escaped technology and maintains its natural integrity. Ecologists consider the grizzly to be a "barometer" of environmental quality, because it cannot survive where man has upset the ecosystem; thus . . . it represents the harmony of the wilderness world. To advocate destruction of the grizzly, then, is tantamount to favoring annihilation of the remaining primeval lands. The grizzly represents in many minds the continuation of an age-old conflict between the domesticated sphere of man and his stock and the wild which always threatens it. In a deep sense, the grizzly epitomizes a culturally ingrained antipathy toward tamed nature. Inextricably part of inherited pioneer tradition, it is an ethos which views the wild as an element to be overcome. The grizzly bear's plight recapitulates America's conquest of the wilderness.

—ELIZABETH LAWRENCE

*211*

PARAGRAPH 2

I have a certain image of a very early water creature, a crude, multicelled entity, crawling out of the salt marshes and becoming the precursor of all of us who walk or fly and take in the air through lungs. I feel sure that it did not just move away from the water with never a look backward. There must have been in it, as there is in many of us still, some voice that urged a return to the water and the ethos from whence it came. Every year I hear that same voice, and my response is unequivocal. I pack the car and leave for the coast. I am not, during these drives to the sea, running away from something—job, home, and family have not overwhelmed me with antipathy. I simply do not feel viable and whole any longer, and I have learned that the only way for me to feel better is to go to the coast.

My destination is a small state park near the confluence of several rivers with the Gulf Coast. There are canals, lagoons, and oyster bars; everywhere there is wildlife. When I move out into the salt marshes and tidal creeks and begin casting for redfish on the incoming tide, I am in my world primeval. Like those ancient creatures of the sea, I move about in and am given life by the salt marshes; when I step again on the land, I am renewed. The effect is tantamount to being cleansed, baptized, made whole and ready for a new life.

## Correct and Exact Words

NAME _____ SCORE _____

DIRECTIONS   In the following sentences, choose the proper word or words from the pairs in parentheses. Cross out the wrong or inexact word or words and write the correct answer in the blank. Use your dictionary freely.

EXAMPLE
Lawns are (manicured, ~~pedicured~~) symbols of American

small-town and suburban life.                            *manicured*

1. A group called the Fruitarian Network (extorts, implores) people to stop mowing lawns.   _____

2. They believe that grass is far from being oblivious (about, to, from) being cut.   _____

3. "We believe that grass has some kind of conscious-ness," says a spokesman. "We (contend, attend) that grass has feelings."   _____

4. The idea that grass has feelings may seem (obstrep-erous, preposterous), but we should not discount the Fruitarians.   _____

5. They are very (oral, vocal) in their protests and deserve to be heard, even protected, in their mi-nority views.   _____

6. In the United States (along, alone) there are some forty-five million lawns.   _____

7. Pieced together, they take up twenty-five to thirty million acres of (real, reel) estate, an area about the size of Indiana.   _____

8. The average lawn of 1,000 square feet costs about $200 to $500 per year to maintain. The same in-vestment in a food garden would (yield, make) more than $2000 worth of fruits and vegetables.   _____

9. So why do we do it? Is our love for lawns the result of our cultural (heritage, heresy) like the necktie or circumcision? _____

10. Or is it a carry-over from a time when we walked (with, on, to) all fours or swung through the trees? _____

11. The cultural argument traces our love of lawns back to the Middle Ages. The nobility (apprehended, comprehended) the utility of lawns and landscaping; they made an approaching enemy visible. _____

12. The purely utilitarian attitude was replaced by the aesthetic, and lawns became a (cymbal, symbol) of prestige. _____

13. Our fascination with lawns may have begun much earlier than the Middle Ages. The ecologist John Falk realized that lawns (recur, occur) around the world. _____

14. "They are (omnivorous, omnipotent, omnipresent)," he says. _____

15. Falk's (current, currant) hypothesis is that humans have lawns because they have an innate preference for savannah-like terrain. _____

16. For more than 90 percent of human history, a savannah was home because humans could avoid or (allude, elude) their enemies on the open plain. _____

17. Falk is also exploring the idea that we may landscape our homes in patterns (reminiscent, acquiescent) of life on the savannah. _____

## 21

**Avoid wordiness but include all words needed to make the meaning or the grammatical construction complete.**

Almost every writer's first draft includes many words that are not needed and lacks some words that are. A careful revision based on close proofreading is the only way to transform a rough draft into an effective piece of writing.

ROUGH DRAFT WITH REVISIONS

According to the most recently developed scenario, a large city

has a microclimate which varies considerably from a country

climate. The city has lower wind velocity. It has polluted air.

It has more fog. And it is overheated.

### 21a  Use only those words or phrases that add meaning to your writing.

Most wordiness in composition results from writers' attempts to achieve what they think is a "high style"—to write sentences that sound brilliant. Too often they fill out their sentences with clichés, roundabout phrasing, and jargon.

WORDY    It is, of course, a well-known fact that a large city's climate varies from a country climate. The conurbation suffers from low wind velocity, polluted air, fog, and overheating.

CONCISE    The climate of a large city usually has lower wind velocity, more polluted air, more fog, and more overheating than a country climate.

Use one clear word instead of a long phrase whenever possible. Following is a list of some more common wordy phrases and their one-word counterparts.

| Wordy | Concise |
|---|---|
| to be desirous of | want OR desire |
| to have a preference for | prefer |
| to be in agreement with | agree |
| due to the fact that | because |
| in view of the fact that | because OR since |
| in order to | to |
| at this point in time | now |
| in this day and age | today |
| with reference to | about |
| prior to | before |
| in the event of | if |

Another kind of wordiness, occurring particularly in student composition, results from the writer's lack of confidence in his/her position. Such wordiness frequently includes expressions like "I think," "it seems to me," "in my opinion," and "would be."

WORDY    In my opinion the tall buildings of the city contribute to the problems of low wind velocity and overheating.

CONCISE    The city's tall buildings lower wind velocity and contribute to over-heating.

### 21b Restructure sentences whenever necessary to avoid wordiness.

Often you can combine sentences through subordination to avoid wordiness. (See also Section **24**.)

WORDY    A city has extensive asphalt, concrete, and stone surfaces, and they can be compared to impervious rocks, and they store and release the summer heat, which accounts for the "baking oven" effect on summer nights.

CONCISE    During the summer the city's asphalt, concrete, and stone surfaces store the day's heat and radiate it at night to create the suffocating "baking oven" effect.

WORDY    The polyphemous moth and the marine medusa are apparently insignificant creatures, and they have been immortalized by great writers. The polyphemous moth is discussed in Annie Dillard's *Pilgrim at Tinker Creek* and the medusa in Lewis Thomas's *The Medusa and the Snail*.

CONCISE    The polyphemous moth and marine medusa are apparently insignificant creatures that have been immortalized by great writers: the moth by Annie Dillard in *Pilgrim at Tinker Creek* and the medusa by Lewis Thomas in *The Medusa and the Snail*. [The *that* clause and the colon reduce the two wordy sentences to one concise sentence.]

Wordiness may also be caused by sentences that begin with *there* or *it*. To eliminate this kind of wordiness, restructure your sentences to use an active verb in place of the form of *be* that inevitably follows *there* or *it*.

WORDY    There is a haze canopy over a city that is produced by chemical particles and dust suspended in the air.

CONCISE    Chemical particles and dust suspended in the air produce a haze canopy over a city.

WORDY    It is obvious that a circulation of fresh air into the city could eliminate the haze canopy.

CONCISE    Obviously, a circulation of fresh air into the city could eliminate the haze canopy.

### 21c Avoid needless repetition of words and ideas.

Repetition of the same word or idea in several consecutive sentences results in monotonous writing. Using pronouns helps as much as anything to avoid this problem.

REPETITIOUS    In order to funnel fresh air into the city, the architect designed clear approach paths. He used canals and long strips of lawn as approach paths.

CONCISE    In order to funnel fresh air into the city, the architect designed clear approach paths—canals and long strips of lawn.

**Note:** Several popular expressions are always repetitious: *each and every, any and all, various and sundry, if and when, combine together, return back.* Other such expressions include *red in color, triangular in shape,* and *city of Cleveland.*

REPETITIOUS    Each and every city has more fog and more cloud cover than the country.

CONCISE    Every city has more fog and cloud cover than the country.

REPETITIOUS    A total of one cubic meter of water vapor is produced by the combustion of one liter of gasoline.

CONCISE    One cubic meter of water vapor is produced by the combustion of one liter of gasoline.

In writing direct quotations many students tend to overwork forms of the verb *say.* Remember that many verbs besides *said* can introduce direct quotations. *Explained, pointed out, noted, continued, described,* and *observed* are only a few.

REPETITIOUS    The EPA spokesman said, "A city's fog and cloud cover increase because of two processes." He later said, "First, the emission of water vapor is greater in towns; and, second, particles suspended in the air provide a large supply of condensation nuclei."

BETTER    The EPA spokesman said, "A city's fog and cloud cover increase because of two processes." He later explained, "First, the emission of water vapor is greater in towns; and, second, particles suspended in the air provide a large supply of condensation nuclei."

**Wordiness and Needless Repetition**                    Exercise 21–1

NAME _____ SCORE _____

DIRECTIONS   Cross out needless words in each of the following sentences. For each sentence needing no further revision, write *1* in the blank; for sentences that need additional changes, even changes in punctuation, write *2* in the blank and make the needed revision. There may be more than one way to revise some sentences.

EXAMPLES

There are various ~~and sundry~~ books on ecology.                    *1*

~~The reason why~~ *o*ne should read books on ecology ~~is learning~~ *to learn* about

the threats to his environment.                    *2*

1. Rachel Carson was a woman who pioneered in ecological studies.    _____

2. She wrote *Silent Spring* in order that she might awaken people to the dangers of insecticide poisoning.    _____

3. In the book it tells about a spring when no birds sang.    _____

4. The reason that the robins disappeared from many areas of the country was that the elms were being heavily sprayed with DDT.    _____

5. The robin population was affected indirectly for one simple reason: the reason was that they ate earthworms that had stored DDT in their bodies.    _____

6. The earthworm's favorite food is the leaf litter from elms that they like better than anything else.    _____

7. Consequently, DDT reached the robins that fed on the infected earthworms for this reason.    _____

8. Robins eat many earthworms a day, and they eat as many as one earthworm a minute.    _____

9. As few as eleven infected earthworms can kill a robin and cause the bird to die.    _____

10. Not each and every robin died as a result of DDT poisoning.    _____

11. Many robins faced extinction for another reason: this was because of sterility induced by the absorption of DDT.    _____

12. One of the saddest pictures Rachel Carson paints in her book is of a robin sitting on its eggs faithfully for twenty-one days without their hatching and this is one of the saddest pictures in the book.    _____

13. Almost simultaneously at the same time people in various parts of the country began to notice a scarcity of robins.    _____

14. At the Michigan State University campus an ornithologist who studies bird life might once have seen 370 robins, but in 1957 he could find only two or three dozen.    _____

15. In 1958 the ornithologist could not find a single fledgling robin on the campus and this is even more depressing.    _____

16. Thus efforts to control Dutch elm disease almost destroyed not only the robin population but it also proved disastrous to many other species of earthworm-eating birds.    _____

17. The robins are used as an example by Rachel Carson in order to illustrate the plight of all living things.    _____

18. It was largely because of her horrifying account of a silent spring without birds that was the reason that the American public became interested in ecology.    _____

19. In the 1960's students all over the country were reading *Silent Spring* and they were discussing it.    _____

20. The book was published in 1962, and it is not a recent book, but it is still one of the most influential ecological studies.    _____

## 22

**Do not omit a word or phrase necessary to the meaning of the sentence.**

**22a Be careful to include all necessary articles, pronouns, conjunctions, and prepositions.** Revised omissions are indicated by a caret (Λ) in the following examples.

**(1) Do not omit a needed article before a noun or another adjective.**

Tanzania's Serengeti National Park is a wildlife refuge and *an* inspiring example of human attempts to preserve endangered wildlife.   [The article *a* precedes a word that begins with a consonant; *an* precedes a word that begins with a vowel.]

**(2) Do not omit necessary prepositions or conjunctions.**

The type *of* animal that is most endangered is the black rhinoceros.   [*Type* is not an adjective here.]

Some Africans do not believe *in* or care about protecting wild animals.   [*Believe about* is not idiomatic phrasing.]

Do not omit *that* when it is needed as a subordinating conjunction.

We learned *that* even the massive elephant is easy prey for poachers.   [*That* introduces the clause that functions as the complement of the sentence.]

The guide said *that* poachers killed about 20 elephants in 1976 but have killed nearly 70 this year.   [Here the conjunction *that* signals the beginning of an indirect quotation.]

*That* may be omitted when the meaning of the sentence would be clear at first reading without it.

We realized poaching could eradicate the elephant population in Serengeti.

## 22b Include necessary verbs and helping verbs.

*been*

Since 1962 Serengeti National Park has ∧ and will continue to be the focal point of

study by the Serengeti Wildlife Research Centre.    [*Has continue to be* is an error

in tense.]

## 22c Include all words necessary to complete a comparison.

*in*

Black rhinos are as scarce in Serengeti as ∧ the United States.

*as*

A poacher's understanding of wildlife is as good ∧ perhaps better than, a biologist's.

## 22d When used as intensifiers, *so, such,* and *too* should usually be followed by a completing phrase or clause.

There are *too* many poachers in Serengeti for the park rangers to control.
The poachers are *such* relentless hunters that they literally will walk their prey to
death.

## Omission of Necessary Words                           Exercise 22–1

NAME _____ SCORE _____

DIRECTIONS   In the following sentences insert the words that are needed to make the meaning or the grammatical construction complete. In the blank, write the words that you have added.

EXAMPLE
A rhinoceros horn is used as a type *of* medicine.                    *of*

1. The black rhino is animal most depleted by poachers.              _____

2. The rhino's horn is prized as a medicine and aphrodisiac.         _____

3. Many Asians have and always will grind it and use it as medicine. _____

4. Horns have been carved may be used as dagger handles.             _____

5. In North Yemen, a highly polished and carved horn forms the handle for curved dagger.  _____

6. The curved dagger which I refer is called a jambiyya.             _____

7. Poachers greater success in Serengeti because of the plentiful wildlife.  _____

8. Park rangers have realized the poachers who are successful travel in very small bands.  _____

9. The poachers have learned travel without comfort.                 _____

10. Camps without fires are safer.                                   _____

11. Park rangers always have and always will associate small fires with poachers.  _____

12. Firearms make noise than primitive weapons.                      _____

13. Poachers believe bows and arrows and spears are
    better.                                            _____

14. Some poachers been trying to use firearms.          _____

15. They make quick raids into and out the Serengeti,
    arriving and departing before park rangers catch
    them.                                              _____

# SENTENCE UNITY                                    su 23

## 23

**In a unified sentence, ideas within the sentence are clearly related; excessive detail, mixed metaphors, and mixed constructions do not obscure the ideas; and subjects and predicates fit together logically.**

**23a Establish a clear relationship between the clauses in a sentence; develop unrelated ideas in separate sentences.**

When you write a compound sentence, you suggest that the ideas in the two main clauses are closely related. Similarly, when you write a complex sentence, you make your reader expect a relationship between the ideas in the main and subordinate clause.

UNCLEAR   Many migratory bird species winter in the tropics, and they are threatened by the clearing of tropical rain forests.

CLEAR   Because many migratory bird species winter in the tropics, they are threatened by the clearing of tropical rain forests.

UNCLEAR   Scientists are concerned about the declining population of songbirds in the United States, and many of these songbirds migrate to Latin America for half the year.

CLEAR   Scientists are concerned about the declining population of songbirds in the United States. Many of those songbirds migrate to Latin America for half the year.

**23b Keep the central focus of your sentence clear.**

Too much subordination or detail, even if relevant, will obscure the central focus of a sentence.

UNCLEAR   Migrant bird species are particularly vulnerable to habitat destruction, and some are territorial, accustomed to returning to the same site each year, so when their home forest disappears, they also disappear, and certain species depend on localized foods, while others may need to interact with nonmigratory tropical species that also disappear when the habitat is destroyed.

CLEAR   Migrant bird species are particularly vulnerable to habitat destruction. Some are territorial, accustomed to returning to the same site each year. When their home forest disappears, they also disappear. Certain species depend on localized foods, while others may need to interact with nonmigratory tropical species that also disappear when the habitat is destroyed.

## 23c Be aware of mixed metaphors and mixed constructions.

UNCLEAR John White, the author of *Songbirds Bye Bye*, has been described as a grain of sand crying out in the wilderness.

CLEAR John White, the author of *Songbirds Bye Bye*, has been described as a voice crying out in the wilderness.

UNCLEAR When White publicized the effects of habitat destruction on songbirds angered the leaders of several Latin American countries.

CLEAR When White publicized the effects of habitat destruction on songbirds, he angered the leaders of several Latin American countries.

OR

White's publicizing the effects of habitat destruction on songbirds angered the leaders of several Latin American countries.

## 23d Avoid faulty predication.

Make the subject and predicate of a sentence fit together grammatically and logically.

ILLOGICAL Bachman's warblers are a serious controversy today. [There is a problem with logic here: *Bachman's warblers* does not equal *controversy*, as the linking verb, *are*, suggests.]

LOGICAL Efforts to preserve Bachman's warblers have generated serious controversy.

ILLOGICAL The source of the controversy is because destruction of their habitat caused their extinction. [*Source* does not equal *because*, as the linking verb, *is*, suggests.]

LOGICAL Because destruction of their habitat caused their extinction, they have become a symbol of the controversy about habitat destruction.

OR

The source of the controversy is the relationship of habitat destruction to their extinction.

ILLOGICAL In the emotional debate over songbirds causes some scientists to lose sight of the best tool for saving the birds—international diplomacy. [The writer has mistaken the object of a preposition, *debate*, for the subject of the sentence.]

LOGICAL The emotional debate over songbirds causes some scientists to lose sight of the best tool for saving the birds—international diplomacy. [Here *debate* is the subject.]

**23e  Define a word or an expression clearly and precisely.**

The use of forms of the linking verb *be—is, are, was, can, be,* and so on—frequently leads to faulty predication, particularly when the linking verb is followed by *when* or *where.* By substituting a nonlinking verb such as *occur* or *is found,* you can often eliminate the error in unity or logic.

ILLOGICAL  An example of John White's theory is when the habitat of Bachman's warblers was destroyed and replaced by sugarcane fields, thereby leading to the warblers' extinction.

LOGICAL  John White's theory explains the extinction of Bachman's warblers as a consequence of their winter habitat being replaced by sugarcane fields.

OR

An example of John White's theory is the extinction of Bachman's warblers because their winter habitat was replaced by sugarcane fields.

**Unity in Sentence Structure**                                    Exercise 23–1

NAME _____ SCORE _____

DIRECTIONS   In the blanks, write *a*, *b*, *c*, *d*, or *e* to indicate whether the chief difficulty
in each sentence is (a) an unclear relationship among ideas, (b) excessive detail and
subordination, (c) mixed metaphors and mixed constructions, (d) an illogical combination of subject and predicate, or (e) unclear or imprecise definitions. Revise the sentences to make them effective.

EXAMPLE
There are many songbirds nesting in my backyard, but I prefer play-

ing tennis, *to watching birds.*                                    _a_

1. The Northern Parula, a migrant warbler with a grey back
   and head, grey wings barred with black and white, a cream
   colored underside, and copper spots on its throat and shoul-
   ders, is endangered.                                             _____

2. It is a delicate bird but which is quite hardy.                  _____

3. The early bird went from the frying pan into hot water.          _____

4. Does anyone know why the author wrote the essay for *Sierra*
   magazine or where did he find the statistics?                    _____

5. The essay apparently believes that vanishing woodlots in
   America also are causing the extinction of songbirds.            _____

6. *Clearcutting* is when all of a forest's vegetation is removed.  _____

7. The woodlot across the street from our house, the one that
   was owned by the Jones family that moved here from Balti-
   more and that built a pizza restaurant, was the nesting ground
   for ten different species of songbird.                           _____

8. An example of the effect of cutting down the woodlot is the
   red-eyed vireo, a warbler that was common in the woodlot.        _____

9. The author uses binoculars to study the few remaining vireos
   and saw an osprey near the lake in 1971.                         _____

10. Migration is where a bird nests in one environment, for example, a woodlot in Georgia, and then in winter flies to a warmer climate, for example, the Amazon basin.    _____

11. One book I read believes that migrating birds must be treated as essential members of two ecosystems.    _____

12. It was a simple observation but which was extremely important.    _____

13. Any change in the first ecosystem, if it is destroyed or if it becomes inhospitable because of some change, perhaps because its insect population drops or a factory is built near it or increased traffic pollutes it, will affect the second, related ecosystem.    _____

14. When a vireo loses its nesting site or winter home causes it to adapt very quickly or die.    _____

15. Such adaptation is where a species, not an individual, gradually becomes accustomed to a new environment.    _____

## 24

**Use subordination to relate ideas concisely and effectively. Use coordination to give ideas equal emphasis.**

Subordination is the method good writers most often use to extend their sentences and to vary the beginnings of sentences. (Subordinated additions to the sentence base are italicized in the following paragraph.)

> *Faced with severe air pollution and health problems,* the Japanese government decided *that it must impose strict controls on industrial emission of wastes.* Between 1968 and 1978 sulfur dioxide emissions were cut by 73 percent *after some 1,200 scrubbers were installed on smokestacks.*

As this example shows, grammatically subordinate structures may contain very important ideas.

The following sentence demonstrates coordination, which gives equal grammatical emphasis to two or more ideas. (See also **12a**, **12c**, and Section **26**.)

> The Japanese chose to accept more government restrictions and more emission control devices in order to have cleaner air and cleaner water and to live longer and better.  [Coordination gives equal emphasis to each word in a pair—*more* and *more, cleaner* and *cleaner, longer* and *better.*]

**24a  Instead of writing a series of short, choppy sentences, choose one idea for the sentence base, or main clause, and subordinate other ideas.**

Because it stands apart from other sentences in a paragraph, a short sentence is often used for emphasis (see Section **29**). But if the paragraph contains only short, choppy sentences, no single idea stands out, and the primary effect is monotony.

| | |
|---|---|
| SHORT AND CHOPPY | The United Nations publishes current information about environmental matters. The publication is called *Earthscan.* It is published in London. |
| SUBORDINATION | *Earthscan,* a London-based news service of the United Nations, contains current information about environmental matters.  [The subordinated part is an appositive.] |
| SHORT AND CHOPPY | British scientists and authors first recognized, named, and described the effects of acid rain. Acid rain is not considered a serious problem by British officials. They also deny responsibility for causing it elsewhere. |
| SUBORDINATION | Although British scientists and authors first recognized, named, and described the effects of acid rain, it still is not considered a serious problem by British officials, who also deny |

responsibility for causing it elsewhere. [The subordinated parts are an adverb clause and an adjective clause.]

**24b  Instead of linking sentences primarily with coordinating conjunctions, such as *and, so,* or *but,* or with conjunctive adverbs, such as *however* and *therefore,* extend most sentences through subordination.**

Coordination of main clauses is helpful in developing a varied style because it gives equal emphasis to separate ideas.

> In order to decrease urban pollution Britain has increased its use of North Sea gas and low-sulfur oil and coal, and it has built taller smokestacks to funnel pollutants into air currents far above the land surface.

But when ideas have a time, place, descriptive, or cause and effect relationship, use subordination to show the connection between clauses while emphasizing the main idea.

> STRINGY  Britain built tall smokestacks to funnel pollutants into air currents far above the land surface, so the air currents carry the pollutants away from Britain to other countries or out to sea.

> RELATED  Because Britain built tall smokestacks to funnel pollutants into air currents far above the land surface, the air currents carry the pollutants away from Britain to other countries or out to sea.  [shows cause and effect]

> STRINGY  West Germany wants to control emission from cars, so it requires cars sold after 1986 to have catalytic converters and to use unleaded gasoline.

> RELATED  To control emission from cars, West Germany requires cars sold after 1986 to have catalytic converters and to use unleaded gasoline.  [shows cause and effect]

**24c  Avoid excessive or overlapping subordination.** (See also **23b**.)

If you overdo or overlap subordination, your reader will have difficulty deciding what the sentence base, or main clause, is.

> UNCLEAR  Jennifer Nunnery, who has been studying old buildings in Europe and who is convinced that their deterioration is rapidly escalating, eating away as much as a tenth of an inch of stone from old buildings and sculptures during the next decade, also is convinced that the rates of lung cancer and heart disease are increasing because of air pollution.

> CLEAR  Jennifer Nunnery has been studying old buildings in Europe and is convinced that their deterioration is rapidly escalating. She predicts that air pollution will eat away as much as a tenth of an inch of stone from old buildings and sculptures during the next decade. She also is convinced that the rates of lung cancer and heart disease are increasing because of air pollution.

**24d Be sure the relationship between the subordinate clause and the main clause is logical.** (See also **23a**.)

ILLOGICAL    Because apple trees no longer bloom in spring in Krakow, Poland, the air pollution there is at toxic levels.   [The air pollution causes the trees to not bloom, not the other way around.]

LOGICAL    Because the air pollution in Krakow, Poland, is at toxic levels, apple trees no longer bloom there in spring.

**Subordination and Coordination
for Effectiveness**

Exercise 24-1

NAME _____ SCORE _____

DIRECTIONS   Combine each of the following groups of short, choppy sentences into one effective sentence. Express the most important idea in the main clause and put lesser ideas in subordinate clauses, phrases, or words. Use coordination when ideas should be given equal emphasis.

EXAMPLE
A flavorist is an expert at creating flavors. The flavors may go into food, drink, mouthwash, and toothpaste. The flavorist needs to have the nose of a bloodhound and the tastes of an oenophile. He also needs a Ph.D. in biochemistry.

*A flavorist is an expert at creating flavors that may go into food, drink, mouthwash, and toothpaste; to create these flavors he needs a Ph.D. in biochemistry, the nose of a bloodhound, and the tastes of an oenophile.*

1. A flavorist works in a laboratory. The lab is filled with hundreds of potions and powders, exotic oils, roots, leaves, dried berries, and seeds. The flavorist combines the variety of compounds to improve on nature.

2. Individual flavors are complicated. Coffee contains more than 800 different flavor compounds. Only a fraction are essential to its characteristic flavor.

3. Scientists need to detect the essential characteristics. They go on location to jam, coffee, or chocolate factories. They use machines to capture the aroma of roasting beans or steaming berries.

4. The flavorists do not always succeed. They have not found a good substitute for coffee or chocolate. There also are no good synthetic substitutes for strawberry or roasted meat.

5. Flavorists call these the Holy Grail of the flavor industry. Their flavors are created by many compounds. The several compounds work in concert to create a flavor hard to reproduce.

## Subordination and Coordination
## for Effectiveness

Exercise 24–2

NAME _____ SCORE _____

DIRECTIONS   Rewrite each of the following sentences to make one effective sentence. Express the most important idea in the main clause, and put lesser ideas in subordinate clauses, phrases, or words. Use coordination when ideas should be given equal emphasis.

EXAMPLE
Most flavors have been characterized and mimicked precisely in the laboratory, and

it is nearly impossible to distinguish the fabricated from the original.

*most flavors have been characterized and mimicked so precisely in the laboratory that it is nearly impossible to distinguish the fabricated from the original.*

1. Some very popular flavors do not even exist outside of their synthetic renditions; they have no natural counterparts at all.

2. Cola is a "fantasy flavor," and cola nuts taste nothing like a cola soft drink, so cola is a purely artificial flavor.

3. Cola and the taste of Dr. Pepper were completely invented, but most work done by the flavor industry does not concentrate on flavor creation, but it emphasizes duplicating natural flavors.

4. Hungarians like the flavor of paprika and Indonesians enjoy the taste of the fruit of the durian tree, and that fruit smells, to the Western nose, something like an expired skunk.

5. Latin Americans like the nutty flavor of cashew, and Indians favor ghee, and it has the flavor of clarified butter, sometimes from yak or buffalo butter, and orange is by far the most favored taste internationally.

## Subordination and Coordination
## for Effectiveness
Exercise 24-3

NAME _____ SCORE _____

DIRECTIONS    Rewrite the following paragraph, using subordination to eliminate the short, choppy sentences and the stringy compound sentences. Use coordination when ideas should be emphasized equally. (Not every sentence must be changed.) You will notice the improvements in style that proper subordination and coordination achieve if you read aloud first the original version of the paragraph and then your revision.

[1]Every culture has its favorite flavors, but flavor preference is not a genetically inherited characteristic, and several scientists around the world have devoted their careers to studying how preferences are acquired. [2]Some scientists have done at least part of their work at Monell Chemical Senses Center. [3]This is a research institution. [4]It is loosely affiliated with the University of Pennsylvania. [5]Visitors to the Monell Center in Philadelphia recognize the building quickly. [6]It has an enormous gilded sculpture of a human nose and mouth. [7]The sculpture perches just in front of the entrance. [8]Inside the building the main order of business is immediately obvious. [9]The halls of the building are pervaded by odors. [10]The smell varies with the particular floor and hallway one happens to be walking through. [11]The overall olfactory effect is memorable. [12]It makes one think of a large cage in which a family of not entirely hygienic hamsters is baking chocolate chip cookies. [13]The Monell scientists have learned that people are born with only a few taste prejudices. [14]For example, they have a preference for sweet and a dislike for bitter, and there is a very good reason for this. [15]In the wild, sweet plants are generally nutritious while bitter ones are often poisonous, so a built-in sweetness preference and a bitterness aversion have helped the species survive. [16]There is little evidence that children are born with any other inherent preferences; humans are neophobic about food. [17]They dislike and distrust any food until they have grown accustomed to it. [18]So do animals.

REVISION

## 25

**Place modifiers carefully to indicate clearly their relationship with the words they modify.**

An adverb clause can usually be moved to various places in a sentence without affecting the meaning or clarity of the sentence.

> *Although the first white colonists considered Australian aborigines to be Stone Age primitives,* anthropologists have shown that the aboriginal way of life was particularly well suited to the harsh Australian environment.
>
> Anthropologists have shown, *although the first white colonists considered Australian aborigines to be Stone Age primitives,* that the aboriginal way of life was particularly well suited to the harsh Australian environment.
>
> Anthropologists have shown that the aboriginal way of life was particularly well suited to the harsh Australian environment, *although the first white colonists considered Australian aborigines to be Stone Age primitives.*

The movement of the adverb clause affects the punctuation of the sentence and the part of the sentence to be emphasized (see also Section **29**). But the sentence has the same meaning, and that meaning is clear whether the adverb clause is an introductory, interrupting, or concluding addition.

Other sentence parts may not be moved around as easily, as the following discussions of various modifiers will show.

### 25a Avoid needless separation of related parts of a sentence.

**(1) In standard written English, adverbs such as *almost, only, just, hardly, nearly,* and *merely* are usually placed immediately before the words they modify.**

MISPLACED    Professor John Watson *nearly* devoted ten years of his life to studying aboriginal creation myths.

BETTER    Professor John Watson devoted *nearly* ten years of his life to studying aboriginal creation myths.

MISPLACED    Complete dedication to the aborigines *only* has guided his work.

BETTER    *Only* complete dedication to the aborigines has guided his work.

**(2) Prepositional phrases are almost always placed immediately after the words they modify.**

MISPLACED    Aborigines continue *in their world* to regard most anthropologists as intruders.

CLEAR    Aborigines continue to regard most anthropologists as intruders *in their world.*

As long as no awkwardness results, a prepositional phrase may be moved to different places in a sentence for variety. (See also **30b**.)

> Watson completely changed, *with his recent book Dreamtime*, our understanding of aboriginal culture.   [The *with* phrase modifies *changed*.]
>
> *With his recent book Dreamtime*, Watson completely changed our understanding of aboriginal culture.
>
> Watson completely changed our understanding of aboriginal culture *with his recent book Dreamtime*.

**(3) Adjective clauses should be placed near the words they modify.**

Unlike the adverb clause, discussed at the beginning of this section, an adjective clause cannot be moved around freely in a sentence without changing the meaning or causing a lack of clarity.

> UNCLEAR   Developing, *which is the aboriginal term for their distant past*, an explanation of "Dreamtime" took Watson nearly two years.   [The placement of the adjective clause now suggests that *developing* means *distant past*.]
>
> UNCLEAR   Developing an explanation of "Dreamtime" took Watson nearly two years, *which is the aboriginal term for their distant past*.   [The placement of the adjective clause now suggests that *years* means *distant past*.]
>
> CLEAR   Developing an explanation of "Dreamtime," *which is the aboriginal term for their distant past*, took Watson nearly two years.

For the sentence to make sense, the adjective clause must be placed immediately after the word it modifies. Other examples would be

> MISPLACED   Watson received help from Professor Kelly Truitt, *who had been introduced to the Dreamtime myths by Professor Truitt*, in being accepted by the aboriginal tribes.
>
> CLEAR   Watson, *who had been introduced to the Dreamtime myths by Professor Kelly Truitt*, received help from Truitt in being accepted by the aboriginal tribes.
>
> MISPLACED   A student seems unlikely to succeed as an anthropologist *who is afraid to examine burial sites*.
>
> CLEAR   A student *who is afraid to examine burial sites* seems unlikely to succeed as an anthropologist.

**(4) Avoid "squinting" constructions—modifiers that may refer to either a preceding or a following word.**

> SQUINTING   The anthropologist Kelly Truitt was asked on May 29, 1973, to study a burial ritual.   [The adverbial phrase can modify either *was asked* or *to study*.]
>
> OR
>
> The anthropologist Kelly Truitt was asked to study a burial ritual on May 29, 1973.   [The reference of the adverbial phrase is still unclear.]

CLEAR        The anthropologist Kelly Truitt was asked to study the May 29, 1973, burial ritual.

**(5) The parts of the sentence base should not be awkwardly separated, nor should an infinitive be awkwardly split.**

AWKWARD    Professor Truitt's study of the burial ritual, after its publication in 1974 as the lead article in the prestigious journal *Nature*, established her international reputation.   [The verb is awkwardly separated from its subject.]

BETTER    After its publication in 1974 as the lead article in the prestigious journal *Nature*, Professor Truitt's study of the burial ritual established her international reputation.

AWKWARD    Truitt intended to, with the study of aboriginal burial rituals, explain why aboriginal burial sites should be protected.   [The prepositional phrases awkwardly split the infinitive *to explain*.]

BETTER    With the study of aboriginal burial rituals, Truitt intended to explain why aboriginal burial sites should be protected.

Although the awkward splitting of an infinitive should be avoided, sometimes an infinitive split by a single modifier is acceptable and sounds more natural.

Truitt was able to *accurately* record the elaborate music that accompanied the burial.

## 25b  Avoid dangling modifiers.

Dangling modifiers are most often dangling verbal phrases which do not refer clearly and logically to a word or phrase in the sentence base. To correct a dangling modifier, either rearrange the words in the sentence base so that the modifier clearly refers to the right word, or add the missing words that will make the modifier clear and logical.

DANGLING    *Breaking through the crust of a dry, dead Earth,* the myth tells of superbeings from Dreamtime who created all humans and animals. [The verbal phrase illogically modifies *myth*.]

CLEAR    *Breaking through the crust of a dry, dead Earth,* superbeings from Dreamtime created all humans and animals.   [The verbal phrase logically modifies *superbeings*.]

DANGLING    *Thinking about the beings from Dreamtime as the aborigines' ancestors and gods,* the myth told that the beings turned themselves into sacred trees, rocks, mountains, and rivers. [The verbal phrase illogically modifies *myth*.]

CLEAR    *Thinking about the beings from Dreamtime as their ancestors and gods,* the aborigines believe that the beings turned themselves into sacred trees, rocks, mountains, and rivers. [The verbal phrase logically modifies *aborigines.*]

OR

The aborigines, *thinking about the beings from Dreamtime as their ancestors and gods*, believe that the beings turned themselves into sacred trees, rocks, mountains, and rivers.

DANGLING    *While studying the May 29, 1973, burial ritual*, Professor Truitt's observations confirmed her theory that the dead were buried in a sacred location inhabited by ancestral superbeings. [The verbal phrase illogically modifies *observations.*]

CLEAR    *While studying the May 29, 1973, burial ritual*, Professor Truitt confirmed her theory that the dead were buried in a sacred location inhabited by ancestral superbeings. [The verbal phrase logically modifies *Professor Truitt.*]

**Caution:** Simply moving the verbal phrase to the end of the sentence does not usually correct a dangling modifier.

DANGLING    *Having returned to the sacred ground of their ancestors and gods*, the aborigines believe that their spirits stay in the ground and await rebirth. [The verbal phrase illogically modifies *aborigines.*]

DANGLING    The aborigines believe that their spirits stay in the ground and await rebirth, *having returned to the sacred ground of their ancestors and gods.* [A reader may still misread this verbal phrase as modifying *aborigines.*]

CLEAR    After the spirits return to the sacred ground of their ancestors and gods, the aborigines believe they remain in the ground and await rebirth.

OR

Having returned to the sacred ground of their ancestors and gods, the aborigines' spirits remain in the ground and await rebirth.

**Note:** Absolute constructions, which have their own subjects, do not dangle. Also, words, phrases, and clauses that modify the entire sentence are not classified as dangling modifiers.

*The relationship between the sacred land and the burial rites having been clarified*, Professor Truitt could argue that the sacred land should be protected. [The verbal *having been clarified* has its own subject—*relationship.*]

*To sum up*, Truitt used her research to change government policy toward the aborigines. [*To sum up*, used as a transitional expression, modifies the entire sentence.]

*When reading about Truitt's accomplishments*, it is hard not to be humbled by her devotion to the aborigines. [The verbal phrase need not modify any one word when a main clause introduced by the expletive *it* follows.]

**Placement of Modifiers**                                    Exercise 25-1

NAME _____ SCORE _____

DIRECTIONS   Below each of the following sentences is a word, phrase, or clause that, if inserted correctly in the sentence, could serve as a clear and logical modifier. Write *1* in the blank if the modifier can be inserted in only one place in the sentence and *2* if it can be inserted in two or more places. Then write the sentence with the modifier placed in a position where it will not cause an unclear or awkward sentence.

EXAMPLE
Sometime in the distant past, in "Dreamtime," superbeings broke

through the crust of a dry, dead Earth.

who were part human and part beast                          ___/___

*Sometime in the distant past, in "Dreamtime," superbeings who were part human and part beast broke through the crust of dry, dead Earth.*

1. These beings caused the sun to shine and the rain to fall.

who created all humans and animals                          _____

2. The creators turned themselves into sacred rocks, trees, mountains, and rivers.

where their spirits dwell to this day                       _____

3. These creators are the ancestors and gods of aboriginal tribes.

according to creation myths                                 _____

4. Their spirits return to the sacred ground of their gods.

when aborigines die                                         _____.

5. The spirits remain in the ground.
   awaiting their rebirth                                    _____

6. The spirits cannot be reborn and are doomed to wander the
   earth in despair.
   if a burial site is defiled                               _____

7. Nonaboriginal peoples have not always respected the beliefs
   or the burial grounds.
   of the aborigines                                         _____

8. Remains have been dug up for both anthropological and
   strictly prurient reasons.
   for more than a century                                   _____

9. A law has been passed in the Australian state of Victoria.
   that may allow aborigines to reclaim the bones of their
   ancestors.                                                _____

10. The law may mean an end to anthropology in Australia.
    however                                                  _____

**Placement of Modifiers**                                        Exercise 25–2

NAME _____ SCORE _____

DIRECTIONS    Rewrite each of the following sentence bases so that the modifier that follows it is clearly and logically related to a word or phrase in the sentence base. Or add
words to the modifier so that it is clear when it is attached to the sentence base. (Include
examples of both methods in your answers.) Be sure to capitalize and to punctuate the
modifier correctly when you attach it to the sentence base (see **12b** and **12d**).

EXAMPLE
Aboriginal leaders have shown little sympathy for the anthropologists' point of view

or for their work.

remembering the desecration of their burial grounds
*Remembering the desecration of their burial grounds,*
*aboriginal leaders have shown little sympathy*
*for the anthropologists' point of view or for their*
*work.*

1. Nineteenth-century anthropologists used skulls to support the notion that

aborigines are an inferior race.

removed from aboriginal burial grounds


2. Aboriginal graves also were robbed.

no scientific purpose


3. For example, the body of an aboriginal woman was displayed at the Tas-

manian State Museum.

died in 1876


4. Recently anthropologists have helped to change the attitudes of non-

aboriginals toward aboriginal culture.

by offering new interpretations of cultural artifacts


247

5. Aborigines of the eighteenth century had thriving commercial networks and surprisingly effective medical care.
   living better than most whites in Australia

6. They ate better and more regularly than white Australians.
   being excellent hunters

7. Aborigines continue to view anthropology as a vestige of colonial exploitation.
   despite these image-enhancing discoveries

8. The relationship between the aborigines and anthropologists puts them at odds.
   one as the studied, the other as the students

9. Anthropologists are now trying to demonstrate the relevance of their work.
   having underestimated the resentment of the aborigines

10. It is possible that aborigines, in an attempt to gain control of their cultural heritage, may instead succeed in burying it forever.
    in the current climate of confrontation

## 26

**Use parallel structure to give grammatically balanced treatment to items in a list or series and to parts of a compound construction.**

Parallel structure means that a grammatical form is repeated—that an adjective is balanced by another adjective, a verb phrase by another verb phrase, a subordinate clause by another subordinate clause, and so on. Although ineffective repetition results in poor style (see Section **21**), repetition to create parallel structure can result in very effective writing. The repetition of a sentence construction makes ideas clear to the reader, emphasizes those ideas (see Section **29**), and provides coherence between the sentences in a paragraph (see Section **32**).

Connectives like *and, but,* and *or* often indicate that the writer intends to use parallel structure to balance the items in a list or series or the parts of a compound construction.

LIST OR SERIES    In 1968, Congress passed the Wild and Scenic Rivers Act, which classifies rivers under three headings: *Wild*—unpolluted, undammed, with primitive surroundings, accessible only by trails; *Scenic*—undammed, with shoreline largely undeveloped, accessible by road; **and** *Recreational*—readily accessible, with some development and preexisting dams allowed.

COMPOUND PARTS    Supporters of the Wild and Scenic Rivers Act *have stopped* dams and dredging on some rivers **and** *have curtailed* development around others **but** *have failed* to save some of the country's most beautiful rivers.

**26a   To achieve parallel structure, balance a verb with a verb, a prepositional phrase with a prepositional phrase, a subordinate clause with a subordinate clause, and so on.**

The following examples are written in outline form to make the parallel structure, or lack of it, more noticeable. Correct parallel structure is indicated by vertical parallel lines.

AWKWARD    Some critics believe that the builders of the Forked Wolf River Dam
seek
    personal gain
rather than
    seeking public good

PARALLEL    Some critics believe that the builders of the Forked Wolf River Dam seek
|| personal gain
rather than
|| public good.

AWKWARD    Despite the damage that the dam will do to the Wolf River Forest, all that people
    read about in newspapers,
    hear about on radio,
and
    what they watch on television
are the economic benefits of the dam to the nearby small towns.

PARALLEL    Despite the damage that the dam will do to the Wolf River Forest, all that people
|| read about in newspapers,
|| hear about on radio,
and
|| watch on television
are the economic benefits of the dam to the nearby small towns.

**26b To make the parallel clear, repeat a preposition, an article, the *to* of the infinitive, or the introductory word of a long phrase or clause.** (Repeated elements of this type are printed in italics.)

Certainly supporters of the Wolf River Dam have been faced
|| *with* mounting public criticism of their motives
as well as
|| *with* recent criticism from government officials whose support they need.

However, they continue to insist that the dam is necessary
|| *to* control flooding in the Wolf River drainage system,
|| *to* stimulate the region's economy,
and
|| *to* provide recreation to an impoverished region.

They also insist
|| *that they* will realize little profit from the project
and
|| *that they* are residents of the area and would not harm it
but
|| *that* if the public does not want the dam, *they* will stop the project.

**26c  In addition to coordinating conjunctions, connectives like *both . . . and, either . . . or, neither . . . nor, not only . . . but also,* and *as well as*—and expressions like *not* and *rather than* which introduce negative phrasing—are used to connect parallel structure.** (These connectives are printed in boldface below.)

The public response to the project is the result
    **not only**
    || of emotional response to the death of a part of nature
    **but also**
    || of careful analysis of the long-term consequences of the project.

**Parallel Structure**                                      Exercise 26-1

NAME _____ SCORE _____

DIRECTIONS   Make an outline, like the outlines used in this section, of the parallel parts of each of the following sentences.

EXAMPLE

The U.S. Army Corps of Engineers says that about 50,000 dams restrain United States rivers but that only 38 percent of all sites with hydroelectric potential in the continental United States have been dammed.

*The U.S. Army Corps of Engineers says*
*that*
*    || about 50,000 dams...*
*but that*
*    || only 38 percent of all sites*

1. The U.S. Geological Survey has other figures: on the discharge of rivers, on water quality, and on changes in drainage systems.

2. Unfortunately, most of the information on America's rivers is spread among various agencies, not concentrated and not easily accessible.

3. The Wild and Scenic Rivers Act was an attempt both to collect all the vital information about the nation's rivers and to protect the rivers from development.

*253*

4. Earlier efforts toward river conservation had been fragmented and ineffective rather than focused and productive.

5. And in earlier efforts, compromise often seemed neither possible nor productive.

6. After a disastrous flood, the residents of a river valley clamor not only for a dam to control the river but also for any other means of control.

7. Conservation goes out the window as citizens become willing to discuss any means of control: dams; channelization, even if aquatic life is destroyed; and diversion of the flow.

8. A drought also has the ability both to make people forget about conservation and to make them begin discussing "improvement."

## Parallel Structure

Exercise 26–2

NAME _____  SCORE _____

DIRECTIONS  Rewrite the following sentences to restore the parallel structure.

EXAMPLE
Virtually all scientific research in the United States is both government funded and it is expensive.

*Virtually all scientific research in the United States is both government funded and expensive.*

1. Developed and named after Fred Robin, the Robin Institute is a think tank for naturalists.

2. Some politicians claim that the expense of protecting the weaver bird for a year now exceeds the expense of a year's food for a family.

3. The machine can be used to cut timber; it also can be used to remove the limbs and slice off the bark.

4. Unlike the nearby Todd Thicket, Alice's Woods is more a copse rather than a forest.

5. Today, having a forest near a city may seem more a luxury rather than a necessity.

6. The city planners insisted that the park be able to do two things: provide an example of unspoiled nature and be a place for safe family entertainment.

7. Not only is the EPA relying on American companies to support new restrictions on industrial pollution but also on foreign investors.

8. Criticism of the city park program was increased after the recent incidents of violence in the park area and began to come from all segments of society.

9. Until all aspects of the park's impact on the city are understood, the planning slows down and it may face the threat of a permanent halt.

## 27

**As much as possible, maintain consistent grammatical structure, tone or style, and viewpoint.**

As you read the following paragraph, notice how many times you must refocus your attention because of an unnecessary shift in number, tense, voice, or discourse.

The three million inhabitants of New Zealand are outnumbered 23 to 1 by sheep.

So when thirty government ministers wanted an economical, homegrown alternative
**number tense**
fuel source, he turns to an obvious choice. Now a whole fleet of trucks and buses
**number**
are getting ten miles per lamb in a successful experiment to produce diesel fuel from

lamb fat. Lamb tallow, the surplus fat from the carcass, is processed into methyl
**tense voice**
estes of tallow, then will blend with regular diesel fuel. The average lamb
**tense**
produced half a gallon of the stuff. Research scientists say there is no problem with
**number** **discourse**
the process and is asking the government can they be allowed to increase produc-

tion.

## 27a Avoid needless shifts in tense, mood, or voice.

SHIFT During the discussion of Frank's new novel that is set in the Grand Canyon, he *listened* carefully but *said* nothing while his wife *listens* carefully and loudly *applauds* every compliment for the novel.

CONSISTENT During the discussion of Frank's new novel that is set in the Grand Canyon, he *listened* carefully but *said* nothing while his wife *listened* carefully and loudly *applauded* every compliment for the novel.

SHIFT Some contemporary nature writers suggest that whales now *be shown* as possessing the best human traits and that man *is* the mindless destroyer. [shift from subjunctive mood to indicative mood]

CONSISTENT Some contemporary nature writers suggest that whales now *be shown* as possessing the best human traits and that man *be depicted* as the mindless destroyer.

SHIFT        Robert Cox *created* a nature novel set along the northern California coast; the most loving, intelligent character *is played* by a whale named Finn.

CONSISTENT      Robert Cox *created* a nature novel set along the northern California coast; a whale named Finn *is* the most loving, intelligent character in the novel.

Be especially careful in writing essays on literary or historical topics to maintain a consistent present tense while retelling a plot or an event.

SHIFT        In early novels whales *are* often *characterized* as soulless monsters that dispassionately *destroyed* men.   [shift from present tense to past tense]

CONSISTENT      In early novels whales *are* often *characterized* as soulless monsters that dispassionately *destroy* men.

## 27b Avoid needless shifts in person and in number. (See also Section 6.)

SHIFT        When *we* read Cox's novel *Souls in Migration*, *one* realizes that the whale attracts all of *our* sympathy.   [shift from first person to third person]

CONSISTENT      When *we* read Cox's novel *Souls in Migration*, *we* realize that the whale attracts all of *our* sympathy.

SHIFT        A *whale* like Finn acts as if *they* are driven by a conscience.   [shift in number]

CONSISTENT      *Whales* like Finn act as if *they* are driven by a conscience.

## 27c Avoid needless shifts between indirect and direct discourse. (See also Section 26.)

SHIFT        Finn always avoids hurting humans, even if they are attacking other whales, so he appears to consider the justice of his actions and to ask *is he doing the right thing by retaliating*.   [shift from declarative word order to interrogative word order]

CONSISTENT      Finn always avoids hurting humans, even if they are attacking other whales, so he appears to consider the justice of his actions and to ask *if he would be doing the right thing by retaliating.*

OR

Finn always avoids hurting humans, even if they are attacking other whales, so he appears to consider the justice of his actions and to ask, *"Am I doing the right thing by retaliating?"*

## 27d Avoid needless shifts in tone or style.

SHIFT        The fictional whale Finn behaves according to admirable rules. As the leader of his pod of whales, he settles disputes among them; as the leader, he also protects them; but the book mainly explores Finn's attempt *to interface with humanity in a positive way.*   [shift from formal style to doublespeak]

CONSISTENT   . . . but the book mainly explores Finn's attempts to communicate with humanity.

## 27e  Avoid needless shifts in perspective or viewpoint.

SHIFT   A whaling ship looks like a military battleship festooned with harpoon cannons and other fearsome weapons; meat cutting machinery, massive cooking vats, and packing machinery make it a floating factory.   [shift from external to internal perspective]

CONSISTENT   A whaling ship looks like a military battleship festooned with harpoon cannons and other fearsome weapons, but an interior of meat cutting machinery, massive cooking vats, and packing machinery makes it a floating factory.

**Shifts**                                          Exercise 27–1

NAME _____ SCORE _____

DIRECTIONS    Indicate the kind of shift in each of the following sentences by writing *a* (tense, mood, voice), *b* (person, number), *c* (discourse), or *d* (tone, style) in the blank. Then revise the sentence to eliminate the needless shift. Assume that the sentences form a paragraph.

EXAMPLE
Tornadoes often accompany massive thunderstorms that meteorol-

ogists call supercells.                                    *b*

1. Dry air is pulled into the supercells by its strong, swirling
   winds.                                                  _____

2. The cells' updrafts reach speeds of 100 miles per hour or more,
   and the updrafts quickly cooled the dry air.            _____

3. As this dry air cools, they sink.                       _____

4. The moist updrafts collided with the sinking cool air and cause
   the cloud to begin to rotate counterclockwise. The result is a
   swirl of air shaped like the swirl of water in a draining bath-
   tub.                                                    _____

5. When one sees this tower of swirling winds, you are impressed
   immediately by its power.                               _____

6. They say that the height of the funnels can reach 25,000
   feet.                                                   _____

7. At the base of the supercell a small, rotating "wall" cloud
   forms roughly 1,500 feet above the ground. We immediately
   wonder why this wall forms and should we fear it?       _____

8. A tornado vortex spirals down from the supercell and become
   visible.                                                _____

9. The vortex reaches down from the supercell, spits out powerful winds, and objects are sucked up from every direction.   _____

10. Witnesses cite objects from large water fowl of the family
    Anakidae to railroad cars being sucked up by a tornado.  _____

*261*

11. No nation on earth has been struck by as many tornadoes as is the United States. _____

12. Over the last 70 years tornadoes have killed more people than all the floods and hurricanes that were combined. _____

13. Tornado Alley, which spans the Great Plains, gets pummeled the hardest. We usually visualize tornadoes sweeping across the flat agricultural land of the plains states. But one seldom expects them in the northeast. _____

14. The most devastating tornadoes, however, hit the heavily populated east and northeast sections of the country, and more damage is done because of the density of population. _____

15. Now do you understand the destructive ability of tornadoes and how do they form from supercell thunderstorms? _____

**Shifts**                                           Exercise 27–2

NAME ——————————————————————— SCORE ——————————

DIRECTIONS   The following paragraphs, which discuss tornadoes, contain eleven need-less shifts in tense, voice, person, number, style, and discourse. Correct each shift by marking through it and writing your revision above the line. Finally, if possible, read aloud the original version and your revision to compare the improvement in coherence when consistent tense, voice, person, number, and discourse are maintained.

Tornadoes burst out of hiding so quickly that there are little time for effective warning. It can stay on the ground for a few seconds or, like some foul black beast rooting about in mortal carnage, it can stay several hours. They can range from a few feet wide or can be measured more than two miles wide. The de-structive path, they say, may be a few feet long or as long as 200 miles. Inside the tornado's funnel, winds can rage at speeds of more than 300 miles per hour. The most fearsome tornadoes travel in packs, one after another, swooping down on unsuspecting hamlets like wolves in the night bent on death, blood, and destruction.

At the National Severe Storms Laboratory in Norman, Oklahoma, meteor-ologists use the Totable Tornado Observatory (TOTO) to track tornadoes. They place TOTO directly in the path of a tornado. A 400-pound cannister of so-phisticated instruments, TOTO can measure wind speed and direction, tem-perature, pressure, and electrical activity. TOTO helps scientists learn how tornadoes behave and how are we to learn to predict them. TOTO was not the only useful machine that meteorologists have. They relied also on rockets launched into a tornado's heart to measure the forces at work. A new radar system also held promise; known as NEXRAD, it can provide a computer image of a storm and examine all of its components.

## 28

**Make each pronoun refer unmistakably to its antecedent.**

A pronoun has no real meaning of its own; rather, it depends on its antecedent, the word it refers to, for its meaning. If a pronoun does not refer clearly and logically to another word, then your reader will not know what the pronoun means. And if a pronoun refers broadly to the general idea of the preceding sentence or sentences, the reader may have to reread a part or parts of the earlier material to try to determine the meaning of the pronoun.

> *They* believed that the most important lesson they had learned could be summed up in one word: "Simplify!" *They* said *this* because *they* thought *it* captured the spirit of *their* attitude toward nature, a spirit of inquiry and exploration.

There are three main ways to correct an unclear reference of a pronoun: (1) rewrite the sentence or sentences to eliminate the pronoun; (2) provide a clear antecedent for the pronoun to refer to; and (3) substitute a noun for the pronoun or, as in the case of *this*, add a noun, making the pronoun an adjective.

> *Joseph Wood Krutch* and *Henry David Thoreau* believed that the most important lesson *they* had learned could be summed up in one word: "Simplify!" *They* broadened the spirit of *this* idea by viewing the world as a place "more to be admired than to be used." [In the second sentence, note that *this* has become an adjective modifying the noun *idea*.]

### 28a Avoid ambiguous reference.

AMBIGUOUS Albert told Ashley that *he* was innately aggressive.

CLEAR Albert told Ashley, "*You* are innately aggressive."
OR
Albert told Ashley, "*I* am innately aggressive."

### 28b Avoid remote or obscure reference.

A pronoun that is located too far from its antecedent, with too many intervening nouns, will not have a clear meaning; nor will a pronoun that refers to an antecedent in the possessive case.

REMOTE In 1929 Krutch penned his book *The Modern Temper*, in which he shocked many readers with the statement that "living is merely a physiological process with only physiological meaning." The effect of *it* was to establish him as an unduly pessimistic writer. [Readers may think *it* refers either to *The Modern Temper* or to *statement*.]

CLEAR    In 1929 Krutch penned his book *The Modern Temper*, in which he shocked many readers with the statement that "living is merely a physiological process with only physiological meaning." The effect of this statement was to establish him as an unduly pessimistic writer.

OBSCURE    When her father's plane landed, Anna was glad to see *him*. [*Him* illogically refers to *plane*.]

CLEAR    When her *father* walked off the plane, Anna was glad to see *him*. [*Him* logically refers to *father*.]

**28c  In general, avoid broad reference.**

Pronouns like *this, it, that, which,* and *such* may sometimes be used effectively to refer to the general idea of a preceding sentence, or even of a preceding paragraph. But such broad reference is easily misused and should generally be avoided. Make sure that each pronoun you use has a clear reference.

BROAD    He was a good naturalist, and he used *this* to explain his ideas about the desert.

CLEAR    He was a good naturalist, and he used *his ability* to explain his ideas about the desert.

OR

He used his ability as a naturalist to explain his ideas about the desert.

**28d  Avoid using *it* in two different ways in the same sentence. Avoid using the pronouns *it* and *you* awkwardly.**

CONFUSING    Although *it* was difficult for Krutch to break away from the man-made world, he left *it* after he began studying Thoreau in 1930. [The first *it* is an expletive; the second *it* refers to *man-made world*.]

CLEAR    Although breaking away from the man-made world was difficult for Krutch, he left it after he began studying Thoreau in 1930.

AWKWARD    In his biography of Thoreau *it* said, "I felt that the time had come when I should take a closer look at the part of my universe which neither I nor my fellows had made." [The pronoun *it* refers clumsily to *biography*.]

BETTER    In his biography of Thoreau, Krutch said, "I felt that the time had come when I should take a closer look at the part of my universe which neither I nor my fellows had made."

AWKWARD    *One* may wonder what changed Krutch's mind. It may surprise *you* to learn that Thoreau's passionate optimism and joy when he observed nature changed Krutch's outlook.

CLEAR    *One* may wonder what changed Krutch's mind. It may surprise *one* to learn that Thoreau's passionate optimism and joy when he observed nature changed Krutch's outlook.

**Note:** Some grammarians feel that *you* is both natural and correct as long as the writer does not shift person in the sentence or the paragraph; other grammarians feel that *you* should be avoided in formal composition.

**28e Use the relative pronoun *which* to refer to things and animals; use *who* to refer to people and to animals with names; use *that* to refer to things and animals and sometimes to people.**

WHICH    Krutch's article, *which* appears in *Blackwoods* magazine, recounts his reaction to reading Thoreau.

WHO    Krutch, *who* wrote the article, earlier had worked as a theater critic.

THAT    The effect *that* Thoreau had on Krutch was to convince him to return to nature, not as a primitivist but as a thinking, feeling man trying to find himself. [*That* is preferred over *which* to introduce a restrictive clause.]

## Reference of Pronouns

Exercise 28-1

NAME _____ SCORE _____

DIRECTIONS   In the following sentences mark a capital *V* through each pronoun that makes a vague reference and enter the pronoun in the blank at the right. Recast the sentence or sentences to clarify the meaning.

EXAMPLE *like those in communes*
Some people try to establish a new relationship with nature by leav-

ing civilization. ~~The communes are an example of this.~~            *this*

1. Even during the nineteenth century there were people who did not appreciate the signs of progress that were most noticeable in the urban areas and who sought to escape it.            _____

2. Henry David Thoreau wanted to escape the smokestacks and the busyness of modern civilization, which is why he went to Walden Pond.            _____

3. Seeking "to confront only the essentials of life," Thoreau knew that if he did not do it while he was young, he would never have the opportunity again.            _____

4. Ralph Waldo Emerson talked with Thoreau about living apart from civilization, but he did not follow his example.            _____

5. In *Walden* it tells about Thoreau's experiences with nature.            _____

6. They say that Thoreau did not spend all his time apart from friends and civilization.            _____

7. This may be true, but Thoreau did spend most of his two years at Walden in contact with only the land and the wildlife.            _____

8. He built his own house and grew most of his food, which gave him a real sense of independence.            _____

9. Today there are people who follow Thoreau's advice. This is because they seek something which, to them, the city has destroyed.            _____

10. Unlike the people who try to improve the city, those who follow Thoreau's example find it futile to work for reform and so decide to escape it. _____

11. Some seek privacy in other, less civilized countries while others go to isolated parts of our own country for this. _____

12. Many communes are hidden away from civilization. Mountains and forests serve as protectors of privacy and independence. They often are inaccessible by car. _____

13. The Hog Farmers' Commune can be reached only on foot, which discourages sightseers and other interlopers. _____

14. Still more independent individuals tell those who live in communes that they seek more isolation than their way of life provides. _____

15. They find contentment only in total separation from other humans. _____

16. One of these rare individuals has lived in Tennessee for many years in a cave which he has decorated with furnishings made entirely by his own hands. He claims this provides all the shelter and comforts he needs. _____

# 29

**Arrange the parts of a sentence, and the sentences in a paragraph, to emphasize important ideas.**

Emphatic word order, used at the proper time, is an effective way to emphasize ideas and add variety to your writing. But emphatic sentence patterns should be saved for ideas that deserve special stress; if you use unusual patterns too often, your style will appear stilted.

**29a Gain emphasis by placing important words at the beginning or the end of a sentence—especially at the end—and unimportant words in the middle.**

UNEMPHATIC    In the desert, Joseph Wood Krutch found pure air, endless beauty, and seclusion, according to his diaries.

EMPHATIC    In the desert, according to his diaries, Joseph Wood Krutch found pure air, endless beauty, and seclusion.

**Note:**   The beginning and the end (again, especially the end) are also the two most effective places to put important ideas in a paragraph or an essay.

**29b Gain emphasis by using periodic sentences.** (This rule is an extension of 29a.)

A sentence that holds the reader in suspense until the end is called *periodic;* one that makes a complete statement and then adds details is called *loose.* The loose sentence, which is more common, is usually easier to follow. But the periodic sentence, by reserving the main idea until the end, is more emphatic.

LOOSE    According to Krutch, "Man endangers his humanity by an almost exclusively technological approach in social, political, and philosophical thought."

PERIODIC    According to Krutch, "An almost exclusively technological approach in social, political, and philosophical thought endangers man's humanity."

**29c Gain emphasis by arranging ideas in the order of climax.**

In a series, place ideas in order beginning with the least important. Present the most important or most dramatic idea last.

UNEMPHATIC    Krutch revealed his acute perceptions of the desert in three books: his masterpiece, *The Voice of the Desert;* the journalistic record, *The Desert Year;* and the ecological study, *Great Chain of Life.*

EMPHATIC    Krutch revealed his acute perceptions of the desert in three books: the ecological study, *Great Chain of Life;* the journalistic study, *The Desert Year;* and his masterpiece, *The Voice of the Desert.*

### 29d  Gain emphasis by using the active instead of the passive voice.

> UNEMPHATIC  In 1955 Krutch's *The Measure of Man was given* the National Book Award for Nonfiction.

> EMPHATIC  In 1955 Krutch's *The Measure of Man received* the National Book Award for Nonfiction.

Gain emphasis also by using action verbs or linking verbs that are more forceful than a form of *have* or *be*.

> UNEMPHATIC  Krutch *was* a pioneer in American ecological study.

> EMPHATIC  Krutch *pioneered* American ecological study.

**Note:**  When the receiver of an action is more important than the doer, the passive voice will make the emphasis clear.

> Krutch's works were immediately accepted as classics.

### 29e  Gain emphasis by repeating important words.

> Krutch thought of himself as a gadfly who was significantly different from other men. He especially felt that he lived in contrast to those men who were frustrated by and alienated from the world about them. Earlier in his life he had experienced a similar frustration and alienation, but his study of natural history became a palliative for his ailments. He wrote, "But from what I believe man actually is, what human life can be, I am certainly not alienated. And that, I think, sets me apart from at least many of those who call themselves both alienated and existentialists."

**Caution:**  Repetition of a word produces only monotony unless the word is important enough to be emphasized. (See also **21c**.)

### 29f  Gain emphasis by using inverted word order or by putting a word or phrase out of its usual order.

> UNEMPHATIC  Smog-enveloped, polluted big cities were symbols of the earth's illnesses.

> EMPHATIC  Big cities, polluted and smog-enveloped, were symbols of the earth's illnesses.

> UNEMPHATIC  Perhaps Krutch could find himself by living in the desert.

> EMPHATIC  Perhaps, by living in the desert, Krutch could find himself.

### 29g  Gain emphasis by using balanced constructions. (See also Section **26**.)

> UNEMPHATIC  In nature Krutch found meaning for his life, but cities were no help.

> EMPHATIC  In nature Krutch found meaning for his life; in cities he found none.

**29h Emphasize an important sentence in a paragraph by making it noticeably shorter than the others.** (See also Section **24**.)

Throughout his career as a naturalist, Krutch contended that "smog, pollution, and the horrors of war" could be eliminated by a technological society only if it had the sense of values to put such objectives above its greater desire for "more speed, more power, and more wealth." Krutch had become a naturalist because he sought in nature something that he felt was missing from his life—a vitality and meaning. Like Thoreau in the nineteenth century, he was enthralled by the "wildness" of nature in contrast with the despoiled cities. Even as he spread the new gospel of ecology across the world, he also was on a mission of personal understanding and personal betterment. In nature he sought to meet himself, face to face.

**Emphasis**                                                   Exercise 29-1

NAME _____ SCORE _____

DIRECTIONS   Rewrite each of the following sentences in emphatic word order. Use the rule indicated in parentheses after the sentence to guide you in revising for emphasis.

EXAMPLE
There are many famous ecologists, one of whom is Rachel Carson. (**29b**)

*Rachel Carson is one of many famous ecologists.*

1. Jan McHarg's book *Design with Nature* is one of the most important of our time, according to most environmental critics. (**29a**)

2. Nature is an ally and a friend when viewed from McHarg's perspective. (**29b**)

3. McHarg proposes that humans improve, modify, and study their environment. (**29c**)

4. The value system of nature must be understood by humans before they can properly react to it. (**29d**)

5. McHarg's thesis was to emphasize designing with nature. (**29d**)

6. McHarg's carefully researched and designed landscapes demonstrate his concept of man in cooperation with nature. (**29f**)

7. Satirizing the American dream, McHarg writes, "Give us your poor and oppressed and they will receive Harlem and the Lower East Side." (**29g**)

8. McHarg wants to establish a balance between humans and nature, preserve natural areas, and encourage people to develop an aesthetic plan to their building. (**29c**)

9. McHarg's writing is sometimes obscure and difficult for a lay person to follow. (**29b**)

10. The following jargon-filled sentence was written by McHarg: "The measure of success in this process, in terms of the biosphere, is the accumulation of negentropy in physical systems and eco-systems, the evolution of appercep-tion or consciousness, and the extension of symbioses—all of which might well be described as creation." (**29d**)

# Emphasis

NAME _____ SCORE _____

DIRECTIONS   Write a paragraph in which you try to emphasize certain ideas by using three or more of the techniques in Section **29**. When you have finished, number the sentences in your paragraph and analyze what you have done to achieve emphasis by answering the questions on the next page.

SUGGESTED TOPICS

your favorite movie about an animal
why you like to canoe, fish, hunt, or hike
your favorite natural setting

PARAGRAPH

ANALYSIS

1. Did you use a short, abrupt sentence to emphasize an idea? If so, which sentence is used in this way? _____

2. Why did you emphasize this idea? _____

   _____

   _____

   _____

3. Which sentences in your paragraph have loose structure? _____

   _____

4. Which sentences have periodic structure? _____

5. Did you use any other techniques to achieve emphasis—for example, inverted word order, balanced structure, repetition of an important word or words? If so, list each technique used and the number of the sentence in which it appears.

## 30

**Vary the length, structure, and beginning of your sentences to make your style pleasing.**

On a few occasions a series of short sentences that all begin with the subject is effective. In general, however, vary the length, structure, and beginning of your sentences to achieve a fluid style.

**30a  Vary the length of sentences, using short sentences primarily for emphasis.** (See also **29h.**)

> A rectangular pit in front of the great Pyramid of Cheops at Giza may hold a scientific treasure more rare than any ancient artifact. Using technology originally designed to sniff the surface of Mars, researchers are planning to analyze the chamber's trapped air for evidence of how the earth's atmosphere may have changed over the centuries. *Inside the pit, 4,600-year-old air waits to yield its secrets.*

**30b  Vary the beginnings of sentences.**

**(1)  Begin with an adverb or an adverb phrase or clause.**

ADVERB *Finally,* scientists could analyze the air in the pit.

ADVERB PHRASE *In 1986,* scientists could analyze the air in the pit.

ADVERB CLAUSE *After scientists drilled a hole into the pit,* they could analyze its air.

**(2)  Begin with a prepositional phrase or a verbal phrase.**

PREPOSITIONAL PHRASE *In the pit* scientists also hope to discover ancient artifacts.

VERBAL PHRASE *Studying the air,* scientists are hoping to detect significant changes in the earth's atmosphere.

**(3)  Begin with a coordinating conjunction, a conjunctive adverb, or a transitional expression when such a word or phrase can be used to show the proper relation of one sentence to the sentence that precedes it.**

COORDINATING CONJUNCTION    Because technology advances so rapidly and because we accumulate data at astounding rates, we sometimes think that there is little to learn about our earth. *But* the experiment with the pit near the Pyramid of Cheops illustrates the knowledge that can be gained when someone asks a question never before asked. In this case, the question is "How does this 4,500-year-old air differ from present-day air?"  [coordinating conjunction]

| | |
|---|---|
| CONJUNCTIVE ADVERB | *Indeed*, this experiment illustrates the value of continued inquis- itiveness and of our ability to turn technology to a great variety of uses. |
| TRANSITIONAL EXPRESSION | Technological advances from the space program have affected much of civilian science. *In fact*, scientists could not hope to pen- etrate the pit and study the air without contaminating it if they did not have a set of drills created by NASA. We should remember such benefits when we consider the value of NASA. |

**(4) Begin with an appositive, an absolute phrase, or an introductory series.**

| | |
|---|---|
| APPOSITIVE | *Flightless and cantankerous birds*, Magellanic penguins live on the Patagonian coast of Argentina. |
| ABSOLUTE PHRASE | *Their environment devastated by cold, wet weather*, the pen- guins have become endangered. |
| INTRODUCTORY SERIES | *Torrential rains, low temperatures, driving winds*—all have served to decimate the population of nestlings. |

## 30c Avoid loose, stringy compound sentences. (See also 24b.)

To revise an ineffective compound sentence, try one of the following methods.

**(1) Make a compound sentence complex.**

| | |
|---|---|
| COMPOUND | The penguins feed on small sardines and silverside fish, and a shift in winds caused the fish to reappear near Patagonia in 1985. |
| COMPLEX | Because of wind shifts in 1985, the small sardines and silverside fish that penguins feed on reappeared near Patagonia. |

**(2) Use a compound predicate in a simple sentence.**

| | |
|---|---|
| COMPOUND | Magellanic penguins are far from the United States, and they are dif- ficult to study, but American volunteers have initiated and partici- pated in most of the efforts to restore the population. |
| SIMPLE | American volunteers have initiated and participated in most of the efforts to restore the Magellanic penguin population, despite the pen- guins' remote location and the difficulty of studying them. |

**(3) Use an appositive in a simple sentence.**

| | |
|---|---|
| COMPOUND | The reaction generated in the hydrogen bomb is called "fusion," and scientists are trying to learn to control it. |
| SIMPLE | Scientists are trying to learn to control "fusion," the reaction gener- ated in the hydrogen bomb. |

**(4) Use a prepositional or verbal phrase in a simple sentence.**

| | |
|---|---|
| COMPOUND | Ball lightning is formed in thunderstorms and it is spherical in shape and floats, ghostlike, in the atmosphere. |

SIMPLE    Formed in thunderstorms, ball lightning is spherical in shape and floats, ghostlike, in the atmosphere.

## 30d  Vary the conventional subject-verb sequence by occasionally separating the subject from the verb with words or phrases.

SUBJECT-VERB    Ball lightning contains enormous power, and scientists hope to harness that power.   [compound sentence]

VARIED    Scientists, aware of the enormous power of ball lightning, hope to harness it.   [simple sentence]

SUBJECT-VERB    The physicist Gerard Dijkhuis uses a submarine battery for power and has generated several small spheres of ball lightning.

VARIED    The physicist Gerard Dijkhuis, using a submarine battery for power, has generated several small spheres of ball lightning.

## 30e  Occasionally, use an interrogative, imperative, or exclamatory sentence instead of the more common declarative sentence.

How can anyone seriously hope to contain lightning, one of Nature's glorious creations? To wish to do so is an unnatural and dangerous ambition.   [a rhetorical question followed by a declarative statement]

Concentrate. Place both your palms against either side of the ball lightning. Prepare to be illuminated.   —*How to Transcend Reality*   [three imperative sentences]

**Variety**                                                    Exercise 30–1

NAME _____ SCORE _____

DIRECTIONS   Analyze the ways in which variety is achieved in the following paragraph by answering the questions on the next page.

[1]Approximately one-half of the 180 major pests in the United States come from beyond its borders. [2]For example, the exotic walking catfish was imported into Florida by tropical fish dealers. [3]Several specimens then literally walked away to freedom, and now they contend with native fish in many of South Florida's waterways. [4]The chestnut blight, caused by a parasitic fungus, was brought into New York City from Asia on nursery plants in 1908. [5]As a result, most of the chestnut trees in the eastern forest were dead by 1950.

[6]Operating on a faster timetable, the sea lamprey invaded the Great Lakes. [7]This predator, which normally lives in the ocean but spawns in streams, had navigated the St. Lawrence River into Lake Ontario but had been blocked from further advance by Niagara Falls. [8]In 1829 the Welland Canal opened, allowing the lamprey to bypass the falls into Lake Erie. [9]Seven years later lampreys were found in Lake Michigan.

[10]In Lake Michigan, the lampreys virtually wiped out lake trout. [11]Can you imagine the consequences? [12]Because lake trout were the primary predators on alewives, the alewife population exploded. [13]Unfortunately, the population increased to critical levels and soon there were massive die-offs. [14]Masses of dead, stinking fish littered the Lake Michigan shoreline. [15]An ecological problem suddenly became a political one.

ANALYSIS

1. Which sentences are shorter than the others? _____

   _____

2. What is the purpose of the short sentences? _____

   _____

3. How many simple sentences are there? _____

   _____

   How many compound sentences? _____

   How many complex sentences? _____

4. In which sentence is the subject preceded by an adverb? _____

   _____

5. In which sentences is the subject preceded by an adverb phrase? _____

   _____

6. In which sentence is the subject preceded by an adverb clause? _____

   _____

7. Which sentence begins with a coordinating conjunction? _____

   _____

8. Which sentences begin with a transitional expression? _____

   _____

9. Which sentences vary from Subject-Verb-Complement word order in the
   main clause by inserting a word or words between the subject and verb?

   _____

10. Which sentence is not a declarative sentence? _____

   _____

   What kind is it? _____

**Variety**                                                   Exercise 30-2

NAME _____ SCORE _____

DIRECTIONS   Write a paragraph in which you use at least three of the methods for achieving variety explained in Section **30**. Because most people are more likely to use varied sentence patterns when they write on subjects that they feel strongly about, traditional views that they can question, or topics that they can treat humorously, you may find one of the five beginnings suggested below useful. After you have finished your paragraph, number your sentences and analyze what you have done to achieve variety by answering the questions on the next page.

SUGGESTED BEGINNINGS

1. I recently devoted a week to studying the habits of a wild animal near my home. I recorded its behavior and my reactions in this journal entry.

2. My favorite animal in literature (or films) is the Black Stallion (or . . . ) because . . .

3. Despite the effect on the environment, the Park Service must keep our parks open to everyone. Every American citizen has the right to see our natural heritage.

4. The recent proposal to build a bridge across the Grand Canyon does not seem preposterous to me. The benefits are obvious.

5. Every family in America could raise its own supply of protein if it would learn to raise fish in a small pool or pen. The proposition is an easy, sensible, profitable one.

PARAGRAPH

PARAGRAPH CONTINUED

ANALYSIS

1. Have you used a sentence or two that are noticeably shorter than the other sentences in the paragraph? _____

2. What type of sentence structure have you mainly used: simple, compound, or complex? _____

3. Which sentences have you begun with something other than the subject?

   _____

4. Does any sentence have a word or words inserted between the subject and verb or the verb and complement? _____

5. Have you used any kind of sentence other than the declarative sentence?

   _____

# LOGICAL THINKING

**log 31**

## 31

### Base your writing on logical thinking. Avoid common fallacies.

Learning to reason clearly and logically and to judge the reasoning of other writers is an essential part of your preparation as a writer. This section will help you to understand inductive and deductive reasoning and to avoid common errors in reasoning called *fallacies.*

### 31a Learn how to use inductive reasoning in your writing.

Ancient peoples watched the sun and moon rise and set each day and studied the progression of the stars against a night sky. The evidence showed, they thought, that the earth was the center of the universe, and for thousands of years they held to that belief.

Inductive reasoning, as in the above example, is based on evidence: people observe or otherwise acquire facts—or what they believe to be facts—and then make a generalization based upon them. But, as the example of the earth-centered universe demonstrates, our reasoning sometimes fails us. When we reason inductively, we must take certain precautions: we must

make sure the evidence is sufficient;
make sure the conclusion fits the facts;
make sure we do not ignore evidence;
make sure we do not present only evidence that supports our conclusion.

### 31b Learn how to use deductive reasoning in your writing.

Suppose you assume that massive fish kills are always the result of some kind of pollution of the water. While you are fishing on a local lake, you notice a great many shad floating dead or dying on the surface of the lake, so you conclude that a local industry or water treatment plant has polluted the lake. This kind of reasoning is based on a logical structure called a syllogism.

*Major Premise* (usually a generalization): Massive fish kills result from pollution of the water.
*Minor Premise* (a specific fact): Today I discovered many dead or dying shad in a local lake.
*Conclusion:* The fish were killed by pollution.

When the major premise and the minor premise are correctly related to form a conclusion, the syllogism is valid. Even if the reasoning is valid, however, the conclusion may be false if one of the premises is false. For instance, suppose massive fish kills can result from something other than pollution. Hundreds, even thousands, of shad may die in a lake because of the natural warming and then cooling of the water. That makes your major premise false; therefore, your conclusion is false. Based on the evidence that you had, your reasoning was valid, but your conclusion was false.

As you use deductive reasoning in your writing, particularly in argumentative papers, think very carefully about your premises to be sure your argument is sound—both true and valid. Also, consider your reader as you frame your premises: how difficult will it be for the reader to accept your premises?

## Deduction

NAME _____

DIRECTIONS Prepare for a class discussion of the premises and conclusions in the following:

1. Major Premise:  All angels are immaterial beings.

    Minor Premise:  All immaterial beings are weightless.

    Conclusion:  All angels are weightless.

2. Major Premise:  One must choose between learning to use a computer and making costly errors.

    Minor Premise:  Anna has learned to use a computer.

    Conclusion:  Therefore, she will not make costly errors.

3. Major Premise:  It's impossible to be both rich and unhappy.

    Minor Premise:  Terry isn't rich.

    Conclusion:  Therefore, he must be unhappy.

## 31c Avoid fallacies.

Fallacies are faults in reasoning. They may result from misusing or misrepresenting evidence, from relying on faulty premises or omitting a needed premise, or from distorting the issues.

**(1) Non Sequitur:** A statement that does not follow logically from what has just been said—a conclusion that does not follow from the premises.

> FAULTY   My senator is concerned about environmental issues; therefore, he will vote against building a dam on the Duck River. [Other issues—for example, the impact of the dam on the local economy and on local politicians—may influence the senator's vote.]

**(2) Hasty Generalization:** A generalization based on too little evidence or on exceptional or biased evidence.

> FAULTY   A snake is a cold, slimy creature. [A snake's body temperature is the same as the temperature of its environment, and it is dry to the touch.]

**(3) Ad Hominem:** Attacking the person who presents an issue rather than dealing logically with the issue itself.

> FAULTY   His arguments for allowing the drilling of oil wells on national park land may sound impressive, but why should we take such comments seriously from a man who isn't even a high-school graduate? [The man's education does not necessarily invalidate his argument.]

**(4) Bandwagon:** An argument saying, in effect, "Everyone's doing or saying or thinking this, so you (or we) should, too."

> FAULTY   Everyone else is dumping chemical wastes in the river, so why shouldn't we? [That others do it does not make it right.]

**(5) Circular Reasoning:** An assertion that restates the point just made. Such an assertion "begs the question" by drawing as a conclusion a point stated in the premise.

> FAULTY   The passenger pigeon is extinct because not one passenger pigeon is alive. [The extinction of the species is the same as all of them dying.]

**(6) Red Herring:** Dodging the real issue by drawing attention to an irrelevant issue.

> FAULTY   Why worry about the dangers of nuclear reactors when thousands of people are starving in Africa? [Starving people in Africa have nothing to do with nuclear reactors.]

**(7) Post Hoc, Ergo Propter Hoc:** "After this, so because of this"—the mistake of assuming that because one event follows another, the first must be the cause of the second.

FAULTY   Halley's Comet passed near the earth in spring of 1986, and that summer we had a severe drought.   [The assumption is that the comet caused the drought, an assumption unlikely to be true.]

**(8) Either ... or Fallacy:**   Stating that only two alternatives exist when in fact there are more than two.

FAULTY   We have two choices: elect a new president or watch our national park system be ruined.   [In fact, other possibilities exist.]

**(9) False Analogy:**   The assumption that because two things are alike in some ways, they must be alike in other ways.

FAULTY   Since the canoes cost the same and are about the same size, one is probably as good as the other.   [Equal cost and size of the canoes cannot ensure that one is as good as the other.]

**(10) Equivocation:**   An assertion that falsely relies on the use of a term in two different senses.

FAULTY   The United States has a right to protect its commercial fishing industry, so it should do what is right and prohibit other nations from fishing in its coastal waters.   [The word *right* means both "a just claim" and "correct."]

**Fallacies**

Exercise 31–2

NAME _____ SCORE _____

DIRECTIONS    Identify the fallacies in the following sentences.

1. In summer of 1986 a nuclear reactor exploded in Russia, and in fall of 1986 the North Sea commercial fishermen netted 22 percent fewer cod than in the previous fall.    _____

2. Baby birds are so helpless because they just can't protect themselves.    _____

3. Why worry about endangered animals when we ought to be worried about people who are starving?    _____

4. Americans are sick of hearing excuses for our failure to protect the environment, but it is a sickness we can cure with more funding. Our national health requires it.    _____

5. We have two choices: ban smoking in public places or fire people who smoke.    _____

6. His arguments against off-shore drilling are much less persuasive because of the problem of alcoholism in his family.    _____

7. The Japanese have begun clear-cutting their forests, and the Germans have employed clear-cutting for nearly twenty years. It is time for us to adopt clear-cutting as our technique for cutting forests.    _____

8. This board is long and straight; therefore, it will be strong.    _____

9. The mountains are the same height and in the same climatic region, so climbing one should be the same as climbing the other.  _____

10. Meteorologists just cannot predict the weather.  _____

## 32

**Write unified, coherent, and adequately developed paragraphs.**

We recognize the beginning of a new paragraph by the indention of the first word—about one inch when handwritten or five spaces when typewritten. A typical paragraph may range in length from fifty to two hundred fifty words, with an average length of about one hundred words. The indention and length of a paragraph are signals to a reader that this unit of discourse will coherently and adequately develop an idea. As we read a paragraph, we expect to learn the controlling idea and understand the relationship that each of the sentences has to that idea. And, finally, we expect the sentences to flow smoothly, so that we do not have to mentally fill in any words or phrases or stop reading at any point to refocus our attention.

### 32a Construct unified paragraphs.

**(1) Make sure each sentence is related to the central thought.**

In the following paragraph the controlling idea appears in italics. The words in boldface echo the controlling idea and help to unify the discussion.

1 *The loss is most pronounced on the nation's farmlands.* **On the farms,** we are **losing** more **soil** than we were **losing** in the years of the Dust Bowl. The U.S. Department of Agriculture reports that one-third of the **nation's cropland** is **eroding** at a rate of more than five tons per acre per year, the "T (or tolerance) value" at which most fields are said to be able to replace **soil.** The General Accounting Office reports that 84 percent of the **nation's farms** have **losses** greater than five tons. In some places, the **losses** are shocking. A million acres in the Palouse area of Washington and Idaho are **losing** an average of fourteen tons per acre, or a twelfth of an inch off the top, each year. Some Idaho **soils** that were originally a foot deep are today only six inches. In western Tennessee, **farms** are **losing** one hundred fifty tons per acre per year. In eastern Washington, **losses on some farms** are said to reach two hundred tons.

In this paragraph, the writer explains that soil loss "is most pronounced on the nation's farmlands." Every sentence in the paragraph relates clearly and directly to that controlling idea. The reader never has to fill in gaps in the ideas or suffer the momentary confusion caused by a sentence that does not continue to develop the main idea.

**(2) State the main idea of the paragraph in a clearly constructed topic sentence.**

A topic sentence embodies the central thought of a paragraph. Notice how the first sentence of paragraph 2 clearly signals the idea to be developed; obviously the paragraph will explain how "a weasel is wild."

2    *A weasel is wild.* Who knows what he thinks. He sleeps in his underground den, his tail draped over his nose. Sometimes he lives in his den for two days without leaving. Outside, he stalks rabbits, mice, muskrats, and birds, killing more bodies than he can eat warm, and often dragging the carcasses home. Obedient to instinct, he bites his prey at the neck, either splitting the jugular vein at the throat or crunching the brain at the base of the skull, and he does not let go. One naturalist refused to kill a weasel who was socketed into his hand deeply as a rattlesnake. The man could in no way pry the tiny weasel off, and he had to walk half a mile to water, the weasel dangling from his palm, and soak him off like a stubborn label.

—ANNIE DILLARD, *Teaching a Stone to Talk*

Often the main idea of a paragraph is stated at the beginning, as in paragraphs 1 and 2, but it may occur anywhere in the paragraph. In paragraph 3 the topic sentence is the fourth sentence.

3    Aboriginal people are not averse to killing crocodiles, for they relish both the eggs and the flesh. But, though they are vulnerable to attack by crocodiles, the aborigines do not believe that the species should be exposed to indiscriminate hunting. Like crocodiles, the aborigines of Australia are themselves victims of modern civilization, which has decimated and spiritually impoverished them. *Perhaps no one else can better understand the helplessness of a creature that stands in the way of civilization's onslaught.* Gerry Blitner, an aborigine leader who serves as chairman of the Northern Land Council, pleads, "Something must be sorted out for the old crocodile, a silent reptile that cannot tell the world what people are doing to him."

When a paragraph progresses from particulars to a generalization, the topic sentence is likely to occur at the end, as in paragraph 4.

4    In America, there are eight thousand snakebites a year, a third of them, says Russell, visited upon zookeepers, private collectors, and others who handle snakes regularly. Many are "dry bites," for snakes voluntarily control the release of venom. (Russell found that 24 percent of 779 rattler bites were venomless.) Only a dozen people die in the United States each year from snakebite. Yet we stay indoors to avoid them. Some magazines will not even publish pictures of them. *Our fears seem extravagant.*

A single topic sentence may serve for a sequence of two or more paragraphs. The first sentence in paragraph 6 unites paragraphs 5 and 6.

5    Our confusions about soil erosion aren't merely economic. A large part of the problem is that we don't naturally think about soil. Soil is, to the human mind, an abstraction. When it performs its intended office, it is covered with greenery, invisible, out of sight and mind. When you see soil, it is usually out of place, muddying the water of a flood, tracked onto the living-room carpet, stuck to one's trousers after a slide into home plate. Or it is something dissected and impaired, a road sliced through a hillside, its mineral matter stripped of organic life, the mere bones bleached and drying in the sun.

6  *In its proper place, soil doesn't fit the natural shapes of inquiry.* It doesn't move. It doesn't have a discernible shape. The minuteness of its constituent particles frustrates the eye. The creatures that dwell inside it are drab and tiny and silent.

Occasionally no topic sentence is necessary because the details clearly imply the controlling idea.

7  Soil holds moisture long after the rain has gone. It lets air circulate freely, and a well-aerated soil may be more than half air space by volume. When you pile up billions of grains of sand, silt, and clay, they rest against one another the way ping-pong balls might rest in a carton, with vast amounts of surface area for things to cling to and grow upon. A cubic inch of soil contains acres of surface area, and is inhabited by billions of creatures. And with all its space and air and moisture, soil is chemically active. Clay particles are electrically charged. They attract certain kinds of molecules and foster novel combinations with other kinds of molecules. Scientists study clay particles as a nursery for evolving organic molecules. Some suggest that life itself may first have evolved in the soil, rather than in the seas— that, indeed, as the Bible says, man was made out of clay.

## 32b Make paragraphs coherent by arranging ideas in a clear, logical order and by providing appropriate transitions.

### (1) Arrange ideas in a clear logical order.

The paragraphs below illustrate several ways to arrange ideas in a paragraph. The choice depends on the context of the writing and on the writer's purpose.

TIME ORDER

8  In the early years of the century, the Babocomari, the San Pedro, and other perennial streams became intermittent, alternating between dry and flash-flood stages. They also began the process of channeling (which lowers the water table) and headward arroyo cutting. Today the Babocomari's streambed is more than fifteen feet lower than it was in 1900, and it is dry near Fairbank. Many of the "cienegas"—tracts of soft, wet land in the floodplains, fed by springs, highly vulnerable to compaction—disappeared, as did wetlands created by beaver dams. So did the beavers, fish, elk, antelope, grizzly bears, wolves, and prairie dogs. So did many of the native grasses, which early travelers said grew as high as a horse's belly. They were replaced by weedy or shrubby invaders, such as mesquite, whitethorn, groundsel, locoweed, snakeweed, burroweed, cocklebur, and Russian thistle.

Paragraph 9 demonstrates space order, an arrangement particularly useful for descriptions.

SPACE ORDER

9  Weasel! I'd never seen one wild before. He was ten inches long, thin as a curve, a muscled ribbon, brown as fruitwood, soft-furred, alert. His face was fierce, small and pointed as a lizard's; he would have made a good arrowhead. There was just

a dot of chin, maybe two brown hairs' worth, and then the pure white fur began that spread down his underside. He had two black eyes I didn't see, any more than you see a window. —ANNIE DILLARD, *Teaching a Stone to Talk*

ORDER OF IMPORTANCE

10    The points that I would emphasize are: First, that this sharp division between mentality and nature has no ground in our fundamental observation. We find ourselves living within nature. Second, I conclude that we should conceive mental operations as among the factors which make up the constitution of nature. Third, that we should reject the notion of idle wheels in the process of nature. Every factor which emerges makes a difference, and that difference can only be expressed in terms of the individual character of that factor. Fourth, that we have now the task of defining natural facts, so as to understand how much mental occurrences are operative in conditioning the subsequent course of nature.
       —ALFRED NORTH WHITEHEAD, *His Reflections on Man and Nature*

Sometimes the movement within the paragraph is from general to specific or from specific to general—as paragraphs 11 and 12 demonstrate.

GENERAL TO SPECIFIC; SPECIFIC TO GENERAL

11    I object to fishing tournaments less for what they do to fish than for what they do to fishermen. They have invaded one of the last refuges of civilized man, transmuted a noble art into something it isn't and shouldn't be, and fouled our perception of wild, lovely life forms. I would not argue that fish tourneys should be banned, even if there were a possibility of this; just that they be recognized for what they are—distractions from what's truly important.

12    There are more than a thousand places like Blackberry Crossing in America today—grown-over places lost on the maps but not forgotten. You are walking up this road through the forest and suddenly here is an old clearing gone scratchy with brambles and staghorn sumac; a bucket, rusted through; the rotted corner post of a barrack; a medallion of cracked concrete; a midden of bottles and cans. Artifacts of the Civilian Conservation Corps and its short-term tenure on the land. Nine years—1933–1942—were all they had to make their mark. Yet they left more than middens. They left billions of nursery trees growing in the cutover forest, and billions of mature trees untouched by fire for all the sweat off their smoke-etched brows. They left lean-to shelters and picnic tables and bridges and campgrounds in the parks. They left new parks. They secured the eroding soil with plantings and check dams. They lifted the sagging face of a national landscape gone limp from abuse and neglect.

One common form of the general–specific pattern is topic–restriction–illustration. The writer announces the topic, restricts or qualifies it, and then illustrates it.

TOPIC–RESTRICTION–ILLUSTRATION

13    The earth holds together, its tissues cohere, and it has the look of a structure that really would make comprehensible sense if only we knew enough about it. From a

little way off, photographed from the moon, it seems to be a kind of organism. Looked at over its whole time, it is plainly in the process of developing, like an enormous embryo. It is, for all its stupendous size and the numberless units and infinite variety of its life forms, coherent. Every tissue is linked for its viability to every other tissue; it gets along by symbiosis, and the invention of new modes of symbiotic coupling is a fundamental process in its embryogenesis. We have no rules for the evolution of this kind of life. We have learned a lot, and in some biomathematical detail, about the laws governing the evolution of individual species on the earth, but no Darwin has yet emerged to take account of the orderly, coordinated growth and differentiation of the whole astonishing system, much less its seemingly permanent survival. It makes an interesting problem: how do mechanisms that seem to be governed entirely by chance and randomness bring into existence new species which fit so neatly and precisely, and usefully, as though they were the cells of an organism? This is a wonderful puzzle.

—LEWIS THOMAS, *The Medusa and the Snail*

In the problem–solution pattern, the first sentence states a problem and the solution follows.

PROBLEM–SOLUTION

14   The air was hot and humid and there was very little breeze. There had to be some way to relax and cool off. Then I remembered the cool, dark place under my grandmother's porch. As a child I had hidden there from my cousins or gone there to be alone and think whenever I was feeling moody. And once again that crawlspace could be a refuge for me. I packed a small cooler with soft drinks, apples, and cheese, grabbed a blanket to sit on and my pad and pencil. I would cool off by sitting still and quiet where I had hidden as a little girl. And I would listen and watch as the hot July day burned itself out.

In the question–answer pattern, the topic sentence asks a question and the supporting sentences answer it.

QUESTION–ANSWER

15   How have the Fish and Wildlife Service and state fish and game department responded to the black duck crisis? One answer, now very much the topic of conversation among those who work with waterfowl, is offered in a 1983 report published by the Humane Society of the United States. To catch its drift you don't have to read past the title: "The North American Black Duck: A Case Study of Twenty-eight Years of Failure in American Wildlife Management." Author John W. Grandy has it that the black duck's predicament results mainly from overhunting, and he attributes wildlife managers' failure to curtail the killing to "bureaucratic inertia, puffy professionals who confuse redrafting regulations with admitting error, and, especially, a lack of toughness."

Many types of development exist, and you will have occasion to create types that combine or modify those represented in the preceding paragraphs. Remember, however, that your goal as a writer is to make your sequence of thought clear.

Transitional devices such as pronouns, repetition of key words or ideas, appropriate conjunctions and other transitional expressions, and parallel structures help create a coherent paragraph. Paragraph 16 exhibits several transitional devices.

**16** Like a pure sound or a melodic system of pure sounds in the midst of noises, so a crystal, a flower, a sea shell stand out from the common disorder of perceptible things. For us they are privileged objects, more intelligible to the view, although more mysterious upon reflection, than those which we see indiscriminately. They present us with a strange union of ideas: order and fantasy, invention and necessity, law and exception. In their appearance we find a kind of intention and action that seem to have fashioned them rather as man might have done, but at the same time we find evidence of methods forbidden and inaccessible to us. We can imitate these singular forms; our hands can cut a prism, fashion an imitation flower, turn or model a shell; we are even able to express their characteristics of symmetry in a formula, or represent them quite accurately in a geometric construction. Up to this point we can share with "nature": we can endow her with designs, a sort of mathematics, a certain taste and imagination that are not infinitely different from ours; but then, after we have endowed her with all the human qualities she needs to make herself understood by human beings, she displays all the inhuman qualities needed to disconcert us. . . . We can conceive of the structure of these objects, and this is what interests us and holds our attention; but we do not understand their gradual formation, and that is what intrigues us. Although we ourselves were formed by imperceptible growth, we do not know how to create anything in that way.
—PAUL VALERY, "Man and the Sea Shell"

In the preceding paragraph Paul Valery explores the difference between our understanding of nature and our feelings about it. Valery uses several devices to achieve coherence.

> *Pronoun Reference:* repetition of *they, their,* and *them.*
> *Repetition of Key Words or Ideas:* the repeated pattern *we can.*
> *Structural Patterns:* the use of parallel or coordinate sentences (or sentence parts)—
> *order and fantasy, invention and necessity, we can imitate, our hands can cut, we are even able* . . . Note particularly the contrast implied in the next to last sentence and the parallel construction used to illustrate this contrast.

Note Valery's use of transitional devices within and between sentences as he reminds us throughout the paragraph of the contrast between knowledge and feeling.

You may find the following list of connectives useful:

1. *Alternative and addition:* or, nor, and, and then, moreover, further, furthermore, besides, likewise, also, too, again, in addition, even more important, next, first, second, third, in the first place, in the second place, finally, last.
2. *Comparison:* similarly, likewise, in like manner.
3. *Contrast:* but, yet, or, and yet, however, still, nevertheless, on the other hand, on the contrary, conversely, even so, notwithstanding, for all that,

in contrast, at the same time, although this may be true, otherwise, none-theless.

4. *Place:* here, beyond, nearby, opposite to, adjacent to, on the opposite side.
5. *Purpose:* to this end, for this purpose, with this object.
6. *Cause/result:* so, for, hence, therefore, accordingly, consequently, thus, thereupon, as a result, then.
7. *Summary, repetition, exemplification, intensification:* to sum up, in brief, on the whole, in sum, in short, as I have said, in other words, that is, to be sure, as has been noted, for example, for instance, in fact, indeed, to tell the truth, in any event.
8. *Time:* meanwhile, at length, soon, after a few days, in the meantime, af-terward, later, now, then, in the past.

Clear writing demands clear transitions between paragraphs as well as be-tween sentences. Notice the transitional devices used in the following para-graphs.

17  Thus, in conceiving the function of life in an occasion of experience, we must discriminate the actualized data presented by the antecedent world, the nonac-tualized potentialities which lie ready to promote their fusion into a new unity of experience, and the immediacy of self-enjoyment which belongs to the creative fu-sion of those data with those potentialities. This is the doctrine of the creative ad-vance whereby it belongs to the essence of the universe, that is, passes into a future. It is nonsense to conceive of nature as a static fact, even for an instant devoid of duration. There is no nature apart from transition, and there is no transition apart from temporal duration. This is the reason why the notion of an instant of time, conceived as a primary simple fact, is nonsense.

But even yet we have not exhausted the notion of creation which is essential to the understanding of nature. We must add yet another character to our description of life. This missing characteristic is "aim." By this term "aim" is meant the exclu-sion of the boundless wealth of alternative potentiality, and the inclusion of that definite factor of novelty which constitutes the selected way of entertaining those data in that process of unification. The aim is at that complex feeling which is the enjoyment of those data in that way. "That way of enjoyment" is selected from the boundless wealth of alternatives. It has been aimed at for actualization in that proc-ess.

Thus, the characteristics of life are absolute self-enjoyment, creative activity, aim. Here "aim" evidently involves the entertainment of the purely ideal so as to be directive of the creative process. Also, the enjoyment belongs to the process and is not a characteristic of any static result. The aim is at the enjoyment belonging to the process.

The question at once arises as to whether this factor of life in nature, as thus interpreted, corresponds to anything that we observe in nature. All philosophy is an endeavor to obtain a self-consistent understanding of things observed. Thus, its development is guided in two ways—one is the demand for a coherent self-consis-tency, and the other is the elucidation of things observed. It is, therefore, our first task to compare the foregoing doctrine of life in nature with our direct observations.
—ALFRED NORTH WHITEHEAD, *His Reflections on Man and Nature*

The transitional expressions—*but, thus, at once*—effectively signal the relationships between the paragraphs; the content of the paragraphs bears out the signal. Other similarly useful expressions are

First . . . Then . . . Next . . . Finally . . .
Then . . . Now . . . Soon . . . Later . . .
One . . . Another . . . Still another . . .
Some . . . Others . . . Still others . . .
A few . . . Many . . . More . . . Most . . .
Just as significant . . . More important . . . Most important of all . . .

### 32c  Develop the paragraph adequately.

Sometimes very brief paragraphs, even paragraphs of one sentence, are appropriate. But most very brief paragraphs are brief because their topics are not developed or because they are not paragraphs at all—they are fragments of paragraphs which actually belong elsewhere in the writing. Analyze the paragraphs below to decide how they are inadequately developed and what revision would improve them.

18    About the time we were old enough to complicate the fishing by taking up the fly rod, the Department of Fish & Game decided to rotenone the river and rid it of carp and other trash fish forever. What they forgot was, you can't do that.

19    Most of the smallmouths, being somewhat less tolerant of poison than carp, simply shrugged their fins and went belly up. The carp, on the other hand, suffered only mild nausea and occasional fainting spells, during which they drifted downstream to revive at, say, Monte Rio or Villa Grande.

20    After that, on the broad inside shallows of bends in the river like the one at Bridgehaven, you could see shoals of carp foraging as if the bottom itself were alive. I thought of this the other day when a friend of mine said to me, "You know why there are so many whitefish in the Yellowstone River? Because the Fish and Game people have never done anything to help them."
—RUSSELL CHATHAM, "Summer, and Other Small Things"

These three paragraphs are paragraphs only insofar as indention denotes a paragraph. Together, however, they form a complete discussion of the idea stated in the first sentence. If you have difficulty developing paragraphs, study carefully the methods of development discussed in **32d**.

### 32d  Learn to use various methods of paragraph development.

Writers do not often write paragraphs that perfectly exemplify a single method of development. Most paragraphs combine two or more of the methods as the writer adapts them to a particular audience and purpose. The models that are presented below will help you, however, to learn the characteristics of each type of development. By studying and imitating the models you are not simply restricting yourself for the moment to a particular type of writing; instead, you are learning to use that type of writing to make yourself a more flexible and confident writer. You will have that type of development in mind the next time you write and will almost unconsciously use it in paragraphs or parts of paragraphs because you know it fits your purpose, audience, and content well.

### (1) Use relevant details to develop the controlling idea.

You always need to know the details that support the idea you are writing about. Occasionally you may not use those details, but knowing them will make it possible for you to write about the idea with confidence. All the types of development discussed in **32d** require that you know and use relevant details.

In the following paragraph, the author explains that though "erosion is a natural process," humans have exaggerated the problem. Soil erosion has accelerated beyond natural replacement rates.

21   Erosion is a natural process. Rainfall washes topsoil into rivers. Deltas plod seaward where the rivers run out of land. Windblown silt polishes the sandstone cliffs of the West. The soil that thus blows and washes away is apt to be replaced as bedrock weathers, plants decay, and dust comes to rest. But human activity accelerates erosion far beyond the replacement rates of nature. Highway construction in Virginia produced two hundred times the erosion occurring on undisturbed lands nearby. Off-road vehicles scour soil and bedrock at an annual rate of thirteen tons an acre from parts of the California desert that cannot replace one year's loss in a thousand years. Sediment washing off construction sites in Maryland yielded losses of six hundred seventy tons per acre, thirty-six times the rate of loss on nearby farms and one hundred times natural rates. Surface mining near Sheridan, Wyoming, increased erosion elevenfold. Logging near Newport, Oregon, quintupled the amount of sediment carried into creeks.

By describing briefly the process of natural erosion and contrasting it with man's effects on soil loss, the writer emphasizes the necessity for conservation techniques and underscores the interdependence between man and nature.

### (2) Illustrate a generalization using several closely related examples or one striking example.

22   A good case can be made for the claim that applied biological control, the science of fighting pest insects and plants with other insects and sometimes with microscopic disease organisms, is today's most exciting and satisfying venture into natural history. It is already a viable alternative to chemicals. In this country, major pests such as the alfalfa weevil, cereal leaf beetle, citrus whitefly, and California red scale are almost completely controlled over large parts of their range by natural enemies that entomologists have imported for the purpose.

### (3) Narrate a series of events.

In paragraph 23, Thomas McGuane recounts in chronological order a series of events that lead to his hooking a permit, one of the most elusive of gamefish.

23    As the sun moved through the day the blind side continually changed, forcing us to adjust position until, by afternoon, we were watching to the north. Somehow, looking up light, Woody saw four permit coming right in toward us, head on. I cast my tarpon fly at them, out of my accustomed long shot routine, and was surprised when one fish moved forward of the pack and followed up the fly rather aggressively. About then they all sensed the skiff and swerved to cross the bow about thirty feet out. They were down close to the bottom now, slightly spooked. I picked up, changed direction and cast a fairly long interception. When the fly lit, well out ahead, two fish elevated from the group, sprinted forward and the inside fish took the fly in plain view.   —THOMAS MCGUANE, "The Longest Silence"

**(4) Explain a process.**

The writer of paragraph 24 explains how scientists who work with biological pest control must identify and relocate insects and organisms as alternatives to the use of dangerous chemicals.

24    These scientists ransack the far places of the earth to find the predators and parasites that are the basic tools of their profession. They must bring them back alive; determine whether it is safe to release them into a new environment; calculate their chances of success against what is often an explosive and mobile population of insects that are considered harmful to humankind's best interests; rear them in numbers huge enough to secure their success; and see that they are able to establish themselves in a land with which they are completely unfamiliar. Someone has aptly called this science "the thinking person's pest control."

**(5) Show cause and effect.**

A paragraph of this type asserts a causal relationship; it must explain why one thing caused another and must do so convincingly. The first sentence of paragraph 25 states the causal relationship. The remaining sentences explain it.

25    And perhaps most important, the loss of soil means the loss of agricultural productivity. Says Richard Cruse, professor of agronomy at Iowa State University, "By removing that top layer, we're removing the cream. It's got the most nutrient matter, the best soil structure for aeration, moisture, and temperature. When we remove that, we're substituting the unweathered parent material. Generally such soil has poor aeration, poor infiltration, and poor structure. It just isn't ready for plant growth." In the southern Piedmont, a six-inch loss of soil reduces crop yields by as much as 40 percent. The Department of Agriculture estimates that soil erosion in the past half-century trimmed enough soil nationwide to reduce crop yields by 40 percent. If erosion continues at present rates in the Corn Belt, corn and soybean yields may decline 30 percent over the next fifty years. Farmers hope to make up for the lost fertility by applying more fertilizer and herbicides. In the past fifteen years, herbicide and pesticide use is up 50 percent, and fertilizer is up 75 percent. But eventually there will not be enough soil to hold plant roots and moisture. It will become too full of clay and too acidic. It may not grow anything.

**(6) Use classification to relate ideas.**

Classification requires grouping ideas or elements into categories. In paragraph 26 the author classifies three major influences on the "destruction of bottomland forests" in the United States.

26 The crucial destruction of bottomland forests has occurred during the past thirty years. The perpetrators have been three powerful entities joined in a mutually profitable alliance: (1) the U.S. Army Corps of Engineers, ambitious to include land reclamation among its flood-control activities; (2) agribusiness, especially large landowning corporations, which had discovered that the soybean could be profitably raised on damp soils providing the land was first drained—at a cost of billions of dollars that taxpayers, not the landowners, have had to pay; and (3) politicians, each eager to have a down-home share of porkbarrel spending.

**(7) Formulate a definition.**

In paragraph 27, Alfred North Whitehead defines the word "nature."

27 Nature is that which we observe in perception through the senses. In this sense-perception we are aware of something which is not thought and which is self-contained for thought. This property of being self-contained for thought lies at the base of natural science. It means that nature can be thought of as a closed system whose mutual relations do not require the expression of the fact that they are thought about. —ALFRED NORTH WHITEHEAD, *The Concept of Nature*

**(8) Describe by presenting an orderly sequence of sensory details.**

Paragraph 28 describes one bird authority's sighting of the horned quan, "one of the most bizarre species he has ever encountered." Notice how the details and careful attention to concrete description help readers visualize the strange bird.

28 That Central American bird authority, Alexander Skutch, finds the horned quan one of the most bizarre species he has ever encountered. To help illustrate this, he describes its slender neck and black head, with "a tuft of black feathers, pointing forward over the nostrils, partly concealing the bird's upper mandible. Its bright yellow eyes stared fixedly at me . . . its bare throat was scarlet; and the whole was surmounted by a tall, slender, truncate spike, covered with bare skin the color of ripe strawberries, that arose from the crown and was tilted backward."

**(9) Analyze the parts of a subject.**

Analysis breaks an object into its elements and examines the relationships among its parts. In paragraph 29 the author analyzes the threats to the ecosystem posed by overindustrialization.

29 As a biologist, I have reached this conclusion: we have come to a turning point in the human habitation of the earth. The environment is a complex, subtly balanced system, and it is this integrated whole which receives the impact of all the separate insults inflicted by pollutants. Never before in the history of this planet

has its thin life-supporting surface been subjected to such diverse, novel, and potent agents. I believe that the cumulative effects of these pollutants, their interactions and amplification, can be fatal to the complex fabric of the biosphere. And, because man is, after all, a dependent part of this system, I believe that continued pollution of the earth, if unchecked, will eventually destroy the fitness of this planet as a place for human life. —BARRY COMMONER, *Science and Survival*

**(10) Compare or contrast to develop a main idea.**

Paragraph 30 demonstrates the analysis necessary for comparison and contrast. Notice that the description focuses first on summer afternoons, then on autumn afternoons, reminding the reader of the comparison by referring to similar examples.

30    I think that even if I did not know the month or time of year, I would recognize the season by studying the afternoon. Late summer afternoons in the South are like no other time of day or year. Between about 4 and 6 P.M. you can feel the straight hot sun cutting through what has been cool shade. The light is sharp, direct, and almost white. The night that follows will be heavy with moisture stolen from the day and even the birds will be silent from the long heat. Late summer afternoons are exhausting. They waste your energy and oppress your spirit. And they burn on long into dusk to remind us of spent effort and of the rest for the earth that will come in the fall. Late autumn afternoons are different. The sun strokes the earth at long angles, warming cool shadows under trees and lighting odd corners. The light is diffused, glancing, a warm, golden color. Autumn nights are cool with a sting of winter under the surface of the air. Such afternoons and evenings soothe us without dulling our energy. They are times for watching the light, poised to hear any bird that sings from high in the air. They are short and lead us to wait and watch as the earth relaxes into winter.

**(11) Use a combination of methods to develop the main idea.**

Combining methods of development, the authors of the following paragraphs serve their readers well by writing clear, complete, and appropriate discussions. Notice how difficult it is to separate the development in these paragraphs.

31    When I saw the dead beaver I knew why the fish were jumping. Even a weekend fisherman would know that the dead beaver had drawn a swarm of bees that were flying low over the ground and water. Being my kind of fisherman, I knew I had the right fly to match them, and I did not think that my brother would. He didn't carry many flies—they were all in his hat band, twenty or twenty-five at the most, but really only four or five kinds, since each one was in several sizes. They were what fishermen call "generals," each a fly with which a skillful fisherman can imitate a good many insects and in different stages from larval to winged. My brother felt about flies much the way my father, who was a fine carpenter, felt about tools—he maintained anybody could make a showing as a carpenter if he had enough tools. But I wasn't a good enough fisherman to be disdainful of tools. I carried a boxful of flies, the "generals" and also what fishermen call the "specials"—flies that imitate a very specific hatch, such as flying ants, mayflies, stone flies, spruce bugs. And bees. —NORMAN MACLEAN, *A River Runs Through It and Other Stories*

32    In the wood, God was manifest, as he was not in the sermon. In the cathedralled larches the ground-pine crept him, the thrush sung him, the robin complained him, the cat-bird mewed him, the anemone vibrated him, the wild apple bloomed him; the ants built their little Timbuctoo wide abroad; the wild grape budded; the rye was in the blade; high overhead, high over cloud, the faint, sharphorned moon sailed steadily west through fleets of little clouds; the sheaves of the birch brightened into green below. The pines kneaded their aromatics in the sun. All prepared itself for the warm thunderdays of July.   —RALPH WALDO EMERSON, *Journals*

## Unity, Coherence, and Development                    Exercise 32–1

NAME _____ SCORE _____

DIRECTIONS   Discuss the unity, coherence, and development of the following paragraphs by answering the questions that follow them.

PARAGRAPH ONE

[1]The South Coast, to locals of Big Sur, means about eighty miles of California's central coastline stretching from the Big Sur River south to Raggedy Point. [2]It's a rough and steeply plunging coastline, as anyone who's driven Wonderful One, the scenic highway, knows. [3]Its piny mountains slam like a diving seabird into the Pacific breakers. [4]It seems to be so isolated and primitive a rock-bitten wilderness that you'd hardly think our hills were priced out of the market and that there could be enough people to wear it out, litter it over or fish it empty. [5]But to the old-timers like me and my fishing pardner Buzz, it has become more and more obvious that the abundance of the South Coast, where we used to gather abalone, mussels and rockfish, is no more. [6]The red abalone are completely gone, the smaller black abalone are so near to extinction it's futile to search for them. [7]There are plenty of mussels because here they are generally overlooked as a delicious seafood, perhaps because the orange and black meat with its attached beard of coarse whiskers is somehow obscene to the unliberated. [8]Even rockfish, like the heavyweight cabezon, or kelp bass, and bony sea trout, have become scarce. [9]If Buzz and I actually gave a damn, it might be a sad story indeed, but over a long period of approaching senility, we've managed to downgrade the goal of catching something below the desire to just go fishing. [10]There's a big and fundamental difference, and it takes many years of climbing up and down the beautiful, breakneck South Coast cliffs before one may achieve this particular satori.   —JACK CURTIS, "The South Coast"

QUESTIONS

1. Which sentence states the controlling idea? _____

2. What are the key words in the controlling idea? _____

_____

_____

*309*

3. What transitional expressions help achieve coherence? _____

_____

_____

4. What is the main method used to develop the controlling idea? _____

_____

_____

PARAGRAPH 2

[1]The symbiotic approach to the problem of the city has an extremely simple and familiar premise. [2]It is that man, in addition to his spiritual identity, is part of nature. [3]He is a biological organism, subject like all other creatures to the laws of nature. [4]This implies that he is constantly affected by his physical environment. [5]Each of us is dependent on it, not only for the material necessities of life (though that is the one relationship most of us recognize) but for health and for the balanced functioning of our senses, and ultimately for emotional well-being. [6]The subjective relationship to the environment—how it affects our senses—is the one we know the least about; but we are beginning to study it and recognize its importance. [7]We know that sounds and lights and forms and colors and movements and the other living organisms in our environment influence, for better or worse, our psychological and physical condition; this is merely another aspect of our participation in nature.   —PAUL VALERY, *Aesthetics*

QUESTIONS

1. Which sentence states the controlling idea? _____

2. What transitional devices are used? _____

_____

_____

3. What devices are used to achieve coherence? _____

_____

_____

4. What is the main method used to develop the controlling idea? _____

_____

_____

## Paragraph Practice: Details

NAME _____

DIRECTIONS    Using *details* as the method of development (see **32d(1)**), write a paragraph on one of the subjects listed below or on one of your own or your instructor's
choosing. First, plan the paragraph, writing out a controlling idea and making a list of
three or more details that will develop the controlling idea. Then compose the sentences
in your paragraph. You may use details from this book (rephrased in your own words,
of course), details from your own knowledge, or, if your instructor permits, details gathered from research.

SUBJECTS

1. a late summer storm
2. a favorite outdoor place
3. a crowded state park
4. the coldest winter you remember
5. the worst kind of climate you can imagine

CONTROLLING IDEA

DEVELOPMENT

1.

2.

3.

**4.**

**5.**

**PARAGRAPH**

**Paragraph Practice: Examples**                    Exercise 32–3

NAME _____

DIRECTIONS    Using several closely related examples or one striking example as the method of development (see **32d(2)**), write a paragraph on one of the subjects listed below or one of your own or your instructor's choosing. First, plan the paragraph, writing out the controlling idea and making a list of three or more examples that will develop the controlling idea. Then compose the sentences in your paragraph. You may use examples from this book (rephrased in your own words, of course), examples from your own knowledge, or, if your instructor permits, examples gathered from research.

SUBJECTS

1. some of the good results of conservation
2. your five favorite animals
3. some of the misuses of natural resources
4. ways you relate to nature
5. your early reactions to the natural world

CONTROLLING IDEA

DEVELOPMENT

1.

2.

3.

*313*

4.

5.

**PARAGRAPH**

**Paragraph Practice: Process Analysis**   Exercise 32–4

NAME _____

DIRECTIONS   Using process analysis as the method of development (see **32d(4)**), write a paragraph on one of the subjects listed below or one of your own or your instructor's choosing. First, plan the paragraph, writing out the controlling idea and making a list of three or more details that will develop the controlling idea. Then compose the sentences in your paragraph. You may use details from this book (rephrased in your own words, of course), details from your own knowledge, or, if your instructor permits, details gathered from research.

SUBJECTS

1. how to enjoy the summer heat
2. how to watch an eclipse
3. how to eat wild foods
4. how to identify poisonous plants
5. how to watch a sunrise or sunset

CONTROLLING IDEA

DEVELOPMENT

1.

2.

3.

4.




5.




**PARAGRAPH**

## Paragraph Practice: Classification                    Exercise 32-5

NAME _____

DIRECTIONS    Using classification as the method of development (see **32d(6)**), write a paragraph on one of the subjects listed below or one of your own or your instructor's choosing. First, plan the paragraph, writing out the controlling idea and making a list of three or more categories that will develop the controlling idea. Then compose the sentences in your paragraph. You may use facts from this book (rephrased in your own words, of course), facts from your own knowledge, or, if your instructor permits, facts gathered from research.

SUBJECTS

1. the best fishing holes
2. the best climbing trees
3. types of dangerous snakes
4. three or four styles of camping
5. your reactions to phases of the moon

CONTROLLING IDEA


DEVELOPMENT

1.



2.



3.

*317*

**4.**

**5.**

**PARAGRAPH**

**Paragraph Practice: Comparison or Contrast**     Exercise 32-6

NAME _____

DIRECTIONS     Using comparison or contrast as the method of development (see **32d(10)**), write a paragraph on one of the subjects listed below or one of your own or your instructor's choosing. First, plan the paragraph, writing out the controlling idea and making a list of three or more points that will develop the controlling idea. Then compose the sentences in your paragraph. You may use facts from this book (rephrased in your own words, of course), facts from your own knowledge, or, if your instructor permits, facts gathered from research.

SUBJECTS

1. two different kinds of hunting
2. summer and winter afternoons
3. early morning and late night
4. two of your favorite bodies of water
5. the attraction of the mountains and the beach

CONTROLLING IDEA

DEVELOPMENT

1.

2.

3.

4.

5.

**PARAGRAPH**

**Paragraph Practice: Definition**                    Exercise 32–7

NAME _____

DIRECTIONS    Using extended definition as the method of development (see **32d(7)**), write a paragraph on one of the subjects listed below or one of your own or your instructor's choosing. First, plan the paragraph, writing out the controlling idea and making a list of three or more points that will develop the controlling idea. Then compose the sentences in your paragraph. You may use facts from this book (rephrased in your own words, of course), facts from your own knowledge, or, if your instructor permits, facts gathered from research.

SUBJECTS

1. a perfect sunset
2. the ideal home in the country
3. nature
4. peace in nature
5. your own instincts of survival

CONTROLLING IDEA

DEVELOPMENT

1.

2.

3.

4.

5.

**PARAGRAPH**

**Paragraph Practice: Cause and Effect**                Exercise 32–8

NAME _____

DIRECTIONS    Using cause and effect as the method of development (see **32d(5)**), write a paragraph on one of the subjects listed below or one of your own or your instructor's choosing. First, plan the paragraph, writing out the controlling idea and making a list of three or more points that will develop the controlling idea. Then compose the sentences in your paragraph. You may use facts from this book (rephrased in your own words, of course), facts from your own knowledge, or, if your instructor permits, facts gathered from research.

SUBJECTS

1. the effects of water pollution on you
2. why there are ticks
3. the effects of a sudden violent storm
4. why a tent is better (or worse) than a motel room
5. why the world of nature makes you feel peaceful

CONTROLLING IDEA

DEVELOPMENT

1.

2.

3.

*323*

4.



5.



**PARAGRAPH**

**Paragraph Practice: Combination of Methods**     Exercise 32–9

NAME _____

DIRECTIONS   Write a paragraph on one of the subjects listed below. First, plan the paragraph, writing out a controlling idea and making a list of three or more points that will develop the controlling idea. Then compose the sentences of the paragraph. When you have finished writing the paragraph, list in the margin the type or types of development you have used. Underline the controlling idea of your paragraph, and make a list of the transitional devices you used to achieve coherence.

SUBJECTS

1. books or television programs that have changed the way you think about the natural world
2. what animals can teach us
3. your personal relationship with the natural world
4. the way you feel about some outdoor place
5. the relationship some friend or relative has to the natural world

CONTROLLING IDEA

DEVELOPMENT

1.

2.

3.

4.

5.

**PARAGRAPH**

**TRANSITIONAL DEVICES**

# 33

**Learn to plan, draft, and revise your compositions effectively.**

The principles that you studied for writing effective paragraphs—unity, coherence, and adequate development—are equally important for writing a whole composition. But even more than for a paragraph, the writing of an essay requires a complex of activities—planning, drafting, and revising—that is seldom linear or neat. Usually composing will require you to engage in the three activities several times as you discover, develop, and create the final form of a composition. Whatever repetition or messiness you experience, you must learn to be patient with yourself at the same time you work to improve. The more aware you become of the conventions of writing and of what works well for you, the better and easier your writing will become.

## 33a  Consider the purpose of your composition.

Although it is sometimes difficult to identify, writing always has a purpose. Once you know what a given composition is supposed to accomplish, the composing process will begin to proceed smoothly.

The purposes of nonfiction writing may be classified as *expressive, informative,* and *persuasive.* Very seldom will you write an extended composition that has only one of these purposes, but the terms will help you describe what you wish to write or analyze what you have written.

Expressive writing emphasizes a writer's feelings and reactions to the world. If you keep a diary or journal or write personal letters in which you recount your responses to your experience, you are engaging in expressive writing.

Informative writing focuses a reader's attention on the objective world, not on the writer's responses to that world. This textbook is a good example of informative writing as it leads you to think about the ideas and actions that help you learn to write. News articles, encyclopedia articles, science reports, and other technical writing that transmits information to a specific audience—all are good examples of informative writing.

Persuasive writing attempts to affect a reader's opinions and/or actions. It relies specifically on evidence and logical reasoning. And, as you attempt to persuade, you are likely to employ expressive and informative writing. Whatever final purpose you decide on, you must have a clear picture in your mind of what you intend to accomplish. Only then can you begin to control your writing.

## 33b  Find an appropriate subject.

In a college setting, an "appropriate subject" is one that meets the needs of the writing assignment. Sometimes your instructor assigns a topic, in which case you can immediately begin considering the needs of the audience (**33c**), what aspects of the topic you want to emphasize (**33d**), and how the composition should be organized (**33e**). Many times, however, you will be allowed to choose a topic: for some students this freedom feels more like an obstacle to succcessful writing than an opportunity. In this case, your personal experience, knowledge, and interests are a good place to start looking for subject matter. You can write an interesting, stimulating paper on almost anything you care about.

Sometimes you will need to choose a topic outside your own experience. For example, a history professor who asks you to write a composition on some aspect of nineteenth-century France will want you to demonstrate your command of certain information rather than your personal experience or feelings. But, again, you can write a better paper if you find an aspect of the topic that interests you.

And, of course, two other vital practical considerations are time and length. If you have to write a paper in a few hours, choose a subject you already know about—not one that requires research. If you have to write a paper of 500–600 words on Napoleon, do not choose "Napoleon's Military Career" as your subject. Choose "Why Napoleon Lost at Waterloo" or "Napoleon's Final Years in Exile." Find a subject appropriate to the amount of time you have and the length the instructor has asked for.

### 33c  Analyze your audience.

In recent years many authors have written books that make challenging scientific subjects available to the general public—Carl Sagan's *Cosmos* and Lewis Thomas's *Lives of a Cell* come to mind. Sagan and Thomas are highly trained scientists who can write very specialized articles or books for equally specialized audiences. They are comfortable with the *jargon* or technical vocabulary that is appropriate for their subject and audience. Fortunately for us, however, they are also comfortable writing for readers who understand little about such technical training and subjects. When they write to us—a general audience—they simply assume that we are curious, interested, attentive readers. They either omit the jargon or translate it into diction we can understand; they explain ideas in terms that we know.

Sagan and Thomas are particularly good at infusing dry, technical information with a human element. Thomas describes a parasite in a human body in terms that make it seem almost demonic. Sagan recounts an experiment designed to test whether life from Earth could survive on Mars: in a "Mars jar" he recreated a Martian atmosphere and injected microbes into it. Some of the microbes, he tells us, "froze to death . . . and were never heard from again"; others "gasped and perished from lack of oxygen"; still others "fried under the ultraviolet light." A few microbes, however, survived by "closing up shop," or by "hiding . . . under pebbles . . . or sand."

Sagan and Thomas succeed as writers—in large part—because they know their audiences. They bring us information in a language that we find vivid and accessible; as a result we as general readers get to see and know what they see and know.

### 33d Explore and focus your subject.

#### (1) Explore your subject.

Once you have a general subject in mind, the following methods, used singly or in combination, will help you explore it.

**Listing** Write down everything that comes to mind. Disregard grammar, spelling, and diction—just write. Here is a typical list one student made as she thought about a very broad subject: nature.

> gardens
> plants
> flowers
> beauty
> food
> summer vegetables
> small backyard garden
> my grandfather's big three-season garden
> he's old
> still works everyday
> Why?
> What does he get out of his work?
> more than food
> satisfaction?
> reason to live?
> What is my grandfather's relationship to his garden?
> to the natural world in general?

The list demonstrates the student's discovery of a possible subject—the answer to the questions "What does gardening mean to my grandfather? What is his relationship with nature?"

**Questioning** Journalists typically ask *who? what? when? where? how?* and *why?* Answering those questions about a topic may help you find your subject.

Look at the preceding list and consider the benefit of asking these questions about gardening and about the grandfather's love for his garden. Such simple questions can help stimulate ideas.

**Applying Perspectives** Think about the grandfather's gardening from three different approaches—static, dynamic, and relative. A *static* approach focuses on what gardening is. A *dynamic* perspective focuses on action and change: What does the grandfather do in his garden? How have his practices changed or developed over the years? A *relative* perspective examines relationships within a system. Think of gardening as part of a larger system—as part of the human impulse to participate in the natural world, to manipulate its cycles and seasons, or perhaps to gain some sense of control over the environment.

**Surveying Development Strategies**    The development strategies discussed in **32d** suggest ways of thinking about a topic. For example,

> *Narration*    What happens during the summer when the grandfather works in his garden?
>
> *Process*    How does he select his vegetables and flowers? How does he prepare the soil? and so on.
>
> *Cause and Effect*    Why does the grandfather work so hard in his garden? How does the work affect him?
>
> *Description*    What does the garden look like in its various stages?
>
> *Definition*    What *is* a garden?
>
> *Analysis*    What does working outdoors with plants and flowers teach the grandfather?
>
> *Classification*    What kinds of gardens are there?
>
> *Example*    What kinds of foods and plants has the grandfather grown before?
>
> *Comparison and Contrast*    What is gardening like? How is growing food like growing flowers or tending ornamental plants? How is it different?

**(2) Limit and focus the subject.**

During the previous discussion of exploring the subject, we also have examined limiting and finally focusing the subject—getting a clear idea of what you want to accomplish for a certain audience in a paper of a certain length. Suppose, for example, we move from the very broad topic, nature, to topics that are more and more limited:

> nature→gardens→gardening as a hobby→the meaning of gardening for my grandfather

The last topic—What does gardening mean to my grandfather?—focuses the subject. You now know the limits of your discussion, and you know what kind of information you must research.

**33e Construct a focused, specific thesis statement containing a single main idea.**

In **33d** we suggested a variety of ways to limit and focus a subject. We finally narrowed the broad subject, nature, into a single specific question: What does gardening mean to my grandfather? The question demonstrates a limited, focused subject. The paper we write will answer the question for ourselves and our reader. At some point in the composing process we need to condense that answer into a single statement that clearly suggests the thesis of the composition—the idea that binds together the discussion. For example,

VAGUE THESIS      My grandfather really enjoys gardening.

IMPROVED THESIS      I believe that growing his own food, watching it develop and ripen, and working in the outdoors have given my grandfather a sense of himself as part of the cycle of life. He has achieved a kind of peace and balance through his relationship to the natural world.

The vague thesis statement is as true as the improved one, but it helps neither the writer nor the reader. The word "enjoys" expresses no clear focus for the writer; therefore, the reader is not sure what to expect. The improved thesis statement focuses by explaining "enjoys": After years of gardening, the writer's grandfather has developed a view of the natural world that puts him in harmony with it.

The thesis statement helps a writer decide how to construct the essay. For example, the writer might tell a story associated with her memory of her grandfather at work in his garden, or she might talk to him about it to develop the ideas of (1) the sense of a cycle of life and (2) the peace and balance symbolized by the grandfather's relationship to that cycle. And, of course, a reader will interpret a thesis statement as an indication of the form and content of the discussion.

Depending on the method of development, the thesis statement may occur anywhere in the essay. Or it may not need to be stated at all. For the reader's benefit, however, the thesis statement usually appears at or near the beginning of the essay. At other points in the discussion the writer may repeat the thesis entirely—although in different terms—or in part. The repetition helps to guide the writing and reading processes.

## 33f Choose an appropriate method or combination of methods of development for arranging ideas, and prepare a working plan.

The strategies for developing paragraphs and possible essay topics also work very well for developing longer pieces of writing. Exemplification, narration, process, cause and effect, classification, definition, description, analysis, and comparison or contrast—one of these or a combination of them can be used for organizing your paper effectively. Review 32d.

Eventually every writer develops a working plan; if you intend to write successfully, you must find one that works well for you and master it. Some writers use a very informal plan; perhaps a list (see 33d) is sufficient for them. They jot down ideas, cross out some, move others to another location in the list, draw lines to suggest connections or overlap. They are comfortable with this relatively imprecise kind of plan, knowing that they will write, revise, write some more, and finally clarify what to say and how to say it. The plan remains extremely flexible.

An informal plan may begin with a list and evolve into an informal outline. The earlier list about nature could evolve into this informal outline.

### Informal Outline

Thesis statement: I believe that growing his own food, watching it develop and ripen, and working in the outdoors have given my grandfather a sense of himself as part of the cycle of life. He has achieved a kind of peace and balance through his relationship to the natural world.

1. Background of how long he has had a garden
2. Description of garden through the years—how it's expanded
3. After retirement, grandfather's devotion to gardening full-time
4. Hybrids, experimentation
5. Balance—day organized to correspond to garden work
6. Health—healthy eating, fresh air, and so on.

A formal outline uses indention, numbers, and letters to indicate levels of subordination.

### Formal Sentence Outline

Thesis statement: I believe that growing his own food, watching it develop and ripen, and working in the outdoors have given my grandfather a sense of himself as part of the cycle of life. He has achieved a kind of peace and balance through his relationship to the natural world.

I. My grandfather has had a garden for fifty years.
   A. Initially he helped my grandmother with flowers.
   B. During the depression, they depended on the garden for food.
II. After he retired, my grandfather devoted himself full-time to growing food.
   A. He needed some hobby to fill his time.
   B. He began to experiment with cross-breeding and hybridization.
III. Gardening became the principle by which my grandfather organized his day.
   A. Mornings were devoted to weeding, insect control, and inspection.
   B. Afternoons were devoted to harvesting vegetables and giving the garden a general inspection for damage and/or pests.
   C. Early evenings were devoted to clean-up, watering, and, if necessary, fertilization.
IV. The garden itself and the way of life it promoted produced an emphasis on overall health at my grandparents' house.
   A. Work was purposeful and pleasant.
   B. Food had value for health—both physical and emotional.
   C. The connection between nature and human life was emphasized.

### Formal Topic Outline

Thesis statement: I believe that growing his own food, watching it develop and ripen, and working in the outdoors have given my grandfather a sense of himself as part of the cycle of life. He has achieved a kind of peace and balance through his relationship to the natural world.

I. Grandfather gardened fifty years
   A. First with flowers
   B. Food during depression

   II. After retirement, full-time gardening
      A. Hobby
      B. Cross-breeding, Hybrids
  III. Organized day according to garden work
      A. Mornings
      B. Afternoons
      C. Evenings
  IV. Emphasis on overall health
      A. Purposeful work
      B. Physical and emotional value of food
      C. Connection between nature and human life

## 33g  Write the composition.

Writers often handicap themselves by assuming that they should write a composition in a certain order—that they should write the first word of the composition first and the last word last. Those writers mistake the order of the words in the completed composition (a product) for the order of the words as they come out in the actual writing (a process). Writing—including all the preliminary steps that we have discussed—usually is anything but straightforward and linear. So the best advice you can give yourself as you begin writing is to begin anywhere you can. Only after you get words on the page can you begin making decisions about revision and altering the content or form of the composition as you wish.

### (1)  Write effective introductions and conclusions.

Introductions and conclusions occupy strategic locations in a composition and strongly affect a reader's reaction to the composition. In general they are also harder to write because they differ in function from the rest of the composition. An introduction is the point of entry that arouses a reader's interest and indicates the subject and strategy of the composition. A conclusion satisfactorily completes the essay; it may summarize, restate certain ideas, contain the conclusion of an argument, or point to the other subjects that could be discussed.

    The introductory paragraph below grabs the reader's attention and indicates the content, and to some extent the tone (the writer's attitude toward the subject), of the discussion that will follow.

> A few mornings ago I rescued a bat from a swimming pool. The man who owned the pool—but did not own the bat—asked me why. That question I do not expect ever to be able to answer, but it involves a good deal. If even I myself could understand it, I would know what it is that seems to distinguish man from the rest of nature, and why, despite all she has to teach him, there is also something he would like to teach her if he could.
>
> —JOSEPH WOOD KRUTCH, "The Individual and the Species"

    In the body of the essay, Joseph Wood Krutch discusses humanity's relationship to the natural world, position *in* that world, and influence *on* it. As the title indicates, Krutch's essay considers humans as individuals and as members of a species. His conclusion includes a warning of the implications of human influence on the natural world.

> One thing is certain. However many of us there may be or come to be, no man and no group of men should have too much power over too many of us. It makes such men or such groups feel too much as though they were nature herself. So careful of the type they are—or claim to be; so careless of the single life they so indubitably become.
> —JOSEPH WOOD KRUTCH, "The Individual and the Species"

In his conclusion, the writer summarizes his comparison and calls for a necessary balance, such as that found in the natural world. This reminds the reader of the essay's thesis and serves to complete the discussion.

In the following introductory paragraph Barry Commoner states his thesis directly and concisely. The conclusion reiterates this and unifies Commoner's discussion. Notice that the last sentence of the conclusion is very similar to the last sentence of the introduction in its implications.

INTRODUCTION Once the problems are perceived by science, and scientists help citizens to understand the possible solutions, what actions can be taken to avoid the calamities that seem to follow so closely on the heels of modern technological progress? I have tried to show that science offers no "objective" answer to this question. There is a price attached to every solution; any judgment will necessarily reflect the value we place on the benefits yielded by a given technological advance and the harm we associate with its hazards. The benefits and the hazards can be described by scientific means, but each of us must choose that balance between them which best accords with our own belief of what is good—for ourselves, for society, and for humanity as a whole.

CONCLUSION Science can reveal the depth of this crisis, but only social action can resolve it. Science can now serve society by exposing the crisis of modern technology to the judgment of all mankind. Only this judgment can determine whether the knowledge that science has given us shall destroy humanity or advance the welfare of man. —BARRY COMMONER, "To Survive on Earth"

The purpose of Commoner's essay is to persuade. By stating his thesis at the beginning, he establishes his point of view immediately. And the conclusion indicates that he believes he has made his point and leaves the reader with the responsibility to act.

As you read essays in magazines, textbooks, or newspapers, look carefully at the introductory and concluding paragraphs. Examine the strategy involved in writing them and try to discover methods that you are comfortable using.

**Caution:** Avoid using clichés in your introduction. Also avoid unnecessary definitions, such as "Webster's defines a quasar as . . ." Finally, do not apologize in either your introduction or your conclusion ("Although I'm no expert on this subject, I . . ."). Apologies undermine the effectiveness of your paper.

**(2) Develop a good title.**

Good titles help establish good first impressions. But they can do much more. They can indicate the tone and content of a composition, and they can pique a reader's interest. The introductory and concluding paragraphs in **33g(1)** give a particularly good example. Commoner's title "To Survive on Earth" should capture any alert reader's attention. The introductory paragraph establishes the problems associated with advanced technology and suggests that survival will depend upon a balance between scientific progress and responsible control of that progress. A less skilled writer might have titled the essay "The Dangers of Science" or "Technology and Danger." Commoner's title shows the process aspect of the problem and its universal scope. The concluding paragraph repeats the idea of destruction and the need for sound judgment, reminding the reader of the essay's title.

**33h Revise the composition.**

Do not think of revision as simply the last stage of composing. Revision plays an important part in every stage of composition—from the first vague notions about the subject to the last proofreading. During the composing process you will often pause to rethink or to see in a different way some aspect of the paper; each of these acts is a part of revision.

There is, however, some danger of being overly conscious of the need to revise as you write. Some writers become so impressed with the inadequacy of what they have written or are about to write that they freeze up, fall victim to a writer's block, and cannot continue. The best advice to give yourself is to write, to get words on the page that you and your instructor can assess. Until you get the words out of your head and onto a piece of paper, there is very little anyone can do to help you improve as a writer.

Below is a list of questions that you will find useful as you revise your papers. Apply them systematically to the final draft of the paper before you submit it for grading. Use the questions on the essay as a whole and on individual paragraphs to help you assess your writing during composition.

# Reviser's Checklist

**The Essay as a Whole**

1. Does the whole essay stick to the purpose (see **33a**) and the subject (see **33b**)?
2. Have you kept your audience clearly in mind? Is the tone appropriate and consistent? See **33c**. Do any terms require definition?
3. Is the focus consistent (**33d**)? Do the ideas in the essay show clear relationships to the central idea, or thesis?

4. Is the central idea or thesis sharply conceived? Does your thesis statement (if one is appropriate) clearly suggest the position and approach you are taking? See **33e**.
5. Have you chosen an effective method or combination of methods of development? See **33f**.
6. Is the essay logically sound both as a whole and in individual paragraphs and sentences? See **31**.
7. Will the introduction arouse the reader's interest? Does it indicate what the paper is about? See **33g**.
8. Does the essay come to a satisfying close? See **33g**.

## Paragraphs

1. Are all the paragraphs unified? Are there any ideas in any paragraph that do not belong? See **32a**.
2. Is each paragraph coherent? Are sentences within each paragraph in a natural and effective order? Are the sentences connected by repetition of key words or ideas, by pronoun reference, by parallel structure, or by transitional expressions? See **32b**.
3. Is the progression between paragraphs easy and natural? Are there clear transitions where needed? See **32b**.
4. Is each paragraph adequately developed? See **32c**.

## Sentences and Diction

1. Have you used subordination and coordination to relate ideas effectively? See **24**.
2. Are there misplaced sentence parts or dangling modifiers? See **25**.
3. Do you find any faulty parallelism? See **26**.
4. Are there any needless shifts in grammatical structures, in tone or style, or in viewpoint? See **27**.
5. Does each pronoun refer clearly to its antecedent? See **28**.
6. Are ideas given appropriate emphasis within the sentence? See **29**.
7. Are the sentences varied in length? in type? See **30**.
8. Are there any fragments? comma splices or fused sentences? See **2** and **3**.
9. Do all verbs agree with their subjects? pronouns with their antecedents? See **6**.
10. Have you used the appropriate form of the verb? See **7**.
11. Are any words overused? used imprecisely? vague? See **20**.
12. Have all unnecessary words and phrases been eliminated? See **21**. Have any necessary words been omitted? See **22**.

## Punctuation, Spelling, Mechanics

1. Are commas (see **12**) and semicolons (see **14**) used where required by the sentence structure? Have superfluous commas been removed (see **13**)?

2. Is any end punctuation omitted? See **17**.
3. Are apostrophes (see **15**) and quotation marks (see **16**) placed correctly?
4. Are all words spelled correctly? See **18**.
5. Are capitalization (see **9**), italics (see **10**), and abbreviations used correctly?
6. Is your manuscript in an acceptable form? Have all words been divided correctly at the ends of lines? See **8**.

### 33i Write well-organized answers to essay tests; write effective in-class essays.

**(1) Write clear, concise, well-organized answers on essay tests.**

The best preparation for an essay test is to ask yourself questions that might be on the test and then to formulate responses to those questions. You may want to write out these responses before you take the test to make sure that they are unified, coherent, and clear.

If you get in the habit of identifying potential test questions before you take tests, you will improve not only as an essay test writer but as a student in general. You will become better at identifying what is important and you will get good practice at formulating essential concepts.

Before you begin writing, plan how you intend to spend the time in prewriting, writing, and revising. Just a few moments of planning will probably prevent your being caught at the end of class furiously trying to scribble one last paragraph.

Be sure you read the instructions and questions on the test carefully. And as you write, be sure you carefully follow the guidelines that are stated or implied in the instructions or questions.

**(2) Write well-organized, clear in-class essays.**

In-class essays require you to use time well. Plan your time; jot down a brief outline of your essay; then quickly decide how much time you will need to allow to prewriting, to writing, and to revision.

If you have in mind the essentials of the Reviser's Checklist (**33h**), you can use them to help you analyze your writing as you write and after you finish.

**Limiting a Topic**                                    Exercise 33–1

NAME _____ SCORE _____

DIRECTIONS   Point out the problems that you might have in writing about the following topics. Evaluate each topic on the basis of its suitability for an essay of 300–500 words written for readers like those in your English class.

TOPICS

1. our earth

2. animal mimicry

3. volcanoes

4. why women should not be naturalists

DIRECTIONS   Choose one of the general topics listed below and plan a limited essay of 300–500 words. Consider your classmates as the audience for your essay. To limit the general topic that you choose, use one of the techniques discussed in **32a** or some other technique that you have found useful. Save the work that you do in limiting the topic because your notes will be useful in future exercises.

TOPICS

1. the moon
2. the seasons
3. natural disasters
4. funding national parks
5. hunting

6. Henry David Thoreau
7. Annie Dillard
8. Charles Darwin
9. nature
10. gardens

**Planning the Composition: The Thesis**                Exercise 33–2

NAME _____

DIRECTIONS    Point out the weaknesses of the following thesis statements. Then use the space below to write your own thesis statement for the limited topic that you chose in Exercise 33–1 or on another topic that your instructor approves.

THESIS STATEMENTS

1. Animal mimicry is interesting.

2. Volcanic activity has been important in the formation of the earth.

3. Nature is peaceful.

4. National parks are very educational.

THESIS STATEMENT

*341*

## Planning the Composition: The Outline     Exercise 33–3

NAME _____

DIRECTIONS     Read the following essay carefully and make a topic outline of it.

A five-year-old boy was murdered on March 27, 1950, in Sarasota, Florida. Perhaps "murder" is not the right word, for Edward Schooley was killed by a circus elephant. "Dolly" had been one of the most docile members of the Ringling Brothers, Barnum and Bailey elephant herd for more than twenty years. But for some inexplicable reason she suddenly turned vicious and trampled to death the child who was offering her a peanut. The president of the circus publicly announced that Dolly would be destroyed, and this was done within three days after the tragedy.

Circus officials received many letters and telegrams from people all over the country complaining that Dolly's execution was unjustified. They apparently felt that a moral issue was involved and that an animal could not be held responsible for its actions. This point of view implies some interesting assumptions concerning animal psychology, but one thing is quite clear. If such an event had happened one or two centuries ago, the animal involved would have received quite different treatment. The law today states merely that dangerous or vicious animals must be destroyed. This represents a fairly recent simplification of older legal codes.

Ancient Hebraic law decreed that the goring ox be stoned to death. Plato's "Laws" directed that if any animal killed a man, except in combat authorized by the State, the nearest kinsman of the victim should prosecute the murderer. The case was tried by a public official, and if the verdict was against the accused, the guilty animal was banished from Greece. Citizens of Rome used to celebrate the anniversary of the preservation of the capital from night attack by the Gauls. On this occasion homage was paid to descendants of the sacred geese whose cries had given warning of the enemy's approach. On the same day a dog was crucified for the failure of its forefathers to give the alarm.

During the Middle Ages the practice of trying and condemning animals was common in Europe and the British Isles and later even in the New World. It was not confined to small villages and backward regions. In 1546 the French Parliament, the highest court in the land, ordered the execution of a cow, which was first hanged and then burned at the stake. Similar legal trials survived until fairly recent times. In 1906 in a small Swiss village a man and his son, accompanied by their dog, robbed a householder, and in the course of the crime the victim was killed. The two men were sentenced to life terms, but the dog was condemned to death because, the court decreed, it was the chief culprit, without whose complicity the crime would have been impossible.

Between A.D. 824 and 1845, there were at least 144 formal prosecutions resulting in the execution or excommunication of animal criminals. When a domesticated animal injured or killed a human being, it was formally arrested and thrown into jail. Then the judge or ruling nobleman of the district appointed one or several attorneys, who were charged with the duty of defending the accused. Public prosecutors and defense lawyers argued each case before the bar, and the evidence was weighed carefully by the judge before he rendered his verdict.

Mass indictments were not uncommon. On September 5, 1379, the village swineherd of Saint-Marcelle-Jenssey left the communal herd in the care of his son. Before his father was out of sight the boy began to tease some nursling piglets, which promptly burst into a cacophony of terrified squeals. Three old sows charged the tormentor, knocked him to the ground, and killed him before his father could intervene. All the pigs were hurried off to jail, and after due process of law, Philip the Bold, Duke of Burgundy, condemned the three murderers to death. Their guilt was so plain that no one protested the decision, but the legal position of the remaining animals was less clear. The prosecutor insisted that they should be punished as accomplices. He called several witnesses,

**Planning the Composition: The Outline**   Exercise 33–3 (continued)

who testified that all of the swine had hastened to the scene of the murder and shown by their gruntings and aggressive actions that they thoroughly approved of the assault. A wholesale execution was narrowly averted when the attorney for the defense pointed out that the punishment of the convicted pigs would doubtless serve as an effective object-lesson to the other swine and would deter them from committing any more offenses against men. The Duke found this argument convincing; and when the three murderers went to the gallows, the rest received a severe warning and were then released.

It was commonly assumed that lower animals possess a moral sense and could reasonably be expected to understand and obey man-made laws. But there were some jurists who held that the animal's owner was at least partially responsible for its actions. On January 10, 1457, a sow was convicted of "murder flagrantly committed" and was sentenced to be hanged. Her six sucklings were originally included in the indictment as accomplices. Positive proof was lacking, however, and they were released to their owner after he had furnished bail for their reappearance in the event that new evidence was uncovered. The man apparently believed in the inheritance of criminal tendencies, because after worrying about the matter for three weeks, he brought the piglets back to court, openly repudiated them, and refused to be answerable for their conduct in the future.

Swine were not the only animals guilty of criminal offenses. Cattle and horses occasionally ran afoul of the law and received precisely the same treatment as human criminals. Not only was the court procedure the same in each type of case; the same methods of execution were employed. The more common forms of capital punishment were hanging, beheading, or burning at the stake. Whenever possible, the animals were dressed in human clothes before the sentence was carried out.

Homicide was not the only crime for which animals were tried and punished. Jail sentences ranging from a few weeks to several years were not uncommon in cases of the willful injury of a human being by dogs, horses, cows, or other animals. In one Russian village a "he-goat" butted an important official while he was fastening his shoe, and as punishment the goat was banished to Siberia.

A German innkeeper's dog showed such poor judgment as to bite the leg of a village councilman. The animal's master was jailed at once, but he complained so vigorously against this miscarriage of justice that the judge ordered his release. After all, the innkeeper argued, why should he languish behind bars while the real culprit went free? Appreciating the logic of this approach, the court arranged for the incarceration of the dog for a period of one year. The sentence was duly served, and the animal shared its cell with two human prisoners.

Medieval methods of dealing with *wild* animals were, of necessity, more complicated. It was often impossible to capture and keep in jail the untamed creatures that sometimes brought harm to men. Nevertheless, the death sentence was occasionally imposed. In 864, the Council of Worms decreed death by suffocation to a swarm of wild bees that had stung a citizen to death. When animal culprits were not available for physical retribution, action of a different sort was possible. Insects and other pests that indirectly harmed a man by destroying his property could, with appropriate assistance from the clergy, be excommunicated. This extreme measure was not usually resorted to until milder alternatives had been exhausted.

It was customary, for example, to implore a swarm of locusts or a colony of rats to depart and cease whatever depredations they may have been committing. In some cases formal provisions for sanctuary were arranged, and the animals were notified by a Crier that they could take and maintain possession of a particular plot of land which had been set aside for their use. Usually the threat of excommunication was employed in an attempt to force the undesirable visitors to move away.

After the Middle Ages the Church grew less willing to participate in such animistic rituals as the excommunication of animals, but laymen continued to rely upon the efficacy of direct appeal to the presumed intellectual and emo-

**Planning the Composition: The Outline**     Exercise 33–3 (continued)

tional natures of lower animals. Sometimes the approach was informal and per-suasive. In an old issue of the *Journal of American Folk Lore* there appears a copy of a letter dated October 30, 1888. It is addressed very correctly to "Messrs. Rat and Co." The writer begins with fervent expressions of his esteem for the rats and mentions his fear that they must find their present quarters at No. 3, Pine Street quite unsuitable for winter occupancy. He points out that the build-ing was intended only as a summer residence and therefore is draughty and poorly supplied with food. By fortunate coincidence there is at No. 36, Sea Avenue a large well-built house where the rats, "can live snug and happy." The cellar is well stocked and a near-by barn contains large stores of grain. (Direc-tions for reaching the address are included.) Having thus demonstrated his good intentions, the author of the published letter politely suggests that the rats take advantage of his well-meant advice. If they fail to do so, the letter concludes, "the undersigned, who owns the property at No. 3, Pine St., will be forced to use Rough on Rats."

The ethical propriety of adjuring the vermin to move to a neighbor's house seems not to have concerned this gentleman. At that, he was only repeating, with minor modifications, the medieval offer of sanctuary. The more attractive the new abode, the better the chances of acceptance. Peasants in some parts of Europe followed a similar practice in attempting to get rid of cabbage worms. It was customary to go out into the garden and invite the worms to depart, calling out, "In yonder village is church-ale." Church-ale signified a festival which, the peasants must have assumed, no lively cabbage worm could possibly resist.

These historical accounts illustrate the universal human tendency to recognize certain similarities between ourselves and lower animals. In scientific jargon the tendency is termed anthropomorphism. It rests upon an implicit belief that other living creatures have the same kinds of psychological experiences as men and women. Probably many of the people who protested the killing of the circus elephant, Dolly, rationalized their objections by thinking of the precipitating event as an "accident." They may have felt that the animal did not "mean" to injure the boy. Regardless of their reasoning, these individuals were reacting precisely as human beings have reacted for many centuries.

Basic human attitudes and beliefs do not change rapidly. The notions that permitted our forefathers to try, convict, and execute animals as though they were criminals are not completely lacking from our own psychology in this modern and supposedly scientific age.

The difference is that our ancestors assumed that animals had a moral sense and that they either lived up to it or not. If an animal was guilty, it must be punished according to the same laws that applied to man. Today, we know a great deal more about the psychology of animals than our ancestors did and are in a position to know much better how a given animal should be treated. We should ask whether the offender is naturally vicious or whether it was goaded to violence by somebody's cruelty or carelessness.

The emphasis today is on proper precautions and laws to ensure public safety. Society demands that a dangerous animal be put where it can do no harm; but it also demands that the animal be treated humanely.

—FRANK A. BEACH, "Beasts Before the Bar"

OUTLINE

**Planning the Composition: The Outline**     Exercise 33-3 (continued)

OUTLINE

*349*

*THE WHOLE COMPOSITION*

**OUTLINE**

# Writing the Composition:
# Introductions and Conclusions

Exercise 33–4

NAME _____

DIRECTIONS   Using the outline that you completed in Exercise 33–3 as a guide, make notes for a new introduction and conclusion to the essay. Write the new introduction and conclusion in the space below.

INTRODUCTION

**CONCLUSION**

**Writing the Composition**                               Exercise 33-5

NAME _____

DIRECTIONS   Write an outline for an essay of 300–500 words on the limited topic you
selected earlier or on a topic that your instructor approves. Remember that your outline
is only a guide and that you can change it, add to it, or subtract from it whenever you
have reason to do so. When you have finished the outline, write a rough draft and evaluate your compositon using the checklist below. Make any changes that are needed.
Then make a final neat copy of your work. Be sure to give your essay a title that is
suitable to the contents of your essay and that will make your audience want to read it.

CHECKLIST FOR A COMPOSITION

1. Is the title both provocative and appropriate?
2. Does the introduction include the thesis statement or a sentence that suggests the thesis? Is the rest of the introduction appropriate, and does it lead
   smoothly into the statement or the suggestion of the thesis?
3. Is the relationship of each paragraph to the thesis clear?
4. Is each controlling idea in the paragraph developed fully enough?
5. Is the essay coherent—that is, does each paragraph flow smoothly into the
   one that follows it? (Compare the first sentence of a paragraph with the
   last sentence of the preceding paragraph.)
6. Does the conclusion make you feel that the composition is complete, that
   the essay has ended where it began with a restatement of the thesis?
7. Are both the grammar and the punctuation of the composition correct?
   (Proofread the paper at least once for any error that you tend to make frequently.)
8. Are all the words spelled correctly?
9. Is there any wordiness that needs to be eliminated?
10. Does the style seem fluid and clear?

COMPOSITION

**COMPOSITION CONTINUED**

**Writing the Composition**

COMPOSITION CONTINUED

**COMPOSITION CONTINUED**

# APPENDIX

| Parts of Speech | Uses in the Sentence | Examples |
|---|---|---|
| 1. **Verbs** | Indicators of action or state of being (often link subjects and complements) | Tom *hit* the curve. Mary *has* won. He *is* a senator. |
| 2. **Nouns** | Subjects, objects, complements | *Kay* gave *Ron* the *book* of *poems.* *Jane* is a *student.* |
| 3. **Pronouns** | Substitutes for nouns | *He* will return *it* to *her* later. |
| 4. **Adjectives** | Modifiers of nouns and pronouns | *The long* poem is *the best* one. |
| 5. **Adverbs** | Modifiers of verbs, adjectives, adverbs, or whole clauses | sang *loudly* a *very* sad song *entirely too* fast *Indeed,* we will. |
| 6. **Prepositions** | Words used before nouns and pronouns to relate them to other words in the sentence | *to* the lake *in* a hurry *with* no thought *beside* her |
| 7. **Conjunctions** | Words that connect words, phrases, or clauses; may be either coordinating or subordinating | win *or* lose in the morning *and* at night We won today, *but* we lost last week. Come *as* you are. |
| 8. **Interjections** | Expressions of emotion (unrelated grammatically to the rest of the sentence) | *Woe* is me! *Ouch!* *Imagine!* |

---

### *Common auxiliaries (helping verbs)*

| | | |
|---|---|---|
| am | had | ought to |
| is | had to | shall |
| are | has | should |
| be | has to | used to |
| been | have | was |
| can | have to | were |
| could | is | will |
| did | may | would |
| do | might | |
| does | must | |

---

### *Forms of the verb* to be

| | | |
|---|---|---|
| am | have been | will *or* shall be |
| are | is | |
| had been | was | will *or* |
| has been | were | shall have been |

---

### *Common indefinite pronouns*

| | | |
|---|---|---|
| another | everybody | nothing |
| anybody | everyone | one |
| anyone | everything | somebody |
| anything | neither | something |
| each | nobody | |
| either | no one | |

[Usually considered singular]

| | | |
|---|---|---|
| all | more | none |
| any | most | some |

[May be considered singular or plural]

---

*Relative pronouns*

| | | |
|---|---|---|
| that | who | whomever |
| what | whoever | whose |
| which | whom | |

*Subordinating conjunctions (or subordinators)*

| | | |
|---|---|---|
| after | if | until |
| although | in order that | when |
| as | since | whenever |
| as if | so that | where |
| as though | that | wherever |
| because | though | while |
| before | unless | |

*Common prepositions*

| | | |
|---|---|---|
| across | for | over |
| after | from | through |
| as | in | to |
| at | in front of | under |
| because of | in regard to | until |
| before | like | up |
| beside | near | with |
| between | of | |
| by | on | |

*Conjunctive adverbs*

| | | |
|---|---|---|
| accordingly | hence | moreover |
| also | henceforth | nevertheless |
| anyhow | however | otherwise |
| besides | indeed | still |
| consequently | instead | then |
| first, second, third, *etc.* | likewise | therefore |
| furthermore | meanwhile | thus |

*Common transitional phrases*

| | | |
|---|---|---|
| as a result | in addition | on the contrary |
| at the same time | in fact | on the other hand |
| for example | in other words | that is |
| for instance | | |

## Principal Parts of Some Troublesome Verbs

| Present | Past | Past Participle |
|---|---|---|
| begin | began | begun |
| blow | blew | blown |
| burst | burst | burst |
| choose | chose | chosen |
| draw | drew | drawn |
| drink | drank | drunk |
| drive | drove | driven |
| eat | ate | eaten |
| fly | flew | flown |
| freeze | froze | frozen |
| give | gave | given |
| lay | laid | laid |
| lie | lay | lain |
| raise | raised | raised |
| ring | rang | rung |
| rise | rose | risen |
| speak | spoke | spoken |
| steal | stole | stolen |
| swim | swam | swum |
| take | took | taken |
| wear | wore | worn |

# Individual Spelling List

Write in this list every word that you misspell—in spelling tests, in themes, or in any other written work. Add pages as needed.

| NO. | WORD (CORRECTLY SPELLED) | WORD (SPELLED BY SYLLABLES) WITH TROUBLE SPOT CIRCLED | REASON FOR ERROR * |
|-----|--------------------------|-------------------------------------------------------|--------------------|
|     | *considerable*           | *con·sid'·er·a·ble*                                   | *a*                |
|     |                          |                                                       |                    |
|     |                          |                                                       |                    |
|     |                          |                                                       |                    |
|     |                          |                                                       |                    |
|     |                          |                                                       |                    |
|     |                          |                                                       |                    |
|     |                          |                                                       |                    |
|     |                          |                                                       |                    |
|     |                          |                                                       |                    |
|     |                          |                                                       |                    |

*See pages 177–95 for a discussion of the chief reasons for misspelling. Indicate the reason for your misspelling by writing *a, b, c, d, e, f,* or *g* in this column.

a = Mispronunciation
b = Confusion of words similar in sound and/or spelling
c = Error in adding prefixes or suffixes

d = Confusion of *ei* and *ie*
e = Error in forming the plural
f = Error in using hyphens
g = Any other reason for misspelling

## Individual Spelling List (cont.)

| NO. | WORD (CORRECTLY SPELLED) | WORD (SPELLED BY SYLLABLES) WITH TROUBLE SPOT CIRCLED | REASON FOR ERROR |
|---|---|---|---|
| | | | |
| | | | |
| | | | |
| | | | |
| | | | |
| | | | |
| | | | |
| | | | |
| | | | |
| | | | |
| | | | |
| | | | |
| | | | |
| | | | |
| | | | |
| | | | |

A
B
C
D
E
F
G
H
I
J